T0361438

Confidently Chill

Confidently Chill is a groundbreaking two-book set comprising an evidence-based medical workbook and a captivating graphic novel.

Delving into anxiety's societal, familial, and individual dimensions, this unique resource offers practical strategies rooted in empirical research, clinical methodologies, and psychological theory.

Seamlessly blending medical expertise with award-winning artistry, *Confidently Chill* promises a holistic journey towards identity formation and lasting healing amidst today's unprecedented challenges.

 **Duygu Balan**, LPCC, is a psychotherapist, certified trauma professional, and author of the best-selling *Re-Write: A Trauma Workbook of Creative Writing and Recovery in Our New Normal* (2023, Routledge). She lives and practices bi-coastally in the San Francisco Bay Area and New York City.

Yener Balan, MD, DFAPA, is a board-certified psychiatrist and the vice president of behavioral health for a major health-care organization. He is the author of a series of critically acclaimed books that have advanced the field.

 **Nadir Balan** is an award-winning illustrator who has been working in the field for two decades. His work has spanned many genres from pop-culture to history to science.

Confidently Chill

Confidently Chill is a groundbreaking two-book set comprising an evidence-based medical workbook and a captivating graphic novel [illegible]

[illegible] anxiety [illegible] societal, familial, and individual dimensions, this [illegible] practical strategies rooted in empirical research, clinical methodologies, and psychological theory.

Seamlessly blending medical expertise with award-winning creative storytelling, *Confidently Chill* promises a holistic journey toward identity formation and lasting healing amidst [illegible] challenges.

Dongen Batan, [illegible] is a [illegible] author and [illegible] and author of the best-selling [illegible] (2023) [illegible] and practices [illegible] in the San Francisco Bay Area and [illegible] City.

Yener Balan, MD, [illegible] board-certified [illegible] the [illegible] president [illegible] national health [illegible] healthcare [illegible] the author [illegible] of critically acclaimed books [illegible] field.

Nadir Balan is an award-winning illustrator who has been working in the field for two decades. His work has spanned many genres from [illegible] to [illegible]

Confidently Chill

An Anxiety Workbook for New Adults

Duygu Balan, Yener Balan, and Nadir Balan

Routledge
Taylor & Francis Group

A PRODUCTIVITY PRESS BOOK

Designed cover image: Nadir Balan

First published 2025
by Routledge
605 Third Avenue, New York, NY 10158

and by Routledge
4 Park Square, Milton Park, Abingdon, Oxon, OX14 4RN

Routledge is an imprint of the Taylor & Francis Group, an informa business

© 2025 Duygu Balan, Yener Balan, and Nadir Balan

The right of Duygu Balan, Yener Balan, and Nadir Balan to be identified as authors of this work has been asserted in accordance with sections 77 and 78 of the Copyright, Designs and Patents Act 1988.

ISBN: 978-1-032-53778-8 (hbk)
ISBN: 978-1-032-53777-1 (pbk)
ISBN: 978-1-003-41354-7 (ebk)

DOI: 10.4324/9781003413547

Typeset in Galliard
by Apex CoVantage, LLC

To our son-shine, Evrim Kai.

You make us happy,

When skies are gray.

Contents

PART II CROSSING THE THRESHOLD

4 Value of Treatment 77

5 Brain, Body, and Behaviors 95

PART IV THE ROAD BACK

Meet the Authors

Duygu Balan, LPCC, is a licensed psychotherapist specializing in familial and intergenerational trauma and attachment wounding. She is a Psychobiological Approach to Couples Therapy (PACT) Level II trained couples therapist and a certified clinical trauma professional.

Duygu is the first author of *Re-Write: A Trauma Workbook of Creative Writing and Recovery in Our New Normal*, 2023. She is a regular contributor to *Psychology Today* and has been featured on CNN, The Times, MSN, *Cooper*, the *Mentally Stronger* podcast, WARM 106.9, the *Attachment Theory* podcast, and *J & Courtney's In It Together* podcast and in *The Washington Times, Medium, Authority* magazine, *The Good Men Project*, and *When Women Inspire*.

Duygu incorporates existential, relational, and humanistic theories and utilizes mindfulness and somatic techniques. She draws from her multicultural upbringing and embodies teachings from her background in dance, yoga, and writing. She believes in the healing power of humor, creativity, and authentic human connection.

Yener Balan, MD, DFAPA, is a board-certified psychiatrist, best-selling author, and speaker and is currently the vice president of behavioral health for a major health-care organization. He is also a distinguished fellow of the American Psychiatric Association.

Yener currently provides health plan oversight and direction to the behavioral health programs as they develop integrated models for the future of health care. His responsibilities include investing in technology, people, and research to drive market-leading performance; engaging patients and families in quality-improvement efforts; implementing processes that focus on proactive interventions and preventions; and engaging with organizations in the community to help shape the growth, education, and training of the workforce.

Yener has years of extensive experience working in high-volume community emergency departments; is an expert in hospital operations and health-care business and management, and has given lectures and workshops worldwide.

Both Duygu and Yener have dedicated many years to assisting their communities with outreach and counseling of the homeless, mentally ill, and substance-using populations on the margins of society.

They believe in the connection of the mind, body, and spirit and use a holistic treatment approach that combines Western therapeutic techniques with ancient healing practices.

Meet the Illustrator

Nadir Balan is an award-winning illustrator who has been working in the field for two decades. He learned the ropes at Marvel in 2002 and has since worked on a large variety of projects in many genres.

He worked with Ray Harryhausen to relaunch the movie franchises *Clash of the Titans* and *Wrath of the Titans*.

With Stan Lee and William Shatner, he won the Outstanding Book of the Year award for his work on *God Woke*.

His art is featured in galleries, and his paintings are in the permanent collection of the New Haven Museum where, as an avid history buff, he gives lectures on painting techniques and World War I.

His work has graced the covers of scientific and academic books ranging from medical to philosophical to theatrical. He recently worked on all three volumes of Dan Fogler's *Moon Lake*, and his comic book work is featured in *Heavy Metal* magazine.

The cover he illustrated for *Re-Write: A Trauma Workbook of Creative Writing and Recovery in Our New Normal* received a Best Book Cover Design award from *Pacific Book Review* in 2023.

A true renaissance man, in his spare time, Nadir moonlights as the operations director at an Ivy League university theater. Whatever time he finds left, he spends helping animals.

Praise for *Re-Write: A Trauma Workbook of Creative Writing and Recovery in Our New Normal* (2023)

The Balans have created an especially useful workbook on recovering from trauma in our post-pandemic world. It is comprehensive, eclectic, interactive and highly educational.

Bruce J. Schwartz, MD
Deputy Chairman & Professor of Psychiatry
Montefiore Medical Center and Albert Einstein
College of Medicine

This timely, interactive book on trauma addresses our current mental health realities in the context of the pandemic and provides hope in the healing journey. *Re-Write* explores adverse childhood experiences, intergenerational trauma, and gaslighting in a culturally sensitive framework that will resonate with readers. Inspirational and accessible, the Balans have produced another must-read book.

Arpan Waghray, MD
Chief Executive Officer, Well Being Trust
Chair, Behavioral Health Committee,
American Hospital Association

This book brings the perspective and skills of two mental health professionals with expertise in the science and treatment of trauma and adversity. Their approach blends mindfulness, thoughtful reflection, narrative writing and creativity supported by clear explanations, easy to follow steps, and interactive exercises. This book is a practical guide for anyone on a healing journey.

Brigid McCaw, MD, MPH, MS, FACP
Clinical Advisor, California ACES Aware Initiative

Duygu and Yener Balan have written a must-read primer for clinicians and comprehensive self-directed treatment manual for individuals who have experienced trauma all in one. Please read this book—and learn practical approaches you can take to support yourself or others on the path to recovery.

Anton Nigusse Bland, MD
Associate Professor of Psychiatry
University of California, San Francisco

Balan and Balan, as therapist and psychiatrist, bring their diverse experiences and wealth of knowledge to an expertly put together and easy-to-understand book on trauma. *Re-Write* provides a timely, evidence-based view on healing and recovery, in the context of empathy and mindfulness. The creative prompts and interactive exercises are designed for individuals and clinicians alike.

Neil Leibowitz, MD, JD
Chief Medical Officer, Beacon Health Options
Former Chief Medical Officer, Talkspace

With so many treatments available to address trauma, it is understandable to be confused as to which treatments are the most effective and where to go to get them. *Re-Write* helps the reader become an informed consumer of mental health treatments which is key in supporting shared decision making. We know that individuals who are knowledgeable about treatment options and engage in a shared decision-making dialogue with their clinician show improved adherence and satisfaction with treatment.

Andrew Bertagnolli, PhD
Assistant Professor, Alliant International University

Re-Write, by Balan and Balan, is a comprehensive book on trauma related stress, and offers expert case examples and writing prompts that invite the reader to reflect and rewrite their own trauma narrative. A must have in every clinician's library, this workbook written with compassion and humor, will bring new insights to many in need.

Carlos Rueda, MD, MBA
Chairman, Department of Psychiatry, St. Joseph's Health-Care System

Re-Write comes at a time when expectations of ourselves, healthcare, and the economy, are rapidly shifting. Trauma is ubiquitous and trauma-inducing shocks (from climate change, political instability, economic disruptions) are projected to increase in frequency. We need to prioritize our minds and brains. This book intertwines evidence-based medicine with self-guided writing prompts and creative exercises. It is a novel approach, and we desperately need new strategies for mental health. Cultural sensitivity and the relevance of trauma-informed care are highlights of this must-read book. Let us hope that it's therapeutic value can achieve impact far and wide. Humanity needs it now and into the future.

Harris A. Eyre, MD, PhD
Lead, Brain Capital Alliance

This a great book! Balan and Balan harness the power of narrative to help patients and their caregivers access the healing process. A must read for families, clinicians and anyone who has struggled with trauma.

Noam Fast, MD

Surprisingly innovative: I remember experiences I was forced to forget, I forgot trauma I kept remembering and I chose to re-write the memories of who I am.

Yannis Angouras
International Health-Care Executive

A practical blend of evidence-based insights, personal and professional experience, and helpful guidance and exercises, *Re-Write* is an important and innovative addition to the toolset for those recovering from trauma.

Patrick Courneya, MD
Chief Medical Officer, HealthPartners

Re-Write is an excellent workbook by Duygu Balan and Yener Balan that is timely, practical, and informative—the years of experience, passion and research culled into one power-packed book. A must read for practitioners as well as individuals affected by trauma.

Uli K. Chettipally, MD, MPH
Founder & President, InnovatorMD

Re-Write balances clinical case examples with theory, and grounds it on experiential and thought-provoking healing techniques. The writing prompts and resources can be used at the individual level, to support loved ones, and clinically as a teaching tool. I recommend this book to anyone interested in gaining an introspective view on self-growth and healing past traumatic pain.

—Jennifer Christian-Herman, PhD
Vice President, Mind Body Medicine/Behavioral Health, Blue Shield California

Dr. Balan has written an exceptionally well-researched, timely, and practical text on dealing with one of the harder to manage issues in Behavioral Health. It is a must read for anyone struggling with trauma themselves or managing it in their practice.

Andy Rink, MD
Partner, Healthcare Foundry

Other Books by the Authors

Kader's Quest. Routledge, 2025.

Re-Write: A Trauma Workbook of Creative Writing and Recovery in Our New Normal. Routledge, 2023.

Big Book of Emergency Department Psychiatry: A Guide to Patient Centered Operational Improvement. CRC Press, 2017.

Acknowledgements

We are grateful to so many people whose kindness and support have breathed life into the pages of this book.

First, we want to extend a very special thanks to Kristine Mednansky for her unending encouragement and her brilliant ideas that have illuminated the journey that led us to write *Confidently Chill*. We are grateful to the entire team at Taylor & Francis, including our editors, designers, and everyone involved in the publishing process!

Thank you to Nicole Baker, whose courage, resilience, and strength have been our brightest light. Thank you to Lydia Rasmussen and everyone at Smith Publicity for your invaluable expertise, patience, and wealth of knowledge!

We extend our gratitude to Kristen Rogers at CNN, whose passion to address important and often underdiscussed topics has inspired us and given our work a global platform.

Thank you to Tyler Woods and the entire *Psychology Today* editorial team for making Duygu's column 'Un-Numb' a unique platform to uncover overlooked topics about the intricacies of the human condition.

Writing this book would have been impossible without the consistency and support from our family of origin and our chosen family. Special thanks to Neslihan Pınar, Barrie Brouse, Joey Akalin, Liya Garber, and Gulden Çakır Ulusoy, who interacted with our work in our day-to-day and have always given us a place to fall back on.

In loving memory of Orhan Toydemir, Duygu's grandfather, who was the definition of unconditional love. Orhan was confidently chill before it was cool and taught us how to gracefully navigate the uncertainties of life. We miss you so much.

We want to thank each other for being each other's home – without the safety, peace, and love, creating would not be possible.

And lastly, we want to acknowledge today's youth, who were born into a world drenched in economic inequality, job insecurity, climate crises, geopolitical strife, and multiple 'once-in-a-lifetime' events and yet are still the most empathic generation and stand for making a difference in the world through interconnectedness, promoting tolerance, celebrating differences, and being open about mental health struggles.

—Duygu and Yener Balan

THE CALL TO ADVENTURE

DOI: 10.4324/9781003413547-1

Chapter 1

Introduction to
Confidently Chill

Welcome!

You chose this book for a reason, and we congratulate you for taking this important step in your healing journey!

1.1 Introduction

This book will take you through our current challenges, the pushes and pulls of our new normal, and the adaptations we have all been working to develop. As the title *Confidently Chill* implies, we discuss the identification and treatment of anxiety and related issues and provide clinical insight and useful evidence-based tools empowering one towards increasing one's chill and confidence.

Anxiety has many evolutionary benefits, and, when managed successfully, it can be a protective force for survival and a source of energy, creativity, excitement, and success. This book will assist in exploring the balance of appreciating life and all it has to offer along the spectrum of experiences.

We wrote this book to build on the resounding success and wide adoption of our prior book *Re-Write: A Trauma Workbook of Creative Writing and Recovery in Our New Normal,* 2023. Our goal continues to be to create these artifacts, to share our experiences and scientific knowledge, and to serve as a critical response tool for the immense stressors we all face. As parents, we want to be able to lead the way by modeling behaviors and creating an environment that fosters healthy growth while allowing for curious inquiry and informed consent. Our intention is for our readers to gain knowledge about themselves and their surrounding influences and to be able to make informed, uncoerced decisions that positively impact their quality of life.

Establishing confidence, asking questions, and making the best decision with the information available at the present moment are invaluable. Then and only then can you make sense of the world around you, advocate for your needs, and live up to your full potential.

DOI: 10.4324/9781003413547-2

Our goal is to ensure you learn enough about your anxiety to reclaim your power and your narrative.

If you are a clinician working with clients who suffer from anxiety, this book will provide valuable evidence-based information to supplement the therapeutic process outside the session. This book will promote the client's accountability for their own mental health and well-being.

If you or a loved one is dealing with anxiety, worry, or fear, *Confidently Chill* will provide you with information and tools to navigate your struggles and regulate your emotions. While you may not be able to control the things that happen around you, this book will help you take control over the things you can control and help you learn to pause and regulate your stimulus response reaction.

We remain in awe of the resilience of humanity and are excited for you to take these next steps as you dive deeper into this book and transform into a better version of yourself and embrace a confidently chill existence.

> **But if these years have taught me anything it is this: you can never run away. Not ever.**
> **The only way out is in.**
>
> **— Junot Díaz, *The Brief Wondrous Life of Oscar Wao***

1.2 Current State

We are in a mental health emergency. Over 90% of people report they are experiencing this crisis in some form. From the increasing mental health needs of adolescents and young adults to the opioid epidemic, it has poisoned everyone's lives.

We are living in a time when change is the only thing we can reliably expect. Our lives have been turned upside down by the COVID-19 pandemic, and the continued impact on our mental health is intense.

At no time in history has there been this rapid an increase of anxiety and depression, caused by the virus and all the consequences that came along with it. Since 2020, there has been a significant increase in anxiety and mood disorders, stress-related illnesses, and substance use and a decrease in life satisfaction. As we enter the fourth year of the pandemic, the evidence of the effect of this psychiatric epidemic continues to grow in the literature.

While we have had to lock down and socially distance as well as work from home, the modalities of school and interacting have all shifted to an ever-present online world.

There have undoubtedly been benefits to being able to access friends and family, as well as medical providers, on a virtual platform. Access in certain avenues of care and communication has improved, but there have been many drawbacks as well. More than 150 million people in the United States still live in federally designated mental health clinician shortage areas. Based on the rate of increase in demand for mental health services, the projected shortage of mental health professionals is expected to increase.

The combination of the pandemic, economic stressors, global wars, radical imposed lifestyle changes, and continuous pervasive fear has caused measurable harm.

According to an article written by Simon et al. (2021) for the Centers for Disease Control and Prevention (CDC) Morbidity and Mortality Weekly Report, there was a significant increase in firearm homicide and suicide rates from 2020 to 2021, coinciding with the beginning of the pandemic. The authors describe the increase as a record high and highlight the need for prevention efforts. Their suggestions include social connections and teaching coping and problem-solving skills.

Suicide is now a leading cause of death among adolescents and young adults. The CDC updated their data with a review released in late 2023 reporting a continued increase in suicide rates. There has been a 20% increase in suicides among US military service members. Drug overdose deaths have significantly increased. Anxiety has tripled. Over half of employees report experiencing daily stress and burnout.

Throughout this book, you will see examples in which we emphasize the value of early identification and treatment. In order to successfully ensure people have equal opportunities to healing, we highlight the need for appropriate and equitable access to mental health care. While this book is one piece of one component of the healing journey, the accessibility to services from a preferred provider is very valuable.

We know that having a personal and meaningful connection with your clinician is critical to healing and recovery. To that end, people must have the opportunity to choose their providers and be matched with their preference, be it ethnic, racial, or linguistic. The impetus is on the health-care providers and teams to ensure a diverse workforce to accommodate individual needs and overcome the initial hurdles to recovery.

Health-care providers, whether clinicians in private practice or in larger group settings, must be up to date in their diversity and cultural sensitivity training. This is critical for efficient communication in a compassionate, empathic environment.

For larger health-care systems, we emphasize the need for equitable pay for clinicians, specifically mental health–care providers. Specialists across the spectrum should be trained in early identification of common psychological issues such as anxiety and depression and have the capacity to either intervene with treatment options or refer to specialty mental health.

We are witnessing a level of confusion in the highly regulated managed care world and the competing financial incentives of mental health startups. For example, there are new regulations in some states that swing the mental health parity pendulum to a degree that requires network adequacy allowing for set time intervals between individual psychotherapy visits. At the same time, we are seeing venture capital–backed mental health startups that have gained serious interest and significant monetary investments claim that text-based, asynchronous chatting with a life coach is just as effective.

Some of these mental health startups even go so far as to suggest that continuity of care isn't important and that people do well with anyone who might answer the text, not necessarily someone who has a therapeutic alliance and a relationship with the client.

While there is much that is still unknown in terms of the reliability of these claims, we remain extremely skeptical. How can the demands for increased individual psychotherapy with the same clinician over time be regulated as a law in some states while asynchronous chat-based text therapy is deemed effective at the same time?

The reality is that the value of these interventions likely lies somewhere in between. Some people might benefit from some of these options some of the time and may need other forms of care at other times.

In the meantime, due to the significant supply-demand mismatch and a continuing rise of anxiety, depression, and stress-related disorders, people continue to turn to their health-care providers. Where applicable, embedding mental health clinicians in offices that care for people in primary care settings such as family medicine, pediatrics, and maternal-child has shown to dramatically reduce stigma and increase initiation of care as well as continuation with treatment.

Depending on the culture and family system, an individual may or may not have initial support from their loved ones. It is crucial to realize this and educate patients on the importance of social support networks during their healing process. Many elements in this book touch on the value of promoting healthy social networks.

As we write this book, there is talk of new variants and an overall increasing incidence of the COVID virus. There continues to be wars in various countries, and the impact of the climate crisis on our day-to-day lives is undeniable. According to CNN, the summer of 2023 reportedly had the highest (global) temperatures in recorded history, and the fervor of an upcoming presidential election in the United States is adding to the intensity of the heat.

Social and digital media continue to erode our attention span and capture our attention through fear and addictive doom scrolling. Fear of missing out is being replaced with a post- burnout nihilism in which non-player character (NPC) trends are going viral, with the explicit message of 'don't think.' The defense mechanism pendulum of denial and refusal to acknowledge has swung so far that people are reinforced to check out rather than searching within.

Confidently Chill represents a tool in our armament of antidotes to combat what seems to be an endless barrage of anxiety, stress, and confusion. We view fostering and maintaining a healthy attitude and hope for the future as a major opportunity. As our identities have changed over the past several years, as well as how we view ourselves and our relationships, we must learn to create new healthy habits that will sustain us long term. In this book, we dive deep into the cost-benefit analysis of our mental well-being as well as recommendations for healthy living.

The creative writing prompts and exercises included in this book have been designed to encourage you to be in touch with your current thoughts and realize the multiple angles from which anxiety and stress affect you. We set the stage by putting things in context, focusing on what you can control, prioritizing self-compassion, and providing skills to become a calmer, more confident version of yourself.

1.3 Stress Diathesis Model of Anxiety

As the intellectually curious person open to rational adventure that you are, we ask you which came first: your anxiety caused by genetics or something that happened to you causing you to become anxious?

The answer to this question lies at the heart of the stress diathesis model.

In the context of anxiety and related disorders, the term *diathesis* describes a person's inborn predispositions that increase their susceptibility to worry and anxiety. These inherent vulnerabilities may include genetics or traits that were passed on from their parents.

The term *stress* denotes external stimuli, life changes, traumas, and issues that one experiences. As discussed at great length in our prior book *Re-Write* (2023), we know that life events can have major psychological consequences, including anxiety and other stress-related disorders.

This model of anxiety refers to the interaction between the stress and the diathesis of the individual and the threshold at which they develop a disorder. As we discuss in

Chapter 2, 'Identifying and Treating Anxiety,' for a set of symptoms to be classified as a pathological disorder, they must significantly interfere with the person's day-to-day life.

The tipping point at which an individual begins to experience serious enough consequences of the stressor is dependent on both the burden of diathesis and the severity of the stress. The intricate interplay between cause and effect is genuinely fascinating, and the more we learn about ourselves, the better equipped we will be to stave off feelings of being overwhelmed and gain control.

1.4 What to Expect

> **The world is indeed full of peril, and in it there are many dark places; but still there is much that is fair, and though in all lands love is now mingled with grief, it grows perhaps the greater.**
> —J.R.R. Tolkien, *The Fellowship of the Ring*

Confidently Chill was written by two expert, best-selling clinicians, with over 40 years of experience taking care of tens of thousands of patients. Both Duygu and Yener have worked in private and public clinical care and in acute-care spaces such as inpatient hospitals, as well as outpatient settings, including community health clinics.

The book has been designed to be user friendly, approachable, and engaging. It can be opened randomly for clinical wisdom and guidance as well as being used in clinical practice with a therapist. This workbook is unique in that it includes interactive elements such as creative writing prompts in the context of current real-world events.

Duygu and Yener Balan have been interviewed dozens of times, and the most common question they are asked concerns the increasing trends of self-diagnosis and online media use. This book serves as an evidence-based, up-to-date resource that teaches:

- Tools and skills to better understand anxiety disorders and how they may impact one's day-to-day life.
- That anxiety can be managed and does not need to be in the driver's seat of one's life.
- Evidence-based clinical treatment options, including psychosocial as well as mediation management options.
- Mindfulness techniques that can be practiced while calm and used when feeling anxious, worried, or stressed.
- Concepts of practicing self-acceptance to foster healing.
- Insights that help develop self-compassion, which can help build relationships with others.
- Principles of autonomy and the extreme value of self-reliance and being resourceful.
- Clinical and practical applications of confidence in the context of the healing journey and self-discovery.

This book is divided into four parts.

The first part, titled 'The Call to Adventure,' comprises the first three chapters: 'Introduction to *Confidently Chill*,' 'Identifying and Treating Anxiety,' and 'Balan 3-2-1 Method.'

- We wrote this in an easy-to-understand and relatable manner, accessible to all readers.
- This section discusses the individual's journey through understanding and healing from stressors that may cause anxiety and can also be used as a supplement to therapy.
- In addition to psychosocial modalities and biological treatments for anxiety, we discuss culturally sensitive approaches to ensuring inclusive and equitable care.
- The Balan 3-2-1 Method, initially introduced in *Re-Write* (2023) is a creative writing experience that draws from mindfulness, bibliotherapy, somatic exercises, meditation, self-compassion, narrative psychology, and psychodrama.

The second part, titled 'Crossing the Threshold,' includes the chapters 'Value of Treatment,' and 'Brain, Body, and Behaviors.'

- We dive deep into the value of treating anxiety and related disorders, as well as the biology of the brain and nervous system to promote better understanding of how our thoughts and behaviors are impacted by anxiety.
- This section offers significant evidence of the value of expressive writing and the return on investment of such therapies.
- We include evidence-based, up-to-date clinical information on the connection between the brain and the body and its impact on our behaviors.
- The interactive exercises empower the reader to be as informed about their mind and body as possible and to try different techniques from the different modalities offered.

Part 3 is titled 'The Ordeal,' and includes the chapters 'COVID, Fear, and Grief,' and 'Un-Social Media.'

- We discuss shared experiences over the past several years, including the impact of the pandemic and associated responses at home, school, and the workplace.
- Included are psychosocial risk factors as well as protective factors for mitigating and overcoming serious anxiety responses.
- We discuss the causes and consequences of social and digital media misuse.
- This part concludes with detailed, evidence-based recommendations for individuals, families, school systems, and workplace environments.

The final part of the book, appropriately titled 'The Road Back,' includes the chapters 'Confidence and Recovery,' 'Safety Planning,' and 'Confidently Chill in Our New Normal.'

- Through stigma reduction and normalizing the experience and symptoms shared by others, this section increases the reader's sense of control.
- Emotional regulation, resilience, compassion, and kindness are among the topics discussed, as well as the power of music, humor, and healthy eating.
- We use our decades of combined clinical experience and expertise to provide an interactive chapter on safety planning that can be completed alone or with a clinical team.
- We talk about our path so far, make recommendations for equitable access to mental health care, and dive into climate change and eco anxiety as emerging issues for today's youth.

The book is rounded out with websites, phone numbers, and additional resources to connect with societies and organizations.

Lastly, we include a section that provides a sneak peek into the graphic novel, written by Duygu and Yener and illustrated by Nadir, titled *Kader's Quest*, which complements the learnings in this textbook.

Our intention is for those seeking increased understanding of their anxiety or the issues their loved ones are facing to use this book as a resource. While it has been written in a way that allows it to be used individually, this book can also be used in sessions for clients who need additional guided treatment or prompts. It can also be used in conjunction with individual as well as group therapy to foster a continuous therapeutic process. Some people ask for and benefit from homework outside sessions, and the writing prompts in this book can be assigned and reviewed later on.

1.5 Writing Prompt

Consider the following prompts as an introduction to thinking about your healing goals and creating your customized journey to overcome your anxieties and become confidently chill.

What are the sources of your anxieties and worries?

_____

_____

_____

_____

_____

_____

_____

Describe what your anxiety feels like.? How does it make you think? Where in your body do you feel it?

_____

_____

_____

_____

_____

_____

_____

If you woke up tomorrow with no anxiety, what would your life be like?

_____

_____

_____

_____

_____

_____

If you weren't spending time worrying, what would you be doing instead?

_____

_____

_____

_____

_____

_____

_____

_____

Chapter 2

Identifying and Treating Anxiety

2.1 Introduction

People talk about being anxious or having anxiety all the time. What does that even mean? How do you know if it is a disorder or a normal reaction to something? In clinical practice, there are set definitions and guidelines that allow the clinician to work with the individual to create a treatment plan to address their symptoms.

Anxiety disorders are among the most prevalent psychological disorders. They are the most common childhood-onset mental health disorders and can cause lifelong issues. If the individual has a history of anxiety disorders in early life, there is a two to three times increased risk of developing an anxiety disorder later in life.

Thankfully, as the stigma of mental illness continues to decrease, many of us are more comfortable talking about our feelings and seeking support and clinical care.

This workbook focuses specifically on anxiety and its impacts on the individual during the height of fear and worry, as well as later in life.

This chapter reviews each of the anxiety disorders and describes how a clinician would diagnose them and what management and treatment options are available. The discussion continues with a detailed description of all psychosocial therapeutic and common first-line medication options that have been approved for use in treating anxiety disorders.

Case examples as well as writing prompts are woven throughout to highlight aspects discussed as well as to allow the reader to pause, reflect, and digest the information provided.

Many diagnoses and their criteria were developed to help organize and subcategorize larger sets of problems. Research requires a way for different people to look at the same set of symptoms and come up with the same name for the problem.

Once a diagnosis is made, the individual and family, if part of the treatment team, will work with the clinician to discuss the next steps.

DOI: 10.4324/9781003413547-3

This is the gold standard we recommend:

- Work with your treatment team to inform you of what they think is going on.
- Keep asking questions until you truly understand the management and treatment options that are available and which ones are recommended for you.
- Take the time to discuss and think about the risks and benefits of the recommended care, including the duration of this path to wellness.
- Then, and only then, spend however long it takes looking at all the presented options and decide how you would like to proceed.

The chapter highlights overlaps between the subcategorized anxiety disorders as well as the value of becoming informed and the realization that there isn't a one-size-fits-all approach.

We encourage the reader to go through each of the descriptors provided. Even if you are only interested in or have been diagnosed with one, which is the only reason you are reading this chapter, consider looking through them to see how arbitrary the borders between some of the diagnoses are and how, in reality, you will understand more about yourself through gaining knowledge and making informed choices.

Please note the subtleties in choice of words when working with your treatment team, as well as throughout this book, such as management versus treatment or response reduction versus cure.

At minimum, the goals for care should include a reduction in symptoms so they don't interfere with the person's day-to-day life anymore.

> **The cave you fear to enter holds the treasure you seek.**
>
> —Joseph Campbell

2.2 Giving It a Name

We all have ways of describing our anxieties, fears, stress, and worries. Review some of the more common descriptors and use the space provided to add your own, including any made-up terms you use.

The feelings associated with anxiousness have been described as:

- Agitation
- Angst
- Anticipation
- Antsy
- Apprehensive
- Aversion
- Avoidance
- Butterflies in the stomach

- Can't catch your breath
- Can't focus
- Catastrophizing
- Choked up
- Concern
- Disconnected
- Disquiet
- Dissociating
- Dread
- Edginess
- Feeling jumpy
- Freaking out
- Frightful
- Having the jitters
- Heart skipping a beat
- Hyped up
- Hypervigilance
- Insecurity
- Lightheaded
- Nail biting
- Nervousness
- Overwhelmed
- Pacing
- Palpitations
- Panic
- Preoccupation
- Queasy
- Racing heart
- Racing thoughts
- Restless
- Rumination
- Scared
- Self-doubt
- Sense of impending doom
- Shaky
- Stomach in knots
- Stressed
- Sweating
- Tense
- Terror
- Trepidation
- Uncertain
- Uneasy
- Worried

Add your own anxiety descriptors:

_____

_____

_____

_____

_____

_____

_____

_____

The evidence suggests that the majority of adults who begin mental health treatment for anxiety-related issues are able to locate the beginning of their anxiety in childhood. More often than not, the concern was associated with a specific phobia.

While our psychology and psychiatry founding fathers, including William James and Sigmund Freud, have written in-depth propositions of the genesis of anxiety, this book will review contemporary evidence-based understandings and treatment suggestions. The value of appreciating the terror of solitude in infancy, as described by James in his 1890 book *The Principles of Psychology*, and Freud's discussion of the birthing experience as being the first source of anxiety in his 1908 book *The Interpretation of Dreams* are ideas we encourage you to explore separately.

We know that anxiety, fear, and worry that begin in childhood are strongly correlated with further burgeoning mental health disorders later in life, including depression and even substance use disorders.

This section details each type of anxiety-related disorder to emphasize familiarity with the signs and symptoms and to encourage early identification and treatment. Studies suggest that early treatment interventions can decrease later life incidence of worsening anxiety by between 30 and 50%.

Any way you choose to look at them, those numbers are a sound investment in improving quality of life and decreasing the cost of the illness burden.

2.3 Writing Prompt

Consider using the space provided to reflect on the writing prompt.

What are some circumstances associated with the onset of your anxiety?

_____

_____

_____

_____

If you trace your anxiety back to when you first experienced it, where do you land?

_____

_____

_____

_____

What are some early memories related to your anxiety?

_____

_____

_____

_____

How did your anxiety serve you?

_____

_____

_____

_____

What have you tried so far to help you through your feelings of anxiety?

_____

_____

_____

_____

2.4 Generalized Anxiety Disorder (GAD)

Imagine everyday anxiety, if it was excessive, directly impacted your day-to-day life more often than not and was difficult to control. That is essentially what the diagnosis generalized anxiety disorder is. Over 5% of people have GAD.

Of note, GAD is highly correlated with depression, which can further complicate the diagnostic picture, and may be more challenging to treat. See information in section 2.27, 'Anxiety and Depression.'

According to the *Diagnostic and Statistical Manual of Mental Disorders* (DSM), for a diagnosis of GAD, the patient must experience excessive anxiety and worry most of the time for at least six months, which has an impact on the person's day-to-day life. For younger people, the impact may show up at school, with performance issues; for others, it may be in the workplace setting.

The worrying must be difficult to control, and the anxiety must be associated with:

- Restlessness, feeling on edge or keyed up
- Having difficulty concentrating
- Being tired/fatigued easily
- Irritability
- Difficulty sleeping, such as falling asleep or staying asleep The sleep problems in GAD, as well as in other anxiety disorders, involve initial difficulty falling asleep due to worry about the previous day or the next day
- Muscle tension, twitching, or other nonspecific aches and pains

With younger people, especially those who may not be able to describe the history of the progression of their anxiety, the clinician must keep in mind things that may present with symptoms of worry and anxiety.

Physical health issues such as migraines, asthma, gastrointestinal issues, and thyroid diseases may have an anxiety component, although they must be worked up and treated separately.

Since the experience of anxiety is so common, there are many different ways individuals cope with it. Denying, suppressing, and ignoring anxiety, however, typically does not work as a long-term solution and may cause specific symptoms to worsen and spread to other parts of one's day-to-day life.

2.5 Writing Prompt

Consider using the space provided to reflect on the following prompt:

When you notice you are becoming anxious, what do you do?

_____

_____

_____

_____

_____

_____

_____

_____

_____

_____

2.6 GAD Management

2.6.1 Psychosocial Options

Cognitive Behavioral Therapy (CBT)

- CBT can be started alone or in conjunction with medication management options for GAD.
- Reports suggest that CBT in combination with medications may work better than either of them alone.
- According to studies, CBT itself works better than treatment, as well as placebo.
- Studies suggest that 10 to 15 sessions of CBT initially work well to reduce symptoms of GAD, then continue using the techniques learned on an ongoing basis to ensure the anxiety doesn't return.
- Treatment gains from CBT are generally preserved for up to a year after treatment.

2.6.2 Complementary Treatments

These are all shown to be effective as first-line complementary treatment options for generalized anxiety disorder. They reduce symptoms of anxiety and have a low barrier to entry, meaning they are fairly easy and inexpensive to try.

Mindfulness Meditation for Anxiety

- Research demonstrates that practicing mindfulness in addition to reducing symptoms of stress and anxiety improves insular functioning and connectivity in the brain.
- Mindfulness has also been shown to be noninferior to first-line medication treatment options.
- In 2013, researchers Hoge et al. conducted the first randomized controlled trial comparing mindfulness-based stress reduction with active control for GAD and confirmed the beneficial effects of mindfulness on anxiety symptoms and that it may also improve stress reactivity and coping.
- Mindfulness has also been shown to improve the understanding of and improve connections to the sensations from inside one's body, called interoception.

Therapeutic Yoga for Anxiety

■ Current literature suggests that therapeutic yoga improves physical and mental health and has significant impacts on the following areas:

- Cardiovascular system
  • Improves blood pressure.
  • Improves circulation.

- Respiratory system
  • Regulates breathing.

- Metabolism

- Improves weight control.
  • Decreases inflammation.

- Immune system
  • Decreases stress hormones and aids in decreasing inflammation throughout the body.

- Musculoskeletal system
  • Deliberate exercise that focuses on balance and strength has a positive and protective effect on muscles and joints.

- Mood, mental health, and wellness
  • Yoga balances the mind and body.
  • Studies suggest therapeutic yoga decreases stress, anxiety, and depression.
  • Improves focus and concentration.
  • Improves memory and attention.
  • Regulates sleep.

A 2021 paper by researchers Simon et al. discusses their randomized clinical trial on the efficacy of yoga versus CBT for treatment of GAD and concludes that yoga is efficacious for GAD, with results supporting CBT as first-line treatment.

2.6.3 Medication Options

Most medication options improve generalized anxiety in research studies compared to placebo. The key is to balance the benefits with the negative side effects and take the medications for only as long as necessary.

Selective serotonin reuptake inhibitors (SSRIs): This class of medication is generally regarded as safe with a low risk of serious adverse effects, although it still must be prescribed and monitored by a clinician.

SSRIs such as sertraline (generic for Zoloft), paroxetine (generic for Paxil), citalopram (generic for Celexa), escitalopram (generic for Lexapro), and fluoxetine (generic for Prozac), as well as serotonin and norepinephrine reuptake inhibitors (SNRIs) such as venlafaxine (generic for Effexor) are typically started first, with some of the others added to either reduce side effects of the meds or help quickly reduce the symptoms of anxiety.

Studies suggest staying on a medication for GAD for around 12 months. The purpose is to give the medicine enough time to work continuously and effectively in the body and brain while the patient gains the tools needed to learn about anxiety and how to keep it at a minimum.

> **Stay afraid, but do it anyway. What's important is the action. You don't have to wait to be confident. Just do it and eventually the confidence will follow.**
>
> —Carrie Fisher

2.7 Panic Attacks

Panic attacks are described in the DSM as a discrete period of intense fear or discomfort that involves a number of physical and mental symptoms that peaks within ten minutes. Diagnostically, four or more of the symptoms are required for it to be categorized as a panic attack.

As many symptoms are physiologic in nature, panic attacks and panic disorder are considered diagnoses of exclusion. It is important to seek a medical workup to rule out physical causes of the symptoms and then focus on the psychological implications.

Elements of a panic attack include:

■ Cardiopulmonary symptoms:

- Racing heartbeat
- Chest pain
- Feeling short of breath
- A 'sense of impending doom' or feeling as if in imminent danger

■ Neurological symptoms:

- Feeling dizzy, lightheaded, or faint
- Sensations of trembling or shaking
- Tingling or numbness (paresthesia)

■ Autonomic symptoms:

- Sweating
- Chills
- Hot flushes
- See Chapter 5, 'Brain, Body, and Behaviors,' for more information on the autonomic nervous system

■ Psychological symptoms:

- Feelings of unreality (derealization)
- Feeling detached from oneself (depersonalization)

- Intense fear of dying
- Fear of losing control
- Fear of going crazy

■ Gastrointestinal symptoms:

- Nausea
- Choking feeling
- Stomach cramps
- Intestinal distress

Untreated, panic attacks can become more frequent and complicated episodes, as well as developing into other specific phobias, such as fear of leaving the home. Panic and severe anxiety episodes can then take over one's day-to-day life, destroying one's quality of life. This can result in avoiding social situations, substance use issues, problems with focus and concentration, and difficulty at school or work.

We have cared for individuals who have had untreated extreme forms of panic resulting in depression and suicidal thoughts. Thankfully, there are safe and effective treatment modalities for panic, described in the next section.

2.8 Panic Disorder

A panic disorder is when a person has recurrent panic attacks. People can experience panic disorder with or without agoraphobia. Agoraphobia is described as feeling fear and anxiety of being in a place perceived to be difficult to escape from or embarrassing.

Of note, agoraphobia can be diagnosed whether or not panic attacks or panic disorder is present.

Clinical, real-world examples include being anxious in the following contexts:

■ Outside of the home, especially when unaccompanied
■ In a crowd, such as a mall
■ In open spaces
■ In a closed space, such as a movie theater or an elevator
■ Traveling by public transportation, such as a bus or plane
■ Standing in line

As with other specific phobias and social anxiety, those with agoraphobia find themselves in a pattern of avoiding situations that increase anxiety.

Clinical examples include the way exercise makes a person feel in their body. For example, increased heart rate may remind the person of how a panic attack feels, so the association is negative. We have cared for many clients with panic disorder who describe their avoidance of increasing their heart rate for fear of feeling the discomfort and retriggering themselves.

A client once described panic disorder as the 'intense fear of having more fear.' Since panic attacks typically come out of the blue, unexpected with no discernable triggers or warning, a person living with panic disorder always feels on edge, in anticipation of sheer terror, and therefore always feels tense, trying to compensate and arrange their lives to minimize the impact if and when a panic attack occurs.

People with panic disorder begin to change their behaviors in preparation for a future panic attack. They may avoid leaving their home, avoid public places and crowds, seek comfort in control, and plan for ways to exit a situation.

People with anxiety and panic attacks may engage in ritualistic, compensatory behaviors such as carrying medications or other safety items with them that bring some calm and sense of control. They engage in repetitive behaviors such as always going to the same grocery store as familiarity and predictability increase the sense of control. Finding healthy behaviors, such as finding ways to distract oneself from the experience such as turning to social or digital media, may be helpful in the short term, although untreated panic disorder often generalizes and impacts wider areas of the person's functioning.

2.9 Writing Prompt

Consider using the space provided to reflect on the following prompts:

How has your life been changed by anxiety and panic?

_____

_____

_____

_____

_____

_____

_____

What behaviors are now different?

_____

_____

_____

_____

_____

_____

_____

What situations do you avoid?

_____

_____

_____

_____

_____

_____

How has anxiety changed your eating habits?

_____

_____

_____

_____

_____

How do you feel about these responses?

_____

_____

_____

_____

_____

_____

_____

2.10 Panic Disorder Management

2.10.1 Psychosocial Options

Cognitive Behavioral Therapy (CBT)

- CBT teaches skills and coping strategies for panic attacks and anxiety, including elements of problem solving as well as relaxation techniques.
- The combination of the tools learned in CBT with mindful relaxation methods including breathing techniques allows people to reframe the experiences they are having and prevent full-blown panic or reduce it in the moment to make the feelings more manageable.

Exposure Therapy

■ This modality is particularly useful for individuals dealing with flashbacks from a traumatic event, as well as with a specific phobia.
■ The theory is that repeated exposure to elements or the entirety of the triggering stimulus in controlled, safe environments with a clinician will, over time, desensitize the individual to the stimulus and evoke less anxiety or panic.

Grounding

■ Grounding is another mode of relaxation and mindfulness that brings all five senses to the forefront of the individual. Anxiety, panic, and flashbacks have the commonality of distorting the experience of time, and grounding allows for regaining control. See later in this chapter for a writing prompt that teaches an example of the grounding technique.
■ According to a 2015 study by Chevalier, even a small number of grounding exercises serve to decrease symptoms of anxiety and improve mood more than relaxation techniques alone.
■ We discuss mindfulness and grounding techniques in depth in our clinical workbook *Re-Write: A Trauma Workbook of Creative Writing and Recovery in Our New Normal* (2023).

Medication Options

■ SSRIs continue to be the first choice for treatment of panic attacks. The Food and Drug Administration (FDA)–approved SSRIs for panic include fluoxetine (generic for Prozac), paroxetine (generic for Paxil), and sertraline (generic for Zoloft).
■ Serotonin and norepinephrine reuptake inhibitors (SNRIs): Venlafaxine (generic for Effexor XR) is FDA approved for panic disorder.
■ Benzodiazepines: As discussed throughout this book, this class of medication brings with it the immediate impact and reduction of symptoms along with the very real risk of developing a habit and dependence.

    – Benzodiazepines such as alprazolam (generic for Xanax) and clonazepam (generic for Klonopin) are FDA approved for panic disorder.
    – These medications should be used on a short-term basis, in conjunction with psychosocial treatment options and with close monitoring by a prescribing clinician.

2.11 Grounding Technique

This grounding skill will allow you to practice being aware of your surroundings. Consider using the space provided to reflect on the following elements and repeat as needed. You may write down your responses and revisit them later or rehearse this technique in your mind.

The purpose is to become comfortable doing this grounding exercise while relaxed so during a time of anxiety or panic, you will remember the method.

Focus on the elements around you right at this moment:

What are FIVE things you can see around you right now?

_____

_____

_____

_____

_____

What are FOUR things you can feel right now?

_____

_____

_____

_____

What are THREE things you can hear right now?

_____

_____

_____

_____

What are TWO things you can smell right now?

_____

_____

_____

_____

_____

What is ONE thing you can taste right now?

_____

_____

_____

_____

_____

2.12 Social Anxiety Disorder

When someone is experiencing fears that include most social situations, it may be termed a generalized social anxiety. Often, the person will realize the amount of concern and anxiety they have about the social situation is out of proportion and exaggerated compared to the reality of the situation.

While there are many protective elements of being sensitive to contextual cues and mimics of others, people with social anxiety are often hyper-responsive. This can lead to feeling increased stress, worry, and fear, resulting in compensatory behaviors. These stress responses then sensitize the person to even more intense stress responses in subsequent situations.

Social anxiety disorder is common, with over 10% of the population suffering from it at any given time.

As in all mental health diagnoses, this anxiety must directly affect the day-to-day life of the person and cause marked distress, impacting their interactions in many domains and their ability to function.

The anxiety must also not be directly caused by a medical issue or alcohol or other substance use.

Examples of social anxiety disorder include:

- Fear of being in unfamiliar social situations. Clinical examples include being anxious eating or drinking in front of someone else or having a conversation with others.
- Fear of giving a speech and the associated anxiety overlaps with social anxiety disorder, as well as specific phobias. (See later in this chapter.)
- Anxiety that the person will be embarrassed or rejected or that others will notice their anxiety, and they may feel humiliated. This may include fear of blushing, or trembling.
- Worry that the social situation may trigger a panic attack.

- Fear of eating in public, choking, or vomiting.
- Clinically, the person will either begin avoiding situations that cause such anxiety or put up with them with serious distress.
- Fear of using public restrooms.
- For younger people or those with developmental issues that may prevent clear verbal communication of inner psychic states, the outward manifestation of social anxieties may include crying, tantrums, or selectively not speaking in social situations.

As with other anxiety disorders, untreated social anxiety has a tendency to spread and impact multiple social activities, resulting in significantly altered behaviors and restrictions in enjoying life and may even lead to depression and self-injurious thoughts and behaviors.

2.13 Social Anxiety Disorder Management

2.13.1 Psychosocial Options

Cognitive Behavioral Therapy (CBT)

- CBT remains the most effective form of therapy for anxiety, including social anxiety.
- Exposure therapy, as discussed earlier, is an effective skill that allows the individual to reduce feelings of anxiety and stress and to build confidence.

Skills Training

- Individual and group-level skills training and education are very effective in treating social anxiety.
- Practicing coping skills and effective communication styles and role playing reduce anxiety while providing a sense of calm and control in connection with others.

2.13.2 Medication Options

The first line of medication treatment of social anxiety disorder includes SSRIs such as paroxetine (generic for Paxil) and sertraline (generic for Zoloft).

For some, SNRIs such as venlafaxine (generic for Effexor XR) may also be an option.

Similar to the treatment of other anxiety disorders, benzodiazepines are also extremely effective at reducing symptoms of social anxiety.

Beta Blockers

- This class of medication is predominantly prescribed for people with heart- and blood pressure–related issues.
- Due to the mechanism of blocking the effects of adrenaline (epinephrine), beta blockers can be used for social anxiety. By reducing the physical symptoms associated with anxiety, such as increased heart rate and blood pressure, the person is able to uncouple those uncomfortable, distressing feelings with the social task, such as public speaking.

- The downside is that beta blockers are very effective at reducing heart rate and blood pressure and should only be used for short periods and infrequently when used for anxiety.

The curious paradox is that when I accept myself just as I am, then I can change.

—Carl R. Rogers

2.14 Specific Phobias

This diagnosis involves extreme, excessive fear and anxiety that comes from something the person is either exposed to, such as an animal or seeing blood; an active behavior, such as vomiting or choking; or a situation such as being in a tall building, flying, or giving a public speech.

For younger individuals or those with developmental disabilities, there are also situations that may trigger specific phobias such as loud sounds or costumed characters.

A person with a specific phobia instantly reacts to being exposed to whatever their trigger is, and the anxiety may become intense and develop into a panic attack. As with other anxieties, the individual either learns to avoid the specific cue altogether or has mechanisms to try to reduce their anxiety.

This specific phobia must bring significant distress to the person and interfere with their day-to-day lives.

2.15 Specific Phobia Management

2.15.1 Psychosocial Options

Exposure Therapy

- The most often recommended and most effective treatment for a specific phobia is exposure therapy. As with other anxieties and phobias, while it is important to know the specific stimulus that triggers the anxious response, it is even more important to get at the root of the avoidance and reactive compensatory behaviors.
- Exposure therapy manages and aims to eliminate the avoidance behavior that can generalize into other aspects of day-to-day life, severely limiting the person's ability to experience and enjoy life.

Medication Options

- Similar to social anxiety, the main treatment for specific phobias is time limited and for a short duration. They include beta blockers, as described earlier, as well as benzodiazepines.
- Caution is always advised in the use of medications that can cause more side effects than positive therapeutic effects, and, in the case of specific phobias, psychosocial, non-pharmacologic options should be tried first.

2.15.2 Other Anxiety and Stress-Related Disorders

Separation anxiety disorder and selective mutism are anxiety disorders that are typically seen in children. Parents and caregivers are at the center of the treatment options once diagnosis is made.

Selective mutism typically develops between ages two and four, and separation anxiety develops around age seven. There is a correlation between separation anxiety disorder in early life and an increased risk of developing panic disorder later in life.

Obsessive-compulsive disorder, acute stress, and posttraumatic stress disorders were classified under anxiety disorders in the fourth edition of the DSM, but in the revised fifth edition, they are in separate diagnostic categories. These diagnoses continue to share overlaps in symptoms and may impact the person's life in similar ways, which is why we include them in this book.

2.16 Obsessive-Compulsive Disorder (OCD)

Diagnostic criteria for OCD include having either obsessions or compulsions that impact the person's day-to-day functioning and cause significant distress. While anxiety disorders impact over a third of the population, the prevalence of OCD is currently around 3%.

The pandemic has added fuel to the flame of people with OCD and those with a propensity towards obsessive and compulsive traits. Decontamination rituals were encouraged through the fear of the unknown in an attempt to seek safety and reassurance, although these pandemic-derived rituals blossomed into communal panic and irrationality.

While some of these reassurance-seeking rituals can provide immediate relief from anxiety and doubt, those with OCD may obsessively imagine they were not sufficient, resulting in the need for further rituals.

Obsessions are defined as:

■ Recurrent and persistent thoughts
■ Intrusive or impulsive thoughts or images that are difficult to control and cause stress, anxiety, and discomfort

Examples of obsessions include:

■ Fear of germs, contamination, getting sick
■ Fear of saying inappropriate things
■ Fear of thinking scary thoughts, such as hurting a loved one intentionally or that a loved one will get hurt in an accident
■ Fear of acting out or being impulsive or sexually inappropriate
■ Concerns about intrusive images or having sexual, violent, or otherwise disturbing thoughts
■ Concerns about violent impulses turned inwards, such as self-injurious thoughts, or aggressivity turned outwards
■ Preoccupation with symmetry, order, or exactness

Compulsions are defined as:

■ Behaviors that are performed in response to a recurrent thought (obsession), with the goal of decreasing the anxiety the obsessions cause. These behaviors may be ritualistic and can be excessive.

Examples of compulsions include:

■ Excessive cleaning, decontamination, or use of gels or hand sanitizers
■ Ritualistically checking and the urge to recheck locks, stoves, or candles
■ Checking whether they hurt themselves or others, intentionally or accidentally
■ Patterns of nail biting or hair pulling
■ Repetitive behaviors such as walking back and forth or repeating a task already completed
■ Creating lists and organizing excessively
■ Superstitious beliefs and self-soothing behaviors that are excessive
■ Repeating specific words, prayers, or lists

2.17 Writing Prompt

Consider using the space provided to reflect on the following prompt:

What reassurance-seeking rituals do you have? Do they intensify under stress? If yes, how?

_____

_____

_____

_____

_____

_____

_____

_____

_____

_____

_____

_____

_____

2.18 OCD Management

2.18.1 Psychosocial Options

Cognitive Behavioral Therapy (CBT)

- CBT is an effective first-line treatment method that helps the person understand and control their obsessive thoughts.
- Forms of CBT for OCD include both imaginal and situational exposure and the prevention of the response triggered by the obsessional thoughts.

Exposure and Response Prevention (ERP)

- ERP is a form of cognitive behavioral therapy (CBT) and is considered one of the main forms of effective management of OCD.
- This form of therapy gradually exposes the person to the stimulus, object, or obsession and teaches them how to resist and cope with the urges to complete the compulsions and rituals.
- Treatment planning for OCD includes coming up with a list of the triggers that cause the person discomfort. They are then ranked in order of no discomfort to extreme discomfort. The treatment goal is to continue to work up the rank order list, be exposed to the stimulus – either imaginal or in real life – and work through the responses in a safe, therapeutic environment.

2.18.2 Medication Options

Finding medical management of OCD that works may take some trial and error and some time before symptoms are reduced. According to the literature, medications for OCD reduce up to 40% of symptoms. For these reasons, it is important to continue to work with a clinician using psychosocial modalities such as ERP while also taking any prescribed medication.

Several antidepressant medications are FDA approved to treat OCD. Among them are clomipramine (generic for Anafranil), fluoxetine (generic for Prozac), fluvoxamine (generic for Luvox), paroxetine (generic for Paxil), and sertraline (generic for Zoloft).

2.18.3 Other Treatment Options

Transcranial Magnetic Stimulation (TMS)

- TMS is an FDA-approved treatment that involves a series of sessions. A device that has an electromagnetic coil that is placed on the person's head. This magnet delivers pulses that stimulate nerve cells in the brain and improve OCD symptoms over time.
- While this treatment option is noninvasive, it is typically used when other treatment options have been tried and not shown the desired symptom relief.

Deep Brain Stimulation (DBS)

- DBS is an FDA-approved, invasive procedure for the treatment of OCD.
- The process involves electrodes, which are implanted in certain areas of the brain of the person suffering from OCD. Electrical impulses are then sent through these electrodes, resulting in decreased OCD symptoms.
- As with most invasive procedures, the general recommendation is to try noninvasive, less intense treatment options before turning to DBS.

> We have advantages. We have a cushion to fall back on. This is abundance. A luxury of place and time. Something rare and wonderful. It's almost historically unprecedented. We must do extraordinary things. We have to. It would be absurd not to.
> —Dave Eggers, *A Heartbreaking Work of Staggering Genius*

2.19 Trauma Disorders

Exposure to a traumatic or stressful event is the hallmark of trauma disorders. Traumatic experiences may include being in a war, being a victim of violence, or experiencing a natural disaster such as an earthquake or a fire.

The consequences of experiencing such a life-threatening traumatic event often occur shortly after the event, although clinically, we have seen the symptoms of posttraumatic stress disorder develop months or years after the exposure. The immediate reaction to a traumatic event may sometimes develop into a diagnosis of an adjustment disorder or an acute stress disorder, which then, after time, may progress into a posttraumatic stress disorder diagnosis.

These disorders include posttraumatic stress disorder, acute stress disorder, adjustment disorder, reactive attachment disorder, and disinhibited social engagement disorder, as well as prolonged grief disorder. For these trauma- and stress-related disorders, there's always a specifier indicating that the symptoms experienced must be separate from normal bereavement or prolonged with grief.

2.20 Adjustment Disorder

The DSM criteria for an adjustment disorder include beginning within three months of exposure to a stressor. Similar to all other psychiatric diagnosis, the symptoms experienced must impact the person's day-to-day functioning.

Symptoms of an adjustment disorder typically begin three months after a stressor and last for up to six months.

Symptoms of adjustment disorders include feeling anxious and agitated, difficulty concentrating, loss of interest, feeling stressed, and difficulty sleeping, as well as possible nonspecific physical symptoms such as headaches, being tired, or body aches.

As can be inferred from this list of symptoms, adjustment disorders can be classified as with depressed mood, with anxiety, with mixed anxiety and depressed mood, with disturbance of conduct, mixed, or unspecified.

Examples of possible causes of adjustment disorder include:

- School issues, such as academic trouble, changing schools, or graduating
- Work-related issues, including performance stress or being passed for a promotion
- Moving to a new area for college or for a career
- Financial stressors
- Life-changing events, such as getting married
- Making a large purchase, such as buying a home
- Having a baby
- Relationship issues, such as breaking up
- Medical or mental health issues
- Getting divorced
- Major climate events, such as a hurricane or volcano
- Unexpected disasters, such as global pandemics
- Living in an unsafe home or neighborhood
- Other shifts in life milestones, including retirement and children moving away
- Death of a loved one

2.21 Writing Prompt

Consider using the space provided to reflect on the following two prompts:

What were some tools that helped you cope during a stressful event or phase of life?

_____

_____

_____

_____

_____

_____

_____

_____

_____

Who was in your support network during that time?

_____

_____

_____

_____

_____

_____

_____

_____

_____

_____

2.22 Adjustment Disorder Management

2.22.1 Psychosocial Options

Psychotherapy

- Talk therapy is effective at exploring the cause and effect of current stressors and provides guidance in coping with the situation and the difficult emotions attached to it.
- Individual, family, and group therapy work extremely well at addressing the symptoms of adjustment disorder, as well as providing coping strategies and promoting resilience.
- Building support networks is a key element of the therapeutic process as it reduces the sense of isolation. Self-awareness allows the individual to make meaning of their experience and prevents negative experiences from having such an impact on the person in the future.

2.22.2 Medication Options

SSRIs and SNRIs are first-line medication treatment options, as are benzodiazepines, although the condition itself is often time limited and responds well to talk therapy.

2.23 Acute Stress Disorder

There are a significant number of overlapping diagnostic criteria listed in the DSM for both acute and posttraumatic stress disorders. The lengthier description is provided later in the book. The main thing to understand about the difference between acute and post-traumatic stress disorder is the time of onset of symptoms and duration of pathology.

Acute stress disorder, according to the DSM, typically persists three days to one month after exposure to the traumatic event. Posttraumatic stress disorder, on the other hand, involves symptoms that last four weeks or longer.

2.24 Acute Stress Disorder Management

2.24.1 Psychosocial Options

Cognitive Behavioral Therapy (CBT)

- Trauma-focused CBT is an effective method of reducing symptoms of acute stress disorder.
- According to a 2008 study by Kornor, early trauma-focused CBT works effectively to lessen the chance the severity will perpetuate a longer, more complicated form of posttraumatic stress disorder.
- Exposure therapy is often used, in addition to other mindfulness techniques such as meditation and breathing exercises to address the acute stress symptoms.

2.24.2 Medication Options

The literature suggests mixed results for treating acute stress disorders with medications such as SSRIs or other antidepressants. Robust, significant positive effects of medications are seen when treating PTSD.

Again, benzodiazepines do help with short-term, acute anxiety, although this not a preferred or recommended long-term solution for anything.

2.25 Posttraumatic Stress Disorder (PTSD)

As mentioned earlier, PTSD results from an exposure to the threat of serious injury, death, or sexual violence. The individual must either have experienced this directly, witnessed it, or learned of the traumatic event of a close family member.

The individual must be experiencing the physical and psychological consequences described here for more than a month, and as mentioned earlier, the disorder must cause clinically significant impairment in the daily functioning of the person.

Hallmarks of PTSD include:

- Flashbacks
- Re-experiencing the traumatic event
- Recurrent, intrusive memories of the event
- Perceptual distortions
- Decreased memory of the event
- Heightened startle responses
- Hypervigilance
- Avoidance-type reactions

- Thoughts that one may not have a future or anything to look forward to
- Sleep disturbances

While the majority of people will experience a traumatic event in their life, the recent pandemic being a global equalizer, not everyone develops PTSD. If you are experiencing thoughts of hopelessness; feelings of a foreshortened future; the desire to be dead; or self-injurious thoughts, ideas, or actions, please go to your nearest emergency department and connect with a mental health clinician.

Research continues into the cause of the resilience and protective factors that mitigate the progression to debilitating illness. For an in-depth review, see our previous book *Re-Write* (2023).

2.26 PTSD Management

2.26.1 Psychosocial Options

Trauma-Focused Psychotherapy

- This form of therapy for PTSD often incorporates elements of CBT as well as exposure therapy. This is typically recommended as the first line unless other factors such as depression are an issue.

Eye Movement Desensitization and Reprocessing (EMDR)

- EMDR is an evidence-based treatment for PTSD that helps individuals process traumatic memories and reduces associated symptoms.
- During EMDR treatment, the person is asked to recall the traumatic event while the clinician moves their finger gradually back and forth in front of the person's face. The client is asked to introspect and acknowledge what they are feeling.
- EMDR allows for the processing of information and helps the person incorporate the traumatic event into a memory that is adaptive. Without retraumatizing the person, EMDR allows for the retelling of the event in a safe environment.
- Desensitization is one of the main mechanisms by which this technique works as it allows the person to focus on the memory while reducing their emotional response to it.

2.26.2 Medication Options

- SSRIs and SNRIs are the main choices for medication management of PTSD.

2.27 Anxiety and Depression

Anxiety and depression are both very common and often occur at the same time. Studies suggest that between 40% and upwards of 75% of people with depression also meet criteria for an anxiety disorder at some point in their lives.

As with any diagnosis, there must be several of the symptoms of depression occurring around the same time for many days in a row, and they must interfere with one's day-to-day life and functioning. According to the DSM, there must be five or more symptoms at the same time during a two-week period that are a marked change from the way the person was before. Similarly, the cause of the changes and symptoms must not be a medical issue or alcohol or other substances.

These diagnostic criteria are important to help the clinician distinguish between issues and to determine what to strive for during treatment. With any mental health concern someone has, we recommend discussing it with a licensed professional mental health clinician or primary care/family practice clinician. The goal is early identification so appropriate interventions can be ensured.

Depression is a serious illness, and, untreated, it can even be fatal. If you or a loved one is having suicidal thoughts or concerns, please call 911, if you are in the United States, or go to your nearest emergency department. We discuss urgent and emergent care of depression and other disorders in *Big Book of Emergency Department Psychiatry: A Patient Centered Guide to Operational Improvement* (2017).

Symptoms of depression include:

■ Feeling sad, with down, depressed mood most of the day, almost every day
■ Sleep difficulties, such as trouble falling asleep or staying asleep
■ Tiredness, feeling decreased energy nearly every day
■ Difficulty concentrating or trouble making decisions nearly every day
■ Changes in eating patterns, including weight gain or weight loss (unintentional, when not trying to change weight or dieting)
■ Changes in energy patterns, described as psychomotor agitation or retardation, every day, that are observable by others
■ Anhedonia – a decreased interest in things that were enjoyable in the past
■ Feeling worthless or having excessive feelings of guilt
■ Thoughts of death, thinking of suicide, having a plan for self-harm, or attempting suicide

Since there are multiple issues occurring simultaneously, the symptoms and the way this combination affects the person can be more severe. Anxiety is a longer-lasting, ongoing problem, and depressive episodes can come and go. People with both have an overlap of issues, oftentimes making the suffering even greater.

Clinically, it may be challenging to clearly separate some of the overlapping symptoms of anxiety from those that are components of the depressive disorder. The individual may have trouble recalling which came first as anxiety and depression can cyclically blend into one another.

More recently, the literature supports the specifier 'anxious distress' from the DSM, which can be diagnosed with depression. Of significance is that, according to studies, between 60% and upwards of two-thirds of people with major depressive disorder meet diagnostic criteria for the anxious distress specifier.

The most common symptoms of this specifier include feeling on edge, difficulty concentrating due to feeling worried, inner tension, and agitation. The DSM requires the symptoms be present most of the time during the major depressive episode and discusses how concentration due to worry, feeling tense, feeling a sense of loss of control, feeling restless, and feeling something bad will happen are part of the diagnostic picture.

Symptoms such as agitation, restlessness, and irritability are common. Difficulties with impairment of memory and attention are also described. People with anxiety and depression often have more trouble functioning in their day-to-day lives. Suicidal ideation is also elevated in people with the two, compared to major depression alone.

Similarly, it may be more difficult to get a proper response to treatment, requiring either higher doses of medications or longer psychosocial treatment.

Risk factors for having anxiety and depression at the same time include:

- Severe anxiety
- Panic attacks
- Long-time anxiety
- Sleep-related issues as
- Female gender
- Family history of anxiety and depression
- Prior trauma
- Decreased education
- Fewer social support structures
- Living alone
- Other socioeconomic issues such as poor quality of life
- Personality traits such as neuroticism

As discussed earlier, the key is appropriate identification and intervention. Since anxious depression is often more complicated in its process and may be more challenging to treat to remission, safety is paramount.

2.28 Bio-Psychosocial Determinants and Risk

This normal anxiety of life cannot be avoided except at the price of apathy or the numbing of one's sensibilities and imagination.
—**Rollo May,** *The Meaning of Anxiety*

The factors that increase the risk of an anxiety disorder are multifactorial and complex. From a bio-psychosocial framework, they can be thought of in categories that include the physical, cognitive, psychological, social, evolutionary, and spiritual, as well as other external factors such as location, historical, and political.

- Age

  - Anxiety disorders are less prevalent and occur at lower frequencies in older individuals.

- Culture

  - A person's background, culture, and country of origin, all influence the way they experience the world and express their emotions.
  - It is critical to appreciate that, within cultural and ethnic groups, individual variations occur, and therefore, the best way to care for someone with anxiety is to be culturally sensitive and pay attention.
  - Later in this chapter, we discuss cross-cultural aspects of anxiety disorders.

- Cognitive factors:

  – As discussed in greater detail in Chapter 5, 'Brain, Body, and Behaviors,' there are a number of ways individuals processes information and emotions that influence the development of anxiety disorders.
  – Hypersensitivity to threats as well as exaggerated responses to perceived threats are associated with increased risk.
  – Difficulty differentiating levels of risk from environmental information and intolerance of uncertainty can cause and are caused by increased anxiety.

- Competitive sports and academics

  – Studies have shown that focus on competition, either in advanced placement academic classes or in organized sports, increases the risk of anxiety.
  – Athletes, especially those in high school and college, are at increased risk due to their competitive nature, their training regimens, and the pressure placed on them.
  – The risk of losing, as well as the possibility of the reward of obtaining a high-paying career or becoming a professional athlete, are increased stressors that lead to higher levels of anxiety.

- Developmental factors:

  – Infants who display heightened distress reactions to new things, as well as young children who excessively avoid new situations, are at increased risk.
  – Behaviorally inhibited children are at increased risk of developing anxiety disorders later in life.

- Diet:

  – Diet in this context refers to anything one eats, drinks, uses, or abuses.
  – The current literature on causal links between diet and developing or worsening anxiety and panic is robust and is discussed in Chapter 5, 'Brain, Body, and Behaviors.'

- Education:

  – Lower levels of education are associated with increased risk.

- Employment:

  – Unemployment, and income insecurity are associated with increased risk.

- Environmental factors:

  – In addition to the neighborhood and surrounding areas one grows up in, exposure to uncertainty and traumatic events including racism and bullying, either virtual or in physical reality, increase risk.

- Repetitive exposure to these issues, coupled with the lack of emotional maturity, resilience, or avenues to process these experiences increases risk.
- Individual traumatic experiences can lead to the development of specific phobias.
- Duration and level of involvement in digital media, video gaming and social media are highly correlated with anxiety and is discussed in detail in Chapter 7, 'Un-Social Media.'

■ Ethnicity-related factors:

- Exposure to racism, bigotry, any form of separation, and humiliation are all known risk factors for developing anxiety and stress-related disorders.
- Studies indicate that the burden of illness in anxiety disorders is greater for those impacted by ethnicity-related stressors.

■ Gender:

- According to a 2011 study by McLean et al., there is a preponderance of women among all the anxiety disorder types examined. They did not, however, note a difference in gender for the mean age of onset of anxiety disorders.
- The persistence of anxiety disorders was also found to be similar between genders.

■ Genetic factors:

- The continued debate of nature versus nurture remains unresolved, especially in the domain of anxiety disorders, although family studies including twin studies indicate a correlation with familial transmission of anxiety disorders. In other words, it is clinically important to understand one's family history of anxiety and other psychological issues to get clues into what may be influencing oneself.
- Clinicians will often ask about family history to develop a differential diagnosis, ultimately working towards a specific diagnosis as well as aiding in creating a treatment plan.
- There certainly is an element of intergenerational passing on of trauma and the resulting anxiety and other psychological comorbidities.
- Studies suggest that specific genetic variants, including in the serotonin transporter gene (5-HTT), impact emotional response and anxiety risk. There are several other genes that are being investigated, although the reality is, at this time, the data and clinical relevance of a specific gene causing an anxiety disorder are unclear.

■ Medical comorbidities:

- Newly diagnosed as well as long-term, chronic illnesses add to the stressors and are known risk factors for decreased resilience and coping skills and development of anxiety disorders. Any physical illness or medical issue is associated with stress for the individual.
- Hospital stays, especially longer ones and those requiring intensive care unit treatment, are associated with increased risk of anxiety, depression, and post-traumatic stress disorder.

– There are specific illnesses, such as thyroid problems and heart and lung issues, that cause anxiety or symptoms like worry, panic, and difficulty concentrating. We discuss these in detail in Chapter 5, 'Brain, Body, and Behaviors.'

■ Occupation:

– Some occupations are known to have an associated increased risk of developing anxiety as well as stress-related disorders. These include police officers, firefighters, first responders, and military personnel.

■ Parenting style:

– Overprotective and anxious parenting styles increase anxiety in children. Attachment anxiety and avoidance increase the risk of developing anxiety and depression. How people develop relationships and their self-perception, coping mechanisms, and ability to create bonds with others are all impacted by parent-child attachment styles.
– Emotionally unavailable, highly critical, and insensitive parenting are also known to increase risk.
– Environments where the child is unable to express their emotions or process their feelings increase risk.
– Depressed and anxious parents and parents struggling with mental health issues and addition pose higher risks of being negligent of their child's well-being or even being abusive. Struggling parents impact the general safety and security of the home and the available food and nutrition for the growing child, as well as modeling unhealthy coping mechanisms.
– Neglect and abuse by anyone, especially a parent/caregiver, are known risk factors.
– Factors that lead to these issues are extremely complicated and are often in combination with socioeconomic, educational, and occupational issues.

■ Place of birth:

– There are studies relating to places of birth and origins of family that increase the risk of anxiety disorders.
– Realizing complex and interconnected risk factors, including place of birth and cultural background, can assist the individual and clinical team in working towards understanding the symptoms in a culturally competent way.

■ Peri-partum:

– This is a term that describes the time during pregnancy right before birth and then after the delivery of the baby. The numerous biological as well as psychological changes during pregnancy put the person at increased risk.
– This is a time of known increased risk of sensitivity to the environment and maladaptive stress responses.
– Anxiety around the time of delivery is also linked with increased levels of

parenting stress. This stress was also reported to have increased during the pandemic, according to the findings in a review article by Arzamani et al. (2022).

–   The prevalence of generalized anxiety disorder in pregnant women was three to four times greater than in others.
–   Pregnant mothers reported the negative impact of social media, as well as the confusion, misinformation, and disinformation, also contributed to their anxiety levels.
–   Stress, anxiety, and other mental health issues during pregnancy may appear as:
    •   Maternal avoidance
    •   Frustration
    •   Decreased follow-up care for themselves and the unborn baby
    •   Sadness
    •   Feeling overwhelmed
    •   Decreased adherence to medications and other recommended guidelines
    •   Passivity
    •   Loss of motivation
    •   Change in appetite or malnutrition
    •   Decrease in reaching out for help, which results in delays in getting necessary preventative care, as well as diagnostic assessments to address symptoms of worry, fear, and stress.
    •   Decreased expressiveness
    •   Worry about the baby

–   Physiologically, stress impacts cortisol production, which is linked to negative outcomes for the mother as well as the unborn baby. The behavioral and other psychological issues described earlier all then impact and may complicate the delivery as well as the developmental outcomes of the baby. They have been associated with low birth weight, as well as neurodevelopmental disorders and other cognitive problems. Of note, mothers diagnosed with or thought to have COVID had a higher rate of early (pre-term) delivery.
–   A research article by Roberti et al. (2022) reviews the impact of the pandemic on postpartum women and the significant increase it caused in their anxiety levels.
    •   The study looked at the positive impact of home visits and how they improved the health of the mother.
    •   These visits served to decrease anxiety levels, decrease feelings of loneliness and isolation, provide support as needed, increase self-confidence, and help with parenting competencies.
    •   Mothers reported feeling the visits helped improve breastfeeding, helped them understand the infant's behaviors, and that they felt heard and supported and were able to express doubts and insecurities.
    •   They also allowed for earlier detection of mental health issues and provided a protective effect.

■   Socioeconomic status:

–   Lower socioeconomic status is associated with increased risk of anxiety.
–   Those born into homes with financial and housing insecurity may also be at risk of food insecurity and decreased access to health care.

– Associated environmental stressors as well as the increased burden of adverse childhood experiences compound the development of anxiety disorders.

■ Sleep:

– Healthy sleep practices and hygiene are critical for a balanced, healthy life. We know that sleep disturbances increase the risk of mental health concerns, including anxiety and depression. Anxiety is highly comorbid with depression, especially with adolescent depression. Severe sleep problems are also a known factor for increased suicidal thoughts and attempts.
– Insomnia (sleeping too few hours) and hypersomnia (sleeping too many hours) are both symptoms of a greater issue and must be taken seriously when they begin to interfere with a person's day-to-day life. For example, sleep problems can be caused by anxiety, and they can go on to cause anxiety.
– Anxiety can impact the quality of sleep as well as the content of dreams. These can then result in the loop described earlier, in which one affects the other.
– Sleep disturbances can also lead to cognitive issues such as poor impulsivity and poor judgment.
– Appropriate sleep impacts our immune system, and disturbances can lead to alterations in the serotonin and inflammatory pathways.
– Getting too few hours of sleep leads to feeling tired during the day and can create a loop of decreased physical activity, causing less restful sleep, causing problems the following day.
– A study by Kim et al. (2022) looked at adolescents, who are at an already high, and increasingly higher, risk of anxiety and depression. According to their results, shorter sleep duration was associated with both suicidal ideation and attempts.

■ Temperamental factors:

– Vulnerabilities including the individual's outlook on life are correlated with increased risk of anxiety and stress-related disorders.
– Survivors of adverse childhood experiences and traumatizing events are also at increased risk.

2.29 Predictors of Negative Outcomes

Predictors of negative outcomes of treatment for anxiety disorders include the following:

■ Duration:

– The longer the anxiety is untreated and longer it lasts, the more difficult it will be for treatment and complete relief of symptoms of the illness.

■ Severity at onset:

– The severity of symptoms of when the anxiety first starts is indicative of how treatment will likely proceed. The more severe at onset, the more challenging it will be to treat and the longer the feelings of anxiety may last.

■ Prior unsuccessful treatment:

  – Past mental health treatment outcomes are another area of concern, as partial or incomplete periods of anxiety and stress prolong the treatment of subsequent anxiety issues and make it more difficult.
  – This is a key reason we recommend people be mindful and aware of their minds and bodies and seek treatment when necessary. Once initiated, continue the work of healing, and stay in treatment until full remission of symptoms is obtained.
  – All too often we hear stories of people who start treatment for their anxiety, start to feel better, and either stop going to therapy or stop taking their medications before clinically indicated because they are doing better and later find the symptoms creeping back into their lives.
  – Anxiety typically doesn't start overnight, and it typically won't be cured overnight either.

■ Socioeconomic status:

  – In addition to lack of access to care and lack of funding, socioeconomic status also tips the scale towards decreased medical literacy and awareness of options.

■ Increased age:

  – The older the individual, according to the literature, the greater the likelihood of medical and other comorbidities. These then impact the person's ability to access care, increase potential medication interactions with treatment recommendations, and decrease the brain's and body's ability to heal.

■ Comorbid issues:

  – Anxiety with depression, as described earlier, is a serious complicator in healing to remission. The 'chicken or the egg' conundrum of whether the anxiety came first resulting in the depression or if mood issues resulted in compensatory unhealthy anxious behaviors and symptoms is an obvious concern as to which to treat and how soon the symptoms will resolve.
  – Substance use, another form of comorbid complicator, makes it increasingly difficult for both the individual and the provider to separate the symptoms of the true disorder from the influence of or withdrawal symptoms from the substance being used.
    • For example, when drinking alcohol, symptoms of anxiety typically decrease, although when the person stops drinking and the alcohol begins to be metabolized and removed from the body, feelings of anxiety amplify and can significantly worsen.

■ Lack of support networks:

  – While support systems, including access to care and availability of loved ones, are critical to healthy recovery, the opposite, in the form of active detractors and negative influences, can make healing more challenging.
  – Domestic violence, now referred to as intimate partner violence, is a known

predictor of negative outcomes in the treatment of anxiety (or anything for that matter) when active abuse continues.

■ Personal beliefs and self-efficacy:

- One's cognitive and interpersonal strengths are clear advantageous predictors of healing appropriately.
- The absence of individual strengths or relational savvy, on the flip side, is more difficult to remedy and may make the treatment of anxiety disorders more challenging.

Some of these circumstances are not immediately modifiable, such as age or severity of symptoms upon initial presentation to treatment, although it is valuable to work towards improving those that are. Literature supports the value of building the person's individual strengths early on in treatment to set a strong foundation for healing as well as learning skills to maintain feelings of wellness.

2.30 Writing Prompt

Consider using the space provided to reflect on the following two prompts:

What are some of your beliefs and values that contribute to your feelings of anxiety or stress?

_____

_____

_____

_____

_____

_____

_____

Now reflect on your values that are protective and help you keep negative feelings and thoughts of worry in control.

_____

_____

_____

_____

_____

_____

_____

_____

2.31 Equity

Studies indicate that racial and ethnic minority populations, particularly adolescents and young adults, are at a disadvantage in receiving care, especially mental health care. Lang et al. (2022) document that African American youth are less likely to be diagnosed and less likely to receive timely care.

While anxiety disorders are the most common and care options are fairly straightforward and efficacious when implemented, the reality of inequities in access and prevalent stigma continues to be a problem.

Risk factors for developing anxieties are correlated with socioeconomic and educational status, as well as exposure to violence and childhood adversity. Research indicates that ethnic and racial minority individuals are at an increased risk of developing anxiety disorders.

Coupling that with the comparatively decreased access to mental health care further exacerbates the short- and long-term effects of anxiety disorders. These individuals with untreated anxiety disorders are then at higher risk of developing depressive disorders, substance use disorders, and other psychosocial concerns, including educational and workplace challenges.

As discussed earlier, the bio-psychosocial determinants and risk factors for developing anxiety include adverse childhood experiences, food and income insecurity, discrimination, and unsafe neighborhoods. Unfortunately, in the United States, ethnic and racial minorities are impacted by these risk factors at a very high rate.

The heart of many of our recommendations includes appropriate access, and in the setting of already-disadvantaged populations, a culturally, racially, and psycho-socially sensitive approach must be taken. Research indicates that due to a number of financial and cultural factors, individuals from ethnic and racial minority groups are less likely to start mental health care and more likely to end treatment before completion.

As the pandemic progressed, we quickly became aware that minority populations were disproportionately affected by the virus and resulting social interventions. Lockdowns, school closures, and impacts on businesses large and small as well as limited access to health care impacted everyone, although, according to research, the impacts on the lives of minority and LGBTQIA+ individuals and families in the United States was dramatically worse.

An article by Weersing et al. (2022) discusses potential strategies to address health-care system disparities. The authors suggest matching clients with providers and community members of the same race/ethnicity, if preferred. In addition to cultural competence, the authors suggest sensitive patient-provider communications to further empathy and understanding of experiences of racism. Goals include recognition of implicit bias, reducing these barriers, and fostering cultural humility.

Skills that are recommended to ensure appropriate diversity, equity, and inclusion involve aspects of sensitivity training and cultural humility, as well as communication skills. To match clients with preferred providers, it is essential to have a diverse workforce.

Diversity in language, culture, country of origin, ethnicity, and religion is extremely valuable in ensuring meaningful connections that can lead to healing and recovery. Even though mental health clinicians are likely to be trained in empathic listening and developing rapport, it is very important to begin the exploration of one's own implicit biases. The ability to learn about oneself never ends, and evaluating oneself in terms of bias is extremely valuable.

2.32 Writing Prompt

Consider using the space provided to reflect on the following prompt:

What is most important to you in life?

_____

_____

_____

_____

_____

_____

_____

_____

2.33 Culturally Sensitive Anxiety Care

The dynamic nature of culture across communities all over the world is important to keep in mind. Especially when caring for clients in diverse areas, it is in everyone's best interest for the clinician to be respectful, intellectually curious, and humble.

Sensitivity to different values and beliefs begins with appropriate education and continues with authentic listening skills. If, as a clinician, you are wondering about something and think a specific intervention will improve the therapeutic relationship and move the client closer to their treatment goals, simply ask them.

In order to foster an open discussion about culture, there must be clear respect for personal boundaries. Personal space and privacy are valued differently, and to improve comfort levels in a session, culturally appropriate language must also be used. Avoid using medical terminology that may alienate the person and use respectful, inclusive language.

Explore communication preferences the client may have and any considerations and accommodations necessary, including translation services. The way people describe their worry, stress, anxiety, and sadness is fascinating and worth paying close attention to, as the flavor and quality of the descriptors will hide many valuable gems in unpacking the issues and helping care for them.

Access to care and personal health-related decision making are all important clues as to client's relationship with seeking help. Consider the impact of racism and racial discrimination on the individual that may have led to hesitancy and mistrust in the health-care system.

Make a note of when and why the person chose to begin their treatment. Understand how family dynamics influence reaching out for care and the social support structures they may have. Be mindful of spiritual or religious factors that may be relevant to the individual and their family.

Coping mechanisms are another important area of focus, based on the client's family, upbringing, and culture. Explore how they experience worry, shame, guilt, anxiety, and trauma.

We chose to write this workbook to help people explore their emotions in the additional forms of the written word and creative exercises. In the United States, for example, symptoms of anxiety, including chest tightness and elevated heart rate, are often feared to be an impending heart attack, as they share common sensations.

Other cultures describe their feelings of anxiety in their body differently and have varying ways of expressing them. If one is open and receptive to these nuances, with minimal judgment, the client will be more likely to share their narrative. As the exercises in this workbook can be done alone or in conjunction with a clinician, the person reflecting on the writing prompts and exercises has an increased chance of learning more about themselves.

While there is an increased pull towards individualism in Western societies, cultures that value the health of the social collective emphasize different parts of their identity and subsequent goals of treatment for their anxiety.

Both of us have cared for people in many different settings, including inpatient acute care, emergency departments, outpatient community clinics, directly on the street, and in many different health care organizations on both the East and West Coasts of the United States. As we speak several different languages and have lived in numerous countries, we are sensitive to the barriers that otherness brings and are extremely cautious about making our clients feel seen, heard, and respected.

2.34 Writing Prompt

Consider using the space provided to reflect on the following prompt:

What did you want as a child that you did not receive?

_____

_____

_____

_____

_____

_____

_____

_____

2.35 Treatment

This book was written and intended for the individual reader, clinical education, and therapeutic encounters as a complementary set of exercises and source of psycho-education. This section adds to the modalities already discussed. Depending on the duration and severity of the anxiety symptoms, the length and types of treatment recommended will vary.

The main purpose of treatment is to reduce and remove the feelings and symptoms that are interfering with one's day-to-day ability to live up to their full potential. For any set of symptoms to be categorized as a disorder/pathology, they must directly impact activities of daily living and one's ability to function in relationships, at work, and in society.

One purpose for writing this book was to encourage people to understand the connection between their psychological symptoms, thoughts, and feelings; the impact on their bodily sensations; and how it impacts their behaviors.

Planning for treatment must be done collaboratively, with expert guidance, so outcomes of care can be based on what the individual wants to get out of therapy. Clinical outcomes are improved significantly by a healthy therapeutic relationship and alliance, trust, and a sense of interpersonal connectedness.

Healing does not occur linearly, and there may be setbacks and frustrating moments. We encourage you to remain patient and persistent so you can give yourself the best possible chance of a healthy recovery. Also give yourself permission to feel the emotions you are feeling and remember they are not permanent. Lastly, be compassionate with yourself to allow room for growth.

2.36 Online Interventions for Prevention

Due to the restrictions on in-person care that began at the onset of the pandemic, online interventions for prevention of mental health problems for adolescents and young adults are a growing area of focus.

The key differentiators are the virtual and sometimes asynchronous application of these interventions for folks at risk. Those most amenable to text-based interactions include cognitive behavioral therapy and interventions that include the family.

According to a systematic review by Noh and Kim (2022), results suggest that these online interventions have a better impact on preventing depression. Their article suggests that a significant impact on the prevention of stress and anxiety through online interventions was not seen, implying need for further research in this area.

2.37 Virtual Reality

For anxiety-specific treatments, some studies have shown positive outcomes for social anxiety. Virtual reality and skills training sessions in that environment can help folks acquire communication skills. Controlled environments have also been efficacious in meeting phobias. The military has more experience with treating posttraumatic stress disorder with virtual reality–based therapies that include exposure therapy.

Some studies have also looked at treating patients with eating disorders in virtual reality environments, similar to exposure and decreasing symptoms of anxiety while working on various responses to food stimuli.

Of note, the modalities employed in virtual reality are similar to those online and in traditional face-to-face treatment. At this time, there doesn't seem to be any increased benefit to the virtual reality modality in terms of outcomes. The real benefits are seen in terms of improved access to care, as well as the ability to create scenarios and worlds that the patient and provider can drop in and out of. This certainly has the benefit of being financially more viable and decreases the need for travel as the patient and provider can be in separate locations.

Self-guided VR applications include meditation apps as well as other relaxation-inducing environments that can be added to other treatment options.

We do know there is a somewhat increased uptake and adoption of online and virtual platforms by adolescents and young adults, so this continues to be an increasing area of focus for mental health research.

Chatbots and Artificial Intelligence (AI)

- The news that mental health apps are increasingly using chatbots and other AI spread when one mental telehealth company disclosed they were testing chatbot features unbeknownst to their users.
- The desire is to close the gap between the current supply of clinically trained therapists and psychiatrists and the increasing demand for mental health care. Also, for many of these for-profit companies, which are beholden to their shareholders, the main goal is to reduce overhead and maximize profits.
- Therapists are expensive. Psychiatrists are very expensive. There aren't enough of them being trained, and it feels as if everyone wants mental health care. The market is speaking, and chatbots and AI will be a very real part of our mental health care very soon. (Author's note: We look forward to this section of the book being cringe-worthy and out of date by the time it gets published, lol.)
- As of the time of writing this book, however, these chatbots are in their (digital) infancy, trying to emulate the feel of interacting with a human, although they often fall short.
- Criticism of interacting with chatbots suggests they lack emotional depth, which makes sense for now. Users report that the same responses are repeated so many times they don't feel authentic, they aren't feeling seen or heard in their suffering.
- As these are, by definition, not human interactions, users report they find it difficult if not impossible to develop a rapport or a meaningful connection with the chatbot.
- There are currently no conclusive reports on outcomes or efficacy as to how they work to reduce anxiety or depression.

■ Similarly, there are no studies on the long-term benefits of these apps at this time.
■ Where chatbots currently can and do add benefits:

  – They are instantly and always available to the user, any time of day. They don't complain; they don't require human resources or ask for a raise or a pension plan.
  – The holy grail for large provider networks and health management organizations is to solve the access-to-care challenge, and these promising options to satisfy and, perhaps one day, improve the care and lives of patients are very exciting.
  – Chatbots can currently remind the user to meditate, exercise, do a mindfulness exercise.
  – They can provide a cue to instill a habit such as doing the creative writing prompts in this book.

Psychosocial Therapies

■ **Acceptance Commitment Therapy (ACT)**

  – ACT is a form of cognitive behavioral therapy that helps foster acceptance of one's thoughts and feelings while committing to doing things based on their goals.
  – Acceptance involves evaluating a situation and working towards understanding what one can and cannot change. This, in turn, works to lower anxiety as the person embraces their thoughts and emotions.
  – As the person learns to recognize that their thoughts and anxieties are their own mental events, they begin to put away unpleasant, unhelpful thoughts and belief patterns.
  – ACT is used to treat anxiety, depression, and stress; engage in healthy relationships; and cope with physical health and medical issues.

■ **Breathing Techniques**

  – Deep breathing, specifically exhaling, triggers the parasympathetic nervous system. See Chapter 3, 'Balan 3-2-1 Method,' which includes detailed information regarding breathing techniques.

■ **Cognitive Behavioral Therapy (CBT)**

  – CBT addresses maladaptive thinking patterns and thoughts and behaviors that may be dysfunctional.
  – The client works with the therapist to address automatic thoughts and beliefs that influence the way they act and feel.
  – For generalized anxiety disorder, CBT may be tried before a medication or at the same time medication is started.
  – If there are concerns regarding depressive symptoms that may interfere with starting CBT, discuss with your provider options such as medication first, so you have the best possibility to benefit from CBT.

 – CBT has been shown to have significant efficacy in treating sports- and other performance-related anxieties. For more information, see Chapter 8, 'Confidence and Recovery.'

■ **Cognitive Behavioral Expressive Writing Therapy**

 – In writing therapy, the individual writes about their anxieties, stressors, and experiences, with the emphasis on self-regulation.
 – Studies support the efficacy of the written form of CBT exercises in reducing symptoms of anxiety, stress, and PTSD.
 – Meta-analyses done by Kuester et al. (2016) and Lewis et al. (2019) support the clinical use of internet-based cognitive behavioral writing therapy.

■ **Group Therapy**

 – Studies suggest that earlier interventions of anxiety disorders, particularly in group settings, have significant impacts on the reduction of symptoms.
 – Groups can be led through discussion and processing experiences, as well as manual based, typically using CBT methodologies and concepts together.
 – Group therapy serves to provide social support, decrease one's sense of being alone, model different experiences and forms of recovery, and improve access to care.

■ **Interpersonal Psychotherapy (IPT)**

 – IPT is structured and time limited to 12 to 16 weeks and focuses on social and interpersonal relationships and symptom recovery.
 – IPT improves social functioning and is an evidence-based treatment that reduces anxiety and depression.
 – A meta-analysis by Bian et al. (2022) details the significant effect interpersonal psychotherapy has on improving mental well-being, specifically anxiety and depression.

2.38 Medication Management

Pills, injections, nasal sprays, or tablets that melt in your mouth (or however else you take your medications) do not get rid of anxiety. They cannot undo your history of trauma. They cannot erase your memories or provide you with enhanced insight or judgment.

Ingesting a medication does not intrinsically instill hope upon you, nor can it find you better relationships.

What medications can do, however, is ease the symptoms of anxiety and depression, allowing for a pathway to benefit from other psychosocial modalities. Medications may even work faster in reducing anxiety symptoms, helping you feel less preoccupied with the anxiety itself and clearing up your mind space to allow for exposure, introspection, narrative treatments, cognitive behavioral therapy, mindfulness, and other treatments to be as optimal an experience as possible. The path to wellness takes time.

The energy that you put into yourself, over time, will allow for better understanding of your triggers, memories, and cues and an ability to appreciate yourself as you build healthy connections between yourself and others.

When developing medication care options for your anxiety, it is very important to remember to start low and go slow. This means starting at the lowest reasonable dose, obviously in discussion with your prescriber, and working slowly to increase it based on your prescription recommendations.

As mentioned before, your anxiety most likely did not start overnight; the concerns and thoughts and stressors and worries have been a part of you and your life for a while, and it will take time, persistence, and ongoing energy to reduce the power your symptoms have over you.

Clinician suggestions for rapid results for your anxiety must be approached with skepticism. Sustainable change happens gradually. There are some medications that can have rapid onset and rapid relief, but they do not cure the underlying dysfunctional belief systems and therefore do not last long.

Also be very mindful of the competing incentives of medication manufacturers and pharmaceutical companies as connecting people with long-term medications rather than having them spend time on talk therapy can be motivated by money and not necessarily by taking care of the root cause of the anxiety.

We similarly see examples in which the cost of long-term individual psychotherapy is much higher than for a 10- or 15-minute medication check once every six months. These competing incentives have very real consequences as they relate to insurance providers, regardless of parity laws in the United States.

Of the medications used most often for anxiety, the SSRIs, detailed elsewhere in this chapter, have been the most successful class of psychiatry medications, resulting in billions of dollars of profit to pharmaceutical companies. Anxiety disorders have increased, and people have increased stress- and worry-related concerns; there's also the reality that people want a quick fix, which is reinforced by clinician schedules, reimbursement rates, and clinician supply and demand. Similarly, benzodiazepines consistently become best-selling medications, with each new version introduced to the market outselling the ones before.

Everything has a side effect. Everything must be taken in moderation, knowing exactly who on your treatment team you feel you can trust and that, ultimately, you are in control. It is your responsibility to be well educated about what is available to you and what you need in order to properly treat your anxiety and stay well in the long term.

2.39 Informed Consent

Any time a prescriber recommends an intervention such as a medication or an invasive procedure, it is critical to know everything about it from every angle and to keep asking questions until you feel comfortable.

Anything we put into our bodies has an effect—good or bad, healthy or not—and the prescriber must allow the choice to be made without coercion, shame, or guilt. Interestingly, people who have higher levels of anxiety also experience a higher number of medication side effects.

It is also important to remember that just because a medication might help eliminate some symptoms, it doesn't necessarily mean that is the diagnosis that you have. In other words, if you've tried a medicine or a class of medication and it helped, it doesn't mean you have the specific diagnosis the medication is prescribed for. It's important to discuss your symptoms with the prescribing clinician for informed consent--related purposes and to make the right treatment decision.

Your bodily autonomy is inherent, and the journey you are on is yours. When you are in control of your treatment plan, you will feel better and be more confident.

In the event you experience a negative side effect, with the information you gathered, you will be prepared for what to expect and will have coping strategies for managing it. Informed consent and being an educated consumer are critical and also serve to demystify the process, allow for hope, and reduce anxiety and fear of the unknown.

Having said all this, thankfully, the most commonly prescribed medications for anxiety are safe, effective, and very well tolerated with minimal side effects.

Please consider the following list of questions we suggest you discuss with your prescriber as talk of medication options becomes a reality.

■ What is the diagnosis or set of symptoms the medication will work towards reducing?
■ How long do you have to take the medication? What happens if you forget a dose? What happens if you stop before the end of the recommended treatment timeframe?
■ If you want to get off the medication, can you do so in a day, or do you have to slowly reduce the dose to avoid withdrawal effects? What are the withdrawal effects? How serious are they?
■ How do you take the medication? Is it a pill, an injection, something that melts under the tongue?
■ How often is the medication taken? Daily? Multiple times a day?
■ Is there a need to increase the dose over time? How will you know when you will need to reconnect with the prescriber to discuss this option?
■ How long will it take for the medicine to start working? Will the effects increase over time? Will you start getting used to the effects and need to keep increasing the dose? Is there a combination of medications that will need to be started while waiting for this medicine to start taking effect?

  – What are the side effects of the medication? How will they impact your ability to function day to day? Will it cause things such as stomach upset and diarrhea? Can it cause drowsiness and affect driving a car?
  – Does it affect the appetite or cause weight gain or loss?
  – Does it have sexual side effects like problems with arousal, erections, ejaculation, or orgasm? Do these effects vary by dose, meaning do larger doses have greater side effects?

■ Does the medication interact with other things you are prescribed? Is it affected by alcohol use? Do vitamins or supplements impact the absorption of the medication or make the side effects worse?
■ Does the medication have any interaction with your dietary choices? If so, go over your diet and either come up with a plan of what to eat and what to avoid or consult a dietician and pharmacist as part of your treatment team.
■ Do the benefits of taking the medication outweigh the risks of not taking the medication?

■ Are there physical side effects or potential problems that can occur requiring close monitoring such as repeat blood tests or checking blood pressure? Discuss the benefits of taking the medication versus not taking it at all. Discuss how often you will need to monitor these physical issues and what exactly you need to be on the lookout for.

■ Does the medication impact the ability to become pregnant? Does it affect an unborn baby? Does the medication pass through the milk to the baby? Will it harm the baby?

■ Does the medication cause addiction? Is it a controlled substance, potentially creating concern when traveling with the pill bottle?

■ What alternatives are available, including options to explore what worked for family members? It is worth bringing up something specific to your family's treatment history that either worked or caused negative reactions?

■ Is there the option of not taking the medication at all? What are the drawbacks of waiting to start it? What other alternatives are there?

■ How expensive are the medications, and will insurance cover them? Are there coupons or cost-reducing measures to help make the medication more affordable?

2.40 Writing Prompt

Consider writing down your current medications and questions you may have about suggested treatment options from your clinician. Include questions about how to take the medication, side effects, risks, and benefits.

_____

_____

_____

_____

_____

_____

_____

_____

_____

_____

2.40.1 Medication Options

Selective Serotonin Reuptake Inhibitors (SSRIs)

■ SSRIs have typically been the preferred first-line medication option for treatment of anxiety disorders.

■ SSRIs are less likely to cause sleepiness, sedation, or other thinking/cognitive problems such as brain fog or feeling like you're in a cloud.

■ SSRIs have significant benefits in anxiety and depressive symptoms. Studies suggest, and our clinical experience corroborates, that SSRIs reduce symptoms in over 50% of people taking them.

■ This means that the rest, unfortunately, may not benefit from symptom reduction if the medications are taken alone. A large percentage of people not benefiting from medications alone may point towards other components at play, such as the placebo effect.

■ Literature suggests that it takes from a couple of days to a couple of weeks for on SSRI to begin showing clinical effects. Your prescriber may suggest also starting a medication such as a benzodiazepine (see later in this chapter) to help with anxiety and side effect reduction while the effects of the SSRIs begin.

■ Since there are so many options in the SSRI category to choose from, discuss with your prescribing clinician the option that is a better fit for you.

■ Things to think about include:

  – Side effects of the SSRIs include sleepiness, initial insomnia, agitation, weight gain, sexual dysfunction such as delayed orgasm, gastrointestinal issues such as nausea or diarrhea, sweating, and dizziness.
  – Drug-to-drug interactions: We know some medications interact with others, and it is important to ensure your prescribing clinician is aware of the other medications and supplements you are on, so you can discuss whether this causes one or the other not to work as well or if it can worsen side effects.

■ Medications such as SSRIs are often used in conjunction with other modalities of treatment for maximal benefit, such as CBT.

■ There are times when an SSRI may not work as well as intended or may not provide any relief of anxiety at all. Options include increasing the dose up to the maximum amount recommended and ensuring enough time has passed since starting the medication. If suboptimal response to the medication continues, recommendations may include switching to another SSRI or an SNRI.

■ Examples include sertraline (generic for Zoloft), paroxetine (generic for Paxil), citalopram (generic for Celexa), escitalopram (generic name for Lexapro), fluoxetine (generic for Prozac), and fluvoxamine (generic for Luvox).

Serotonin and Norepinephrine Reuptake Inhibitors (SNRIs)

■ Similar to the SSRIs, SNRIs are considered first-line medication management options for anxiety disorders and have similar benefits in reducing anxiety in clinical studies.

■ Side effect profiles are similar to the SSRIs mentioned earlier, including sedation, weight gain, sweating, sleep issues, sexual dysfunction, and gastrointestinal issues.

■ Studies suggest that venlafaxine (generic for Effexor) may cause an increase in blood pressure, and blood pressure should be monitored while on it.

■ Your prescriber may suggest another medication to reduce the side effects of the SNRI, at least initially, until your body gets used to the SNRI.

Benzodiazepines

- Benzodiazepines reduce anxiety. They are, however, almost too good at reducing anxiety, and, as with anything that is so effective so quickly, there is always a catch – a downside that must not be ignored.
- Benzodiazepines are habit forming and can cause 'dependence,' which is a nice way to say they are addicting.

  - It is important to be humble and to ensure all your questions are answered (see section on informed consent) when being offered them to reduce anxiety.
  - As any addictive substance, the user develops a tolerance for the medication, which means, over time, the dose they started on may not be as effective at reducing the anxiety as it was, necessitating an increased dose to get the same effect.
  - They also have withdrawal effects, so if one decides to reduce or discontinue benzodiazepine use, this must be done under the guidance of a prescriber to minimize the unpleasant and potentially dangerous effects of withdrawal.
  - Since these serious issues are associated with them, benzodiazepines are controlled substances and are monitored and scrutinized at a higher level.

- Examples include lorazepam (generic for Ativan), diazepam (generic for Valium), and clonazepam (generic for Klonopin).
- Side effects include drowsiness, decreased coordination, and memory issues such as amnesia. Long-term use of benzodiazepines has been associated with cognitive impairment, memory issues, and physical changes to the brain.
- Benzodiazepines interact with other medications as well as alcohol, which can lead to respiratory depression and even death. Alcohol affects the body in a similar way to benzodiazepines, and the two should never be used together.
- Some benzodiazepines work very quickly, but because they also leave the body quickly, and the effects go away, the person may feel withdrawal, requiring additional doses.
- Think of the benzodiazepines as literally cutting off the anxiogenic stimulus from the anxiety response. While reenacting fear from a memory or severe anxiety that inhibits day-to-day life is problematic and may benefit from a benzodiazepine, current real-time concern and fear, as well as physically responding in an actual fear-inducing situation, such as swerving a car, is lifesaving and may be inhibited by the use of a benzodiazepine.
- These days, prescribers are more reluctant to start someone on this class of medications due to the issues described, although if one is on them, respect them for what they can and cannot do.
- Similar to the SSRIs, they can help start a psychosocial therapy modality, ease painful areas, and open the door to learning coping and healing mechanisms.
- Benzodiazepines are sometimes offered when someone first starts an SSRI or SNRI because benzodiazepines work very quickly and very well. They are also used in the initial phase to help reduce the difficulty in falling asleep.

Other Medication Options

- Hydroxyzine is an antihistamine, and therefore, side effects include sedation.

  - Hydroxyzine can also help with anxiety issues as well as difficulty falling and staying asleep. It is not habit forming and is preferred over benzodiazepines when the person may have an alcohol use issue.

- Buspirone (generic for Buspar) is typically well tolerated and is not habit forming. Buspirone helps reduce symptoms of anxiety at similar rates as benzodiazepines. It is sometimes started alone or at the same time as an SSRI or SNRI.
- Antipsychotic medications:

  - Several studies have reviewed the use of antipsychotic medications for anxiety.
  - Examples include quetiapine (generic for Seroquel) and aripiprazole (generic for Abilify).
  - While the side effects of inducing sleep and relaxation through their sedative properties have been noted, these are not typically first-line options for anxiety disorders.
  - Side effects of antipsychotics include weight gain, imbalance in blood sugar levels, sedation, fainting, heart-related problems, and sudden heart attacks.
  - Antipsychotics work well for psychotic symptoms such as hallucinations.
  - Certain antipsychotics also have serotonergic properties that may alleviate depressive symptoms. As mentioned earlier, they aren't first line options for anxiety disorders on their own and have side effects that are quite serious. They are used for treatment resistant anxieties, which means that the person has tried other medication options that did not work well enough.
  - Regarding side effect risk to clinical benefit ratio, as with any medication, please speak with your prescribing clinician as to exactly which aspects of the anxiety and related stress you may be prescribed one of these classes of medications.

2.41 Conclusion

As you gain a better understanding of how you got to this point, where you currently are, and the goals you have for the future, you will continue to build confidence and give yourself the best possible healing journey.

When treatment goals are developed collaboratively and you feel you are being seen for who you are, you will develop the tools needed to successfully face your challenges.

Chapter 3

Balan 3-2-1 Method

3.1 Introduction

Originally introduced in *Re-Write: A Trauma Workbook of Creative Writing and Recovery in Our New Normal* (2023), the Balan 3-2-1 Method allows for reflection, preparation, and creative expression while developing healthy routines.

This chapter will discuss the methodology that we developed over the years. The Balan 3-2-1 Method has been designed to be easily understood, remembered, and used.

The Balan 3-2-1 Method is available for use by clinicians and individuals, and we request that proper credit be given when it is used.

The counting down from 3 to 2 to 1 intentionally brings the focus to the core of the person practicing the method. The three simple instructions in each writing prompt are repeated throughout the book.

We provide space to write your thoughts and responses to the prompts, as well as reminders of the structure of the method. This chapter elaborates on each component of the method and can be referenced as needed.

There are three parts to the method that work synergistically and are recommended to be done in the order described. The first part, three, reminds the clinician or individual of the three elements of setting the environment. The second part is to begin focusing on the writing prompt itself, by diving deeper into two thoughts, two sentences in response to the primed clinical exercise. The last part, one, is to bring the exercise to a close with one affirmation, an intent. Each part will be expanded on later in this chapter.

DOI: 10.4324/9781003413547-4

3.2 Balan 3-2-1 Method Overview

We include writing prompts as guidelines for reflection that can be completed at your discretion. There are three components to this method:

3: The body, the setting, and the breath are the initial elements that set the stage for healing. Prompts are included to promote mindfulness throughout the process.

2: The prompts continue with an area for two thoughts to be reflected on and written.

1: The final space available is for one intention or affirmation to be written.

Reframing exercises are known to be beneficial, especially for feelings of anxiety and worry. Consider reframing the negative feeling into something like excitement or positive anticipation.

As you work towards labeling the feelings as anxiety, as per the last chapter, and are able to realize you have much more control over mind and body, as per Chapter 5, 'Brain, Body, and Behaviors,' you will use the energy to your benefit.

For example, if you are feeling anxious about an upcoming play you will be onstage for, imagine instead that you are feeling excited about how people will enjoy your performance and that you are looking forward to doing well, as you and your colleagues have rehearsed and are well prepared.

> **The place to improve the world is first in one's own heart and head and hands, and then work outward from there.**
> **– Robert M. Pirsig, *Zen and the Art of Motorcycle Maintenance***

3.3 Balan: *Three*-2-1

Everything starts with our minds and our bodies. Our intention in structuring this method is to set the foundation for beginning these writing prompts. These steps are additive and work towards an optimal environment for success.

The three elements are:

■ The body
■ The setting
■ The breath

3.4 Balan: *3*-2-1: The Body

This section is specifically designed to remind you to intentionally prepare your body to be in sync with and receptive to the exercises presented. Consider a warm shower or a comfortable sweater. You can simply wash your face or brush your hair.

The purpose is to prioritize taking care of yourself and bringing this to the forefront of your attention. Consider repeating, "My body matters; this is what I am doing for my body."

These writing prompts and exercises are your time to perform self-care that is genuinely about you, knowing full well you may have other people depending on you. This is your time, and everyone will benefit when you care for yourself.

3.5 Writing Prompt

Consider using the space provided to reflect on the following prompts:

What does self-care look like to you?

_____

_____

_____

_____

_____

What do you do to prioritize self-care?

_____

_____

_____

_____

_____

3.6 Balan: *3-2-1*: The Setting

As we set our inner environment, intentionally focusing on our body, we must ensure our external environment is also conducive to calmness and healing.

These writing prompts that incorporate mindful breathing and intentionality are typically completed in under ten minutes, although readers have told us they have benefitted from taking even more time to reflect on them. The setting you choose for these exercises must be safe, with as few distractions as possible.

We recommend reducing as many of your devices and digital distractions as possible. Perhaps write outside, away from your home office or reminders of your infinite to-do lists.

A mini-mindfulness tool we suggest is writing your current to-do items down on a piece of paper and setting it aside. Know that it will be waiting for you when you are done with your writing prompt. Having the list physically exit your brain and land on the page and actually separating the page from where you will be allow for some freedom to devote mental energy to self-care.

Find a special blanket to sit on the grass with or a favorite candle to light. Similar to the little things we intentionally provide for our bodies, we must also reflect on our setting to ensure we feel comfortable and as content as possible.

Consider listening to music that matches your current mood or perhaps your intended mood. You can also sing a song you love to begin grounding yourself as you harmonize with your environment. We can access preverbal memories and emotions through music that we may not have the ability to access otherwise.

As you may have suspected, these grounding techniques are simple enough to complete yet have great benefits. Look around you and notice the things that are within arm's length and those that are a bit further away. Notice the temperature and the sounds of your environment.

Some cultures value having physical representations of loved ones and family elders in their environment. This can be a photograph or an altar with items that allow you to honor the individual. Alternately, you can have something small in your pocket that soothes you and helps you release stress. This can be a small keychain, a crystal, or a toy that symbolizes or reminds you of your family, a fun vacation, or your friends.

Another grounding exercise that many people enjoy is lighting a candle and mindfully focusing on that as it adds to the backdrop of the work you will be doing. Watch the movement of the flame. Focus on the colors. Can you see the blue light? What does the candle smell like? What kind of memories, sensations, or emotions come up? Can you feel the emanating heat?

As you practice these techniques, they will become easier to connect with and sustain over time. Distractions that were difficult to ignore will become easier to set aside, and your experience will continue to improve. Remember: practice makes permanent.

3.7 Writing Prompt

Consider using the space provided to reflect on the following prompt:

How can you create a calm, healing environment for yourself?

_____

_____

_____

_____

_____

_____

_____

_____

_____

_____

3.8 Balan: *3-2-1*: The Breath

The final part of setting the internal and external environment to ensure an appropriate foundation to heal through the writing exercises is the conscious effort we recommend putting into your breathing. We will be covering several types of techniques. Try them and use the ones that work best for you.

Chapter 5, 'Brain, Body, and Behaviors,' discusses the neurological pathways of trauma and response and how the act of breathing in involves the parasympathetic nervous system. As you breathe in, your heartbeat slows down, and other elements of the parasympathetic nervous system activate. Essentially, think of the things that activate as those that are opposite to and incompatible with the fight-or-flight mode.

Shallow, rapid breaths are a symptom of and can induce or worsen anxiety, panic, and stress. Deeper, controlled breathing elicits calm, reduces signs and symptoms of nervousness and worry, and allows the mind and body to relax. The concept is that you want to regulate your breathing initially so your body knows you are safe.

Think about your own breathing during different times of the day and in different circumstances. Think about how your breathing patterns might change and how that directly affects the way you feel. Even in a situation that might not be associated with anxiety itself, such as working out at the gym or soccer practice, the sensation of increased breathing and pulse rate might be associated with worry and fear in people with anxiety disorders.

As you are increasingly mindful of the speed and depth of your breath, you will be able to have more control over it and also be able to regulate your own emotional responses.

The techniques described here improve both mental and physical responses to stress. Specifically for young adults, students, and those in the workplace, these techniques significantly reduce anxiety, whether related to taking an exam, applying for a job, or public speaking.

For each of the following techniques, we recommend you be in your setting of choice, free of distraction and comfortably sitting down. If your body and setting permit, consider sitting cross legged. Alternately, sitting in a chair with your legs comfortably hanging down is fine. Ensure that you have a proper backrest so you are not slouched over or bending your neck or spine in a way that may cause strain or harm.

Try incorporating one or more of the following techniques as part of the Balan 3-2-1 Method. Consider doing the breathing exercise for two minutes each time to start with. As your body and mind become more comfortable with the technique, you can gradually increase the time by a minute or two more.

3.9 Breathing Techniques

3.9.1 Deep Breathing

This may be the most basic yet most versatile of the techniques to significantly reduce feelings of anxiety while bringing on a sense of calm. Routine breathing is automatic, requiring no effort or conscious thought. Deep breathing involves a more conscious effort.

To begin, sit comfortably and close your eyes if that might help you focus better. This technique involves breathing in through the nose and exhaling through the mouth. Inhale deeply and slowly as you feel your lungs expand and your belly rise as your lungs fill with air. Hold your breath for one or two seconds, and then slowly exhale through your mouth.

Repeat this cycle for several minutes, focusing on the sensation of the breath entering and exiting your body and how it makes you feel.

3.9.2 Writing Prompt

Consider using the space provided to take down notes on how you felt during and after trying the **deep-breathing** method.

_____

_____

_____

_____

_____

_____

_____

_____

_____

_____

_____

3.10 Diaphragmatic Breathing

This breathing technique is recommended by the American Academy of Child and Adolescent Psychiatry. This mode of breathing is well tolerated and has many valuable mental and physical rewards.

To begin, place one hand on your belly and the other hand on your chest. Take a couple of moments and breathe to see how both hands feel as you inhale and exhale. Breathe slowly and notice your lungs and your belly expand. When you exhale, slow the flow of air through your mouth by making it into the shape of a small 'O.'

Breathe in and out several times like this, each time focusing on expanding your belly and slowly exhaling. Focusing conscious thought and energy like this will yield significant positive outcomes. The value of having your hands on your belly and chest is to emphasize and reinforce the breath going towards your abdomen in deeper, longer breaths.

This is in contrast to shallow breaths that enter and exit quickly at the level of the chest and are associated with states of anxiety, stress, and fight or flight. Breathing slowly and mindfully helps improve the body's ability to balance and recover after stressful events. Increasing the amount of oxygen in the body and decreasing stress and cortisol help long-term reduction of anxiety and the ability to heal and recover.

As we recommend with any behavioral change, practice makes permanent. If this is a breathing technique that you enjoy, and you find calms you better or more sustainably than the others, consider doing so for a couple of minutes longer each time you sit down for a writing exercise.

Not only is there no downside to this but your mind will also incorporate deep breathing and associate it with the reduction of stress, anxiety, and traumatic feelings.

3.11 Writing Prompt

Consider using the space provided to take down notes on how you felt during and after trying the **diaphragmatic-breathing** method.

_____

_____

_____

_____

_____

_____

_____

_____

_____

_____

3.12 4-7-8 Breathing

This technique is also known as 'fourfold breath' and involves recommended time intervals during which you focus on inhaling, holding your breath, and then exhaling. Obviously, this is just an example, and everyone's body and lungs are different. The 4-7-8 is simply an easy way to remember the technique, and if any of the time intervals are too long or create discomfort, stop. You can modify the time intervals to whatever feels comfortable. **Please check the below sequence once.**

4: To begin, inhale through your nose for four seconds and notice your lungs filling and your diaphragm expanding.

7: Then hold your breath for seven seconds.

8: Lastly, exhale through your mouth for eight seconds. Try to completely exhale the breath during that time, and then repeat this cycle for one or two minutes.

3.13 Writing Prompt

Consider using the space provided to take down notes on how you felt during and after trying the **4-7-8 breathing** method.

_____

_____

_____

_____

_____

_____

_____

_____

_____

3.14 Writing Prompt

Consider using the space provided to reflect on the following prompt:

What was it like trying these breathing techniques? Which technique do you plan on using again?

_____

_____

_____

_____

_____

_____

_____

_____

_____

_____

3.15 Balan: 3-*Two*-1

The second step in the 3-Two-1 method serves as a prompt to anticipate the upcoming written tasks. Throughout this book, we offer writing prompts and cues corresponding to the section and themes being addressed.

In response to the writing prompts, you'll find designated space to articulate your reflections. The use of two is intentional – the number is deliberately kept low to prevent a sense of being overwhelmed and to establish clear parameters within the framework of the process.

You are encouraged to express two reflections. These could manifest as two brief sentences or extend into two paragraphs. The emphasis lies not so much on the volume or content as on engaging in the process itself, liberated from external disruptions. Our aim is to foster a concentrated effort towards healing.

3.16 Balan: 3-2-*One*

The last section is to reflect on and conclude the prompt with a final thought. You can write one affirmation, one wish, a desired outcome, an intent, or a hope. This may be in the form of something you have and are grateful for or something you wish to acquire or strive to incorporate into yourself. We encourage you to reflect on tangible and abstract aspects of what you are grateful for, including interpersonal connections.

Dive into an exploration of your inner qualities – these may include appreciation for your journey of self-awareness, acknowledgement of integrating your past, or your ongoing process of personal awakening.

Examples of statements you can repeat to yourself, say out loud, or write in the prompt section include:

I am grateful for the strength within me.
I appreciate the abundant love and support that surround me.
I am empowering my past hurt self and am worthy of love.
I am grateful for the capacity to learn and grow into the person I am becoming.

Think about what you would like for yourself, and always frame the thoughts through a positive lens.

3.17 Writing Prompt

Consider using the space provided to reflect on the following prompt:

What is an intention or wish you have for yourself?

_____

_____

_____

_____

_____

_____

_____

_____

_____

Whether you think you can or you think you can't, you're right.
—Henry Ford

3.18 Balan 3-2-1: Summary

Overall, consider the Balan 3-2-one Method a guideline, with suggested prompts that can be completed in whatever timeframe you desire. There are three parts to the method:

3: The body, the setting, and the breath are the three elements that set the stage for healing and allow the body and mind to align as you begin the creative writing exercise. Prompts are provided with space to write them down and will differ based on the topic being discussed. The purpose is to set the stage for mindfulness and bring attention to the process itself. As mentioned, there are no correct or incorrect ways of completing any of the exercises.

2: The prompts continue with an area for two thoughts to be reflected on and written.

1: The final space available is for one intention or one affirmation to be written.

You can do the prompts in the book in whichever order you choose and take as long as you feel is necessary. Some people have told us they like to read the prompts and think about them during the day before coming back to the book and entering their responses. However you find the process to be most useful, we encourage you to use that method and be receptive to your thoughts and needs.

Being is not passive; it takes focused awareness.
—Maureen Murdock, *The Heroine's Journey*

3.19 Analysis

Writing down what you think and feel has innumerable benefits, as discussed in Chapter 4 'Value of Treatment.' This section discussed suggested modes in which one can analyze their writing or work with a treating provider.

The written words act as a historical artifact that is bound within the frame of when it was written and how you were feeling and thinking at that time. Specific to anxiety-related issues, it can serve as a benchmark to see how often you were anxious about something and to recall how often those things actually became a reality. It serves as foundation to assess future growth and healing and to see how far, over time, you have gone in your healing journey and learning to deal with your anxieties.

When you have completed the writing, you can choose to share it with a loved one or your therapist, keep it to yourself, or destroy it altogether. Elements of what you put down to pay attention may include grammar, style, use of tenses, chosen pronouns, point of view, narrative style, included emptions, descriptors, creative elements, areas you chose to elaborate on, and areas you omitted or skipped on purpose. Consider looking at patterns after you have completed a couple of writing prompts to see if there is a larger theme or connections can be made.

Whether you choose to analyze your writing after the fact or not, you should congratulate yourself for being so diligent and making an effort to work on yourself!

3.20 Writing Prompt

Within the framework of the Balan 3-2-1 Method, consider your responses to the following:

What is one thing you wish people understood about you?

3: With intention, set your internal and external environment.

■ The body: What mindfulness techniques are you choosing to allow your body to heal?

_____

_____

_____

_____

■ The setting: How are you intentionally influencing your setting?

_____

_____

_____

_____

■ The breath: Which breathing technique will you use as you prepare for this exercise?

_____

_____

_____

_____

2: What are your thoughts and feelings in response to the writing prompt?

_____

_____

_____

_____

_____

_____

_____

_____

_____

1: What is your one intent or affirmation in the context of the writing prompt?

_____

_____

_____

_____

3.21 Writing Prompt

Within the framework of the Balan 3-2-1 Method, consider your responses to the following:

What areas would I like to heal?

3: With intention, set your internal and external environment.

■ The body: What mindfulness techniques are you choosing to allow your body to heal?

_____

_____

_____

_____

■ The setting: How are you intentionally influencing your setting?

_____

_____

_____

_____

■ The breath: Which breathing technique will you use as you prepare for this exercise?

_____

_____

_____

_____

2: What are your thoughts and feelings in response to the writing prompt?

_____

_____

_____

_____

_____

_____

_____

_____

_____

1: What is your one intent or affirmation in the context of the writing prompt?

_____

_____

_____

_____

3.22 Writing Prompt

Within the framework of the Balan 3-2-1 Method, consider your response to the following:

How would you know somebody loves you?

3: With intention, set your internal and external environment.

■ The body: What mindfulness techniques are you choosing to allow your body to heal?

_____

_____

_____

_____

■ The setting: How are you intentionally influencing your setting?

_____

_____

_____

_____

■ The breath: Which breathing technique will you use as you prepare for this exercise?

_____

_____

_____

_____

2: What are your thoughts and feelings in response to the writing prompt?

_____

_____

_____

_____

_____

_____

_____

_____

_____

1: What is your one intent or affirmation in the context of the writing prompt?

_____

_____

_____

_____

CROSSING THE THRESHOLD

DOI: 10.4324/9781003413547-5

Chapter 4

Value of Treatment

4.1 Introduction

Asking questions is the key to learning – as we improve our thinking, we understand our emotional reactions and enhance our ability to communicate. Anyone suffering from anxiety and stress-related issues understands the value of treatment. This chapter discusses not only the benefits of symptom reduction but also the improvement in quality of life for the individual and those around them.

In a time when fact seems indistinguishable from fiction, this book strives to incorporate multi-modal care options to hone the reader's focus on self-discovery that will help make sense of their external reality.

This chapter presents the benefits of creative and expressive writing from a physiological, mental, emotional, personal, and financial perspective. The techniques we provide can be used alone, with family members, or with a therapist as part of a treatment plan.

We discuss improved mental health and the impact it has on school and work performance and present the value employers will realize through increased productivity and satisfaction.

Learning these tools and techniques involves time and energy, and the reward is made evident through confidence and success. Our intention throughout this book is that the reader will come away with an improved capability of inquiry in their quest to be more confident and self-reliant.

The payoff of persistence despite resistance and setbacks is immense, and we applaud you for exploring your own mind. We look forward to hearing from our readers how these methods have impacted them.

In the fields of observation chance favors only the prepared mind.
– Louis Pasteur

DOI: 10.4324/9781003413547-6

4.2 Prevalence

Everything, including mental health statistics, has become demarcated with a very clear boundary of before COVID (BC) and after COVID (AC).

■ The first couple of years of the pandemic, around 2020, 40% of people reported at least one mental health–related issue.
■ There was a 30% reported prevalence of anxiety and depression; 25% of people reported an increase in stress and trauma related to the pandemic.
■ People reported an increase in substance use to cope with the stress of the lockdowns.

– Opioid use increased, as did fatal opioid overdoses, specifically during lockdowns.
– Alcohol-related deaths increased over 25% during the first year of lockdowns alone.

■ According to a British report by the Office for National Statistics in 2020, 36% of disabled adults experienced moderate to severe depression symptoms.
■ There was an enormous increase in those who had seriously contemplated suicide in the previous 30 days, according to many studies, with even higher rates in those aged 18 to 24.
■ Rates in Hispanic and Black populations have been even higher.
■ Unpaid caregivers and 'essential workers' reported a tripling of anxiety disorders.

4.3 Workplace and Economic Impact

In 2006, according to the *American Journal of Psychiatry*, the estimated economic burden of anxiety and depressive disorders in the United States amounted to 321 million days of work lost, at a cost of close to $50 billion dollars a year!

The study by Barlow in 2004 showed that only 25% of the cost of the illness burden pertained to the costs of treatment. Stress-related disorders, including posttraumatic stress disorder, have been estimated to cost over $3 billion dollars a year.

Even before the pandemic, over 60% of people with mental health–related issues were not receiving adequate or any level of clinical care. As discussed throughout this book, we know that, unfortunately, that number has increased over the years, given the significant increase in need due to the pandemic and its related societal implications.

Untreated mental health issues are linked to a higher risk of other medical and psychiatric issues, as well as an increased risk of dying prematurely.

4.4 Expressive Writing Therapy

One of the key strategies in working towards healing is to identify what the issues are. Being able to describe and name what we are thinking and how we are feeling is important in communicating our current state and to determine if we have made progress in decreasing negative feelings and improving our mental health and well-being.

Throughout this book, we provide interactive prompts that allow the user to reflect and document through expressive writing. The techniques and guidance provided are tailored to help the reader understand and work towards healing. The numerous physical, mental, emotional, personal, and financial benefits of this type of self-reflection and expressive writing are included in this section.

Expressive writing therapy is evidence based and can decrease feelings of anxiety, worry, and fear. Those with more severe symptoms may not benefit as much from this modality of treatment as those with less severe symptoms of anxiety. Those with more complex needs often require multiple forms of care, which may include working with a prescriber and other clinicians.

We formulate our understanding of our worlds with language, and how we think about things and label and create associations all shape our feelings and behaviors. We can analyze and change how we think, and the exercises included in this book provide the guidance and structure to do so.

Thinking about our options, solving problems, and seeing them written down on the page in front of us help create a reality in which there may be a healthier path. We can then choose and reinforce what we would like to see, feel, and think in our day-to-day lives.

■ **Physiological Benefits**

- Expressive writing therapy has been shown to decrease states of arousal, enhance recovery from stress, regulate breathing, and decrease blood pressure. It has been shown to decrease the inflammatory response and cortisol while improving immunity.
- As one gains increased control over their reactions to bodily sensations and cues, understanding and mastery develop. These benefits help decrease the need for urgent health-care visits and has been shown to ultimately decrease avoidable emergency department visits, costs, and stress.
- Gaining insight into one's identity and values through expressive and creative writing allows for an improvement in health, dietary intake, and physical exercise. Activities of daily living are reviewed and revised according to one's values, resulting in the ability to track actions towards outcomes.

■ **Mental and Emotional Benefits**

- Expressive writing has been shown to clinically change the way one looks at themselves and understands the world around them.
  - This cognitive restricting allows the person to re-write their own narrative.
  - It reduces symptoms of anxiety and worry, as well as the negative thoughts and behaviors that are colored by anxiety and worry.
  - As the person increases their understanding of their ability to control these emotions, they improve their writing abilities, re-write their perceptions of their experiences, and, in a cyclic manner, positively reinforce their healthy habits.
- Journaling and writing exercises allow for the anxieties, difficulties, to-dos, shame, guilt, and worries to all be placed on paper, creating a distance between the individual and what is on the page. Over time, the ability to be present in the here and now allows for mindfulness and a calm engagement with one's surroundings.

- Creative writing gives voice to suppressed or blocked memories.
- According to a study by Meshberg-Cohen et al. (2014), expressive writing is correlated with the benefit of decreasing anxiety, depression, and trauma-related symptoms in patients who also have substance use disorders.
- Ritzert et al. (2016) describe the benefits of acceptance and commitment therapy (ACT)–based self-help bibliotherapy as a low-cost intervention for people with anxiety related stressors, with clear symptomatic improvement.
- Journaling and expressive writing exercises such as those throughout this book allow the person to place their anxieties and worries onto paper so they can leave them there and come back to them at a later time.
  - This creates a distance in both time and space between the anxious feelings and any reactionary thoughts or behaviors. When you get back to the thing you wrote that you were anxious about, may seem less intense or not important at all anymore. It also allows you to reinforce to yourself that life goes on, and there are outcomes in which you can and will live peacefully without being under the intense grip of anxiety.
  - Writing thoughts down also allows for a higher, more mature level of dealing with negative feelings when you choose to return to whatever caused the anxiety.
  - It also serves as a benchmark from which to assess any progress made over time.
- Expressive writing enhances resilience and provides a new foundational habit to mitigate future stress responses.
  - When we are emotional or dysregulated, it is easy to fall back into old patterns and habits of coping.
  - As we gain mastery of understanding how anxiety impacts us and how we can use that energy for healing, we buffer against falling back into old unhealthy routines.
- Going back and reading what was written may help reveal parts of ourselves that we have forgotten, repressed, or otherwise pushed aside.

■ Academic and Career Benefits

- Expressive writing and associated mindfulness techniques have been shown to decrease stress and improve sleep quality.
- Implementing these strategies has been shown to improve productivity at school and work, decrease time off, and improve satisfaction overall.
- Workplaces that implement mental health promotion programs show significant returns on investment in decreases in employee burnout, improved retention, and decreased health-care utilization costs.
- Being able to be present and remain focused at school or work improves graduation and career advancement potential.
- When using these techniques with a client, expressive writing exercises have been shown to increase patient satisfaction and therapeutic rapport.
- Especially post pandemic, the lines between our personal lives and work lives have blurred as those fortunate enough to be able to work from home have increased. Be wary of extreme capitalism disguised as balanced altruism when people talk about 'work-life integration.' This likely means 'work all the time,' with no distinction between who you are and the life you exchange for a paycheck. When true boundaries can be set through self-awareness and confidence, true work-life or school-life balance can be met.

4.5 Characterizing Your Anxiety

An important next step after identifying the type of anxiety you are suffering from is to become familiar with how you interact with your anxiety and how it interacts with you. This way of thinking will help you develop insight and foster self-awareness.

Anxiety rating scales such as the Generalized Anxiety Disorder 7-Item (GAD-7) scale and the Hamilton Anxiety Rating Scale (HAM-A) are evidence-based questionnaires to assess how severe anxiety is at any given time. These screening tools and scales are important in tracking the progression of treatment and guiding treatment-planning decisions with your clinician.

In addition to using these scales when prompted by your care providers, we also encourage you to think about how your anxiety is a part of your day-to-day existence. Is it a transient visitor that randomly comes and goes, or does it always live within you?

Characterizing your anxiety can be a playful yet powerful element of gaining control, confidence, and hope about living with anxiety. When thinking about the attributes and traits of your anxiety, consider the associated physical sensations, including touch, sight, smell, sound, and maybe even taste.

Imagine if your anxiety was a small monkey that had a life of its own yet was also a part of your journey. This 'Anxiety Monkey' is a cartoon of itself, intended to get you think about your own relationship with your anxiety.

The Anxiety Monkey may perch on your shoulder and visit you when you know it will: for example, during times that cause you worry and stress. You may feel it climbing up your leg and back, then wrapping its tail around your shoulder.

At level 1, is your Anxiety Monkey playful and energetic, or is it angry or distracting? Can other people see your Anxiety Monkey at this level?

Use this opportunity to think about and list your anxiety-provoking situations, from least to most.

Examples of things that cause you anxiety may include:

- Asking someone out
- Being called on in class
- Being perceived as socially awkward
- Being with someone you have a crush on
- Climate change
- Eating in public
- Feeling you're not dressed appropriately
- Giving a presentation
- Going on a plane ride
- Going to a job interview
- Going to a new yoga class
- Going to a party
- Having a long to-do list
- Having forgotten something at home
- Having to say 'no'
- Health-related concerns
- Joining a sports team
- Not being attuned to the local customs
- Not belonging to a certain group
- Not knowing something
- Receiving a compliment
- Running into someone you know
- Taking a test
- Thinking about losing someone you love
- Thinking about natural disasters
- Using a public bathroom
- Visiting a new college campus
- Waiting for a text or someone's response
- Other: write other situations, thoughts, or experiences that you know cause you anxiety:

_____

_____

_____

_____

When your Anxiety Monkey gets to level 2, it may be more intense, cause more distress, and be even more visible to others.

If you were to meet someone for the first time and anxiety was a part of your life, how would you introduce your Anxiety Monkey?

_____

_____

_____

_____

_____

What are some qualities of your Anxiety Monkey?

_____

_____

_____

_____

_____

Who gets to see your Anxiety Monkey?

_____

_____

_____

_____

_____

How do other people see your Anxiety Monkey?

_____

_____

_____

_____

_____

Where does your Anxiety Monkey go?

By level 3, your Anxiety Monkey is clearly distressed, off the rails, and barely contained. It is seriously impacting you and your decisions and behaviors. Not only are you distracted by it yelling in your face and digging its claws into your shoulder but you also can't seem to focus, and you just want to run away and hide. The problem is that your Anxiety Monkey is there with you and in no shape to be calmed any time soon.

What infuriates your Anxiety Monkey? What makes it go off the rails?

_____

_____

_____

_____

_____

Who brings your Anxiety Monkey out the most?

_____

_____

_____

_____

_____

How can you keep your Anxiety Monkey contained?

_____

_____

_____

_____

_____

Who calms your Anxiety Monkey the most?

_____

_____

_____

_____

_____

What does your Anxiety Monkey serve you?

_____

_____

_____

_____

_____

4.6 Pros and Cons of Anxiety

We developed a pros and cons list of anxiety and stress-related issues so they can be compared with the value of treatment, and a decision can be made as to how to proceed.

Our intention is for readers to be highly educated consumers and make decisions based on what they need and the goals and systems they create. See Chapter 9, 'Safety Planning,' for more information on developing goals, values, and systems.

Pros

- Anxiety is a future-oriented emotion and can provide readiness for a future event. It allows one to creatively think of possible scenarios and options that may be ahead and to work towards being in the right place at the right time to take advantage of those opportunities.
- According to studies, the future orientation of anxiety, combined with a reflective, introspective view, allows people to be better at planning for the future, more organized, and more goal oriented.
- Anxiety motivates adaptive responses to real threats. Anxiety-driven behaviors may lead an individual to plan and prepare for future threats and events.
- Anxious individuals have been described as having attentional bias towards perceiving threats; they may be sensitive to environmental and relationship-level potential threats. This has a protective factor in that it may influence the person to change their behavior, alter their situation, and avoid the consequences of the threat.
- People with anxiety tend to also be more aware of their bodies, and they sense signals and cues.

  - They are more likely to visit doctors for checkups and reassurance and have more frequent interactions with their care teams in general.
  - Unfortunately, people with high levels of anxiety are also at an increased risk of having heart attacks (Olafiranye et al. 2011), although, because they are so in tune with their symptoms, they typically catch the signs and seek out medical care earlier. This, in turn, leads to these behaviors resulting in increased life expectancy.

- According to a study by Coplan et al. (2012), their team found an association between increased intelligence and anxiety.

■ Increased anxiety specifically relating to preparing for and taking an exam has shown a correlation with increased performance.

■ Anxiety can lead to creativity, self-development, and self-expression. The energy of the imagination can be harnessed for positive and constructive endeavors.

■ Studies show that anxious employees are better, more productive employees.

– From a purely short-term, capitalistic, systemic perspective, this is a true 'pro.'
– They make fewer errors in tasks that require sustained attention and are more thorough in their work product.
– According to a study done in 2005 at the University of Wales, anxiety was cor-related with an increase in functioning and self-discipline.
– In the longer term, however, the unsustainability of an anxiety disorder and its impact on the workforce ends up being a true 'con,' with significantly more financial downsides.

■ Anxiety can put things in perspective. As we realize that the feelings of worry and avoidance of threat are likely all in the context of not wanting to die and that, ulti-mately, we all will die, we can use that energy to live our best possible lives.

■ Those with anxiety, according to an article by Fani et al. (2012), have an ability to perceive threats in ambiguous or uncertain situations better than those with-out anxiety. This is explained by the attention bias of people with anxiety towards potential threats in their environment. While we include this in the 'pro' section for having anxiety, the reality is that exaggerated physiological responses to potential threats can be a harbinger of anxiety disorders.

■ Anxious people take fewer risks, reducing risk-taking behavior in general.

■ The desire to avoid feelings of worry, anxiety, and shame has been linked with increased pro-social behaviors, including increased ethical decision-making.

■ People with lower levels of anxiety, on the other hand, have higher rates of divorce.

4.7 Writing Prompt

Consider using the space provided to reflect on the following three-part prompt:

1. Describe a time you were under stress and felt anxious.

_____

_____

_____

_____

_____

_____

_____

_____

_____

_____

2. Reflect on your thoughts, feelings, and actions in response to the experience.

_____

_____

_____

_____

_____

_____

_____

_____

3. In what ways were your responses useful and protective?

_____

_____

_____

_____

_____

_____

_____

_____

_____

Cons

- Early life stress, including anxiety and depression, is associated with later life physical and mental health outcomes.
- Patterns of emotional maladjustment are a risk factor for worsening symptoms of anxiety.
- Anxiety increases interpersonal stress and difficulty developing and maintaining relationships.
- The sensitization model of stress and anxiety, as described in studies, is where early and frequent stress in life adds up so that later on, even small amounts of a stressor may lead to mental distress.

  - In other words, people who experience stress over a long period of time are less likely to tolerate additional stressors.
  - There are, however, competing findings that suggest a strengthening effect of cumulative stressors so, when confronted with new stress and anxiety, the person may exhibit a lowered response.
  - The critical things to remember are that the experience is highly subjective, and the age of stress onset and the intensity of the stressor are variable and will impact people differently.

- Anxiety may impact a person's day-to-day life and ability to perform at school or work. When an individual is always on and always in alert mode, it is exhausting and takes away from energy that could be spent on other things.
- Anxiety may cause sleep disturbances, resulting in concentration and attention difficulties.
- It may complicate other mental health issues such as depression. See Chapter 2, 'Identifying and Treating Anxiety,' for detailed information on anxious depression.
- Studies show that stress, anxiety, and impaired mental health can impact the healing of wounds, as well as immunity in general. Increased level of stress results in inflammatory states (see Chapter 5, 'Brain, Body, and Behaviors,' for more information regarding the interaction of cortisol and negative physical health consequences), which itself is linked to metabolic and cardiac illnesses.
- Anxiety has been linked with an increased perception of pain.
- Increased use of health care. According to studies, those with anxiety-related issues are five times more likely to consult their doctor for a medical or psychological complaint. Similarly, they are six times more likely to be psychiatrically hospitalized.
- Increased use of medications.
- More chronic illnesses.
- Physical and medical health costs:

  - Poor physical functioning.

- School, work, and career costs:

  - Delayed return to work.
  - Increased likelihood of quitting.
  - Increased incidences of getting laid off or fired.
  - Decreased productivity.
  - Decreased attention.

- Financial costs:

  - General cost of medications and therapy.
  - Costs of things to cope with or suppress the feeling, such as alcohol or other drugs; trying different fads or apps.
  - Increased costs associated with cleaning supplies and other things for ritualistic behaviors.

- Mental health and emotional costs:

  - Thinking about, talking about, and worrying about anxiety is exhausting.
  - Anxiety can be intolerable, make the person suffering miserable.

- Relationship costs:

  - Anxiety takes time away from family and loved ones.
  - Anxiety impacts friendships.
  - Missed events.
  - Feeling shame or embarrassment.

- Autonomy and freedom costs:

  - Anxiety may reduce one's ability to travel, resulting in:
    - Decreased driving.
    - Decreased use of planes, trains, and public transportation.
    - Decrease in going outside or to parks or malls.
  - Missed opportunities.
  - Fear of missing out (FOMO).

- Dietary costs:

  - Anxiety may alter an individual's relationship with food.
  - Changes in diet and preferred food types.

- Health-care system costs:

  - Anxiety-related issues often result in increased health care utilization and costs overall.
  - May result in lowered patient satisfaction.

4.8 Shades of Anxiety

Anxiety can color the way we think about and interpret the world. The language we use to describe ourselves and our experiences affects how we think and feel.

Negative descriptors and pessimistic views bring the person down, and others react accordingly. Negativity and looking for the worst in people and things become self-fulfilling prophecies that are reinforced as the negative is experienced to the exclusion of all the good and positive in the world.

4.9 Writing Prompt

Use the space provided to answer the following writing prompts:

Think of something or someone you love and think is the best. List everything positive about this thing or person and the wonderful ways they make you feel.

_____

_____

_____

_____

_____

_____

Now, using the same person or object you just wrote about, list everything you think could be better or you may not necessarily like. Think about all the areas of opportunity for this person or thing to improve.

_____

_____

_____

_____

_____

_____

The first part of this writing prompt was likely easier to complete than the second half, concerning the 'not so great' aspects of something or someone you just spent time thinking and writing wonderful things about.

When we fall into biases of all good or all bad, we don't allow for all the shades in between to be seen. In doing so, we also fail to allow for the many opportunities for improvement to blossom. Living with anxiety over a long period of time begins to reinforce the negative and, especially in aspects of obsessions and compulsions, may solidify patterns of behavior and thoughts that may worsen the anxiety itself.

The reality is that nothing is always perfect or always terrible. Life isn't always easy or always difficult. Even anxiety itself is sometimes more intense and sometimes may seem to go away. Appreciating this from a cognitive perspective allows the individual to remind themselves when things seem darker and less straightforward. Think about the mental energy it just took to write about several sides of the same example. Imagine living under the shade of negativity, anxiety, and worry and the immense amount of energy it takes. Constant states of awareness and searching for threats are exhausting and damaging to one's health and well-being.

Re-writing the experiences of our experiences and deliberately choosing to name and identify aspects of ourselves and our history in a framework that allows for self-compassion and healing is the path we need to be on. As we work on the way we describe ourselves and our experiences, it will also impact the way we talk in public and to our close friends and family.

Language is extremely powerful and has the strength to change cultures and societies and, most certainly, our individual lives. Think of the term 'new normal,' which was used within days of the announcement of the pandemic in early 2020. Everyone—all media outlets, schools, and businesses—kept saying 'new normal,' a term we had never heard or thought of before.

The new normal brought with it many extremes in behaviors and had the impact of demarcating the past from our new reality. The expectation was that this would be it: there would be no going backwards to the way things were.

Chapter 6, 'COVID, Fear, and Grief,' goes into great detail about all the way the pandemic changed our mental and physical lives forever. The point of discussing this here is that those people that had the ability to discern the power of the messaging of words and the ability to appreciate the anxiety and fear that came along with a definite change but were uncertain as to what the new normal would be and had a better ability to assess and make healthy decisions.

As discussed throughout this book, when cognitive, operational, rational decisions need to be made, we are at our best when we can remain as emotionally neutral as possible. Shades of anxiety or sadness invariably taint the picture and can send an individual or an entire society off course, with irreversible consequences. If one thinks that there is no option, that everything is and will be terrible, they manifest that, see the worst in all situations, and are reinforced that things indeed are terrible. Alternately, one can choose to zoom out and look for the positive and the inherent potential in situations.

> **One must still have chaos in oneself to be able to give birth to a dancing star.**
> **—Friedrich Nietzsche**

4.10 Writing Prompt

As we build our mental framework and comfort level in realizing we have the ability to impact how we think and feel by the choices and actions we take, we empower ourselves and can re-write the circumstance to convey positive thoughts and potential opportunities.

Consider the mental model of appreciating the energy that anxiety provides as a force that can instead be used for creativity and excitement.

For example:

"I am worried about this job interview."

Can be re-written in our minds as:

"I am excited about this job and will do my best at the interview."

Use the space provided to think of what you are anxious about.

_____

_____

_____

_____

Now, re-write your thoughts and feelings in a way that allows the positive and potential to be appreciated.

_____

_____

_____

_____

A seemingly straightforward exercise such as the one provided here can allow the time between the emotion of anxiety and the negative thinking to further separate. As the reaction to the emotion is distanced, we have the ability to spend mental energy on taking apart the thoughts, thinking about how bad something can actually be, and what the worst-case scenarios are. When we have this gap between emotion and reaction, we will likely realize that even our worst imagined outcomes are not so bad after all.

Recall the last time you flew on an airplane. When boarding the plane, waiting on the runway, you can see people and cars at their normal size and scale on the ground. Think of those as your day-to-day anxieties. They are real, life-size, in your frame of vision and very clearly in front of you. As the plane takes off and you are zooming away from the planet, you still see the cars and buildings but no longer the people, and then you see the buildings less and less, until you cannot distinguish anything on the ground as you are so far up in the sky.

The anxieties we know to be real and in our faces are only there temporarily and are only there based on one level. When we move or zoom out, they begin to become smaller and even disappear from sight. We know the buildings and cars still exist, but we cannot see them at the moment.

As we perform this mental exercise over and over again and build our confidence recalling positive prior experiences, we can increase our sense of calm. Acknowledging and managing anxiety does not mean anxiety disappears forever. It allows the anxiety to be out of our point of view, away from focus while the calm and confidence washes over.

Chapter 5

Brain, Body, and Behaviors

5.1 Introduction

In this chapter, we will discuss the specifics of how the biology of the brain and body work together. We also discuss how our behaviors are impacted by what we think and feel.

To better understand anxiety and the many ways it may show up in our lives, we discuss known causes of anxiety, including what we eat, our environment, and much more. In addition to our structural organs, such as our brains and nervous system, anxiety is influenced by our society, the predominant stressors at the time of our upbringing, and the way we view the world, as well as our personalities.

As we discuss the brain and biological mechanisms, we review the function and impact anxiety has on the way we experience relationships and the world around us. The connection between the mind, body, and spirit has been acknowledged for centuries.

Did you know that the Latin origin of the word *anxiety* comes from the base word *angere* which means to choke, to cause pain, to afflict, to vex? Throughout this chapter, as well as the entire book, we weave together the intricacies of how our brains and bodies are connected and how they impact our behaviors, choices, and relationships.

While we may not always be aware of how much energy our brains expend, the reality is that we have evolved to be consistently monitoring and mindful of our surroundings. From the periphery of our eyesight to foreign smells to sudden noises, our brains are wired to detect patterns and shifts from the norm. A key part of survival and continuing our legacy as humans is maintaining safety and preventing and avoiding physical and mental harm.

We will begin by discussing the autonomic nervous system, which comprises the sympathetic and the parasympathetic nervous systems, and how these systems complement one another in ensuring we have the best possible chance of reacting and protecting ourselves.

We continue the chapter with physical symptoms, foods, and other environmental causes of anxiety and stress. We then discuss sleep hygiene and provide a template for analyzing your sleep habits with recommendations to improve them.

DOI: 10.4324/9781003413547-7

By all means let's be open-minded, but not so open-minded that our brains drop out.

—Richard Dawkins

5.2 Writing Prompt

Within the framework of the Balan 3-2-1 Method, consider your response to the following:

Am I ready to choose a new approach for my anxieties and worries?

3: With intention, set your internal and external environment.

■ The body: What mindfulness techniques are you choosing to allow your body to heal?

_____

_____

_____

■ The setting: How are you intentionally influencing your setting?

_____

_____

_____

■ The breath: Which breathing technique will you use as you prepare for this exercise?

_____

_____

_____

2: What are your thoughts and feelings in response to the writing prompt?

_____

_____

_____

_____

_____

_____

_____

_____

_____

_____

1: What is your one intent or affirmation in the context of the writing prompt?

_____

_____

_____

5.3 Autonomic Nervous System (ANS)

The autonomic nervous system can be remembered by the four F's it is involved with. Fight, Flight, Fear, and F#$% (the F word that impolitely means to have sex).

The ANS is involved with blood circulation, muscle tone, endocrine activity, cognitive arousal, hormonal activity, and emotions.

5.3.1 ANS: Sympathetic Nervous System

The classic fight-or-flight response is the main function of the sympathetic nervous system. As mentioned earlier, arousal and bursts of energy to protect the self occur even before we are consciously aware of a perceived threat. This arousal occurs before we are even aware of what we are doing or how we are responding to the perceived threat. (See the section on signal pathways and amygdala function.)

During periods of anxiety, anger, or feeling in danger, the sympathetic nervous system is activated. This brings on unpleasant thoughts and feelings. The following is a description of exactly how and why these things occur.

When the sympathetic nervous system is activated, the following bodily changes occurs:

■ Alertness increases.
■ Pupils dilate.

  – This allows for increased awareness.

■ Hearing improves.

- Similar to the increased vision, this increase in the ability to hear and detect changes and threats allows for improved awareness of surroundings.

■ Metabolism elevates.

- There is an increase in blood sugar, which allows for increased energy when fighting the threat or running away if necessary.

■ Heart rate elevates.

- This allows for increased circulation to parts of the body, such as our muscles, so they receive the blood, oxygen, and nutrients they need.

■ Breathing becomes faster and shallower.

- This results in more oxygen being sent to the brain.

■ More blood is able to circulate throughout the core of the body as blood vessels dilate, providing nutrients to muscles, improving the opportunity to either fight the threat or run away.

- Blood vessels in our extremities, such as our arms and legs, constrict, allowing more blood and nutrients to be available to our big muscles. When this happens, the skin on our body may appear pale, which is a common response to anxiety.
- In connection with increased metabolism, circulation to muscles and sweating increase.

■ Since a burst of energy is needed to fight or run away, unnecessary bodily functions, such as digesting food, decrease.

- The purpose is to conserve energy for areas of the body that need it the most.
- Saliva in the mouth decreases, resulting in the feeling of having a dry mouth when anxious or scared.
- There may also be the sensations of needing to vomit, urinate, or have a bowel movement. These are adaptive responses in that they reduce/remove immediately unnecessary processes such as digesting, to allow the fight-or-flight response to be optimized.

■ The stress hormone cortisol is released.

- Cortisol is a hormone that allows you to be alert and extremely aware of your surroundings. It helps with recognizing threats encountered before and prevents you from finding yourself in the same situation again. The learning that occurs with threats and the accompanying anxiety and unpleasant feelings allow future responses to be protective, in the form of fight or flight. See the section on cortisol for more information.

These responses throughout the body go back to their normal baseline once the perceived threat is no longer present. In other words, the heart rate goes back to normal, breathing rate goes back to normal, and blood sugar and cortisol levels return to baseline. When this fight-or-flight mechanism is triggered in the face of real danger, the person is able to make protective decisions.

Unfortunately, during chronic stress, it is harder for the body to go back to baseline, resulting in physical and mental problems. In addition to being exhausting to live in a constant state of stress, it reduces one's ability to concentrate and create memories of life events and decreases the overall quality of life.

Increased blood pressure, high blood sugar, and high cortisol levels over a long period of time are harmful, cause the body and brain to have impaired reactions to stress and anxiety, and can cause adverse medical issues as well.

As discussed in greater detail in Chapter 6, 'COVID, Fear, and Grief,' in our current circumstances, with significantly increased stressors such as the pandemic, wars, climate crisis, and economic unrest, our bodies are unable to go back and forth healthily in and out of the anxiety states. We have seen a dramatic increase in stress-related disorders, which we covered in our prior book *Re-Write* (2023), as well as the anxiety disorders discussed in this book.

5.3.2 ANS: Parasympathetic Nervous System

The parasympathetic system involves resting and digesting. The parasympathetic nervous system serves to save energy by slowing down various functions in the body, which allows for the following:

- Pupils constrict.
- Heart rate decreases.
- Breathing slows down.
- Metabolism goes back to baseline.
- Muscles relax.
- Digestion resumes as the parasympathetic nervous system signals that it is OK to spend energy on movement throughout the gastrointestinal tract.
- Penile erection is facilitated as the nerves and blood vessels to the penis are influenced by the parasympathetic nervous system.

5.4 Limbic System

The limbic system comprises structures that play key roles in memory and emotions. The main physiological components of the limbic system include the following:

- Amygdala
- Thalamus
- Hypothalamus
- Hippocampus

The limbic system processes incoming stimuli and ensures we are responding to perceived threats. If, for example, the amygdala or the hippocampus—parts of the brain that ensure sympathetic responses are elicited in the face of threats—are overactive, we experience anxiety, worry, and even terror. This can occur even if an actual threat is not present.

The limbic system functions to recall events and details based on their emotional aspects, as well as our own intrinsic drives and motivations. Routine reactions, including anxiety, are normal and healthy. When they are elevated, the feelings described earlier, including increased heart rate, sweating, shallow breathing, and the activation of fight or flight, accompany the memory of the threat, triggering the cyclic discomfort of anxiety.

As emotional regulation is also impacted by the limbic system, the complex behaviors and emotions that involve pleasure and reward seeking are affected as well. Similar to the example of learning stressors that cause anxiety and the fight-or-flight reaction, the limbic system also facilitates the reinforcing behaviors of satisfaction and reward. See the sections on serotonin and dopamine for detailed information on the reward pathways and how they impact our behaviors.

5.5 Thalamus

The thalamus receives information from our senses and serves as a relay and connection hub for other areas of the brain. Sensory information from our eyes, mouth, ears, nose, and what we touch and feel all connect and relay through the thalamus.

Elements of consciousness, alertness, and states of being awake and asleep are functions of the thalamus. The thalamus plays a role in concentration and learning and helps sort between what needs to be paid attention to and what does not.

Under extreme stress, memories may become fragmented as stimuli that enter the thalamus are disrupted, resulting in a disrupted ability to recall traumatic events.

5.6 Amygdala

The amygdala processes sensations from the thalamus. Perception of the stimuli received results in a behavioral and emotional response. For example, stimuli that suggest danger or a threat influence the individual's response, such as anxiety, fear, or running away.

The amygdala then sends the information to the cortex to determine what the threat is. The cortex is where the brain attempts to discern if the loud banging outside is a monster or the wind blowing branches against the house.

If a threat is detected by the cortex via the amygdala, that information is sent to the hypothalamus and then to the pituitary gland, then the sympathetic nervous system, and then to the adrenal glands, resulting in the fight-or-flight response.

The amygdala plays a role in the intensity of our emotions as well. There is literature to suggest that intense positive emotions are also processed and that (classical) conditioning is developed via the amygdala. When something that was not connected to an intense negative response becomes connected to such a response when they are experienced together, the brain links them. These associations include the sights and sounds of the event, which can later trigger the threat response, even when there is no imminent danger.

When an individual has been the victim of trauma or there have been chronic stressors in their lives, the amygdala becomes chronically activated, as if the threat is ever present. This triggers the same pathways described earlier, resulting in chronic states of increased stress hormones, including cortisol and adrenaline. For example, people with anxieties, including those with a history of posttraumatic stress disorder who experience flashbacks, will have the activation of the fight-or-flight responses, even in the absence of an actual physical threat.

For more information, we recommend reading our prior book *Re-Write: A Trauma Workbook of Creative Writing and Recovery in Our New Normal* (2023), which goes into trauma-related stressors in great detail.

5.7 Hypothalamic Pituitary Adrenal (HPA) Axis

The HPA axis is made up of the following:

- Hypothalamus
- Pituitary gland
- Adrenal glands

The HPA axis is involved in responses to the perception of threats and other stressors. Signals and information go from the hypothalamus to the pituitary gland, then the adrenal gland, resulting in neurotransmitters and other hormones being secreted.

Chronic stress and an overactive HPA axis can lead to difficulty returning to a baseline level of calm. This can then lead to anxiety, depression, and other stress-related disorders. We go into the biological and immune system damage chronic stress causes later in this chapter.

5.8 Hypothalamus

The hypothalamus receives emotionally encoded information from the amygdala. It then sends that information as well as corticotropin-releasing factor to the pituitary gland. The pituitary gland then releases adrenocorticotropin hormone, which triggers the release of adrenaline and cortisol. This allows for increases in heart rate, breathing, and available sugar in the blood.

The hypothalamus is responsible for regulating stress, the endocrine system, body temperature, sleep, and sensations of hunger and thirst.

5.9 Adrenal Glands

The adrenal glands are small and triangular shaped and rest above each kidney. They are another critical area in the body's response to anxiety and stress, protecting us from danger.

They are responsible for the secretion of epinephrine (adrenaline), norepinephrine, and cortisol during the perception of stress, in response to signals sent from the pituitary gland.

During chronic states of stress, especially when the HPA axis is stimulated inappropriately, serious physical and mental health damages occur.

5.10 Hippocampus

The hippocampus is important in forming and consolidating new memories, as well as in emotional regulation.

5.10.1 Memory Formation and Consolidation

The hippocampus receives signals from the thalamus and from the senses and helps store them as memories. Critical pieces of information, including what went on during an event, when it happened, how it happened, and how our mind and body perceived it, are all processed by the hippocampus. Signals from the hippocampus also go to the anterior cingulate cortex and then to the prefrontal cortex.

The information received from our senses adds context and connections to other memories and influences how the memory is encoded and consolidated into a long-term memory. Higher-intensity memories such as traumatic events or highly anxiogenic periods are encoded with richer information and can be recalled in greater detail.

Spatial memory is another contextually processed and long-term memory function of the hippocampus. It refers to the ability to recall an event or a place in relation to other things.

5.10.2 Emotional Regulation

The hippocampus interacts with the amygdala and prefrontal cortex and works to regulate the emotional response to stimuli.

People with anxieties, including PTSD, may develop distorted understanding of input from their surrounding environment, resulting in misinterpreting stimuli as threats and danger. Under these circumstances, the hippocampus associates these intense feelings of fear and anxiety with the memories that are being formed. These memories then increase the sensitivity to stimuli, which can trigger the amygdala, resulting in a cyclic loop of worsening worry.

5.11 Prefrontal Cortex

The prefrontal cortex allows for information processing, planning, and responding behaviorally in context-appropriate ways. The prefrontal cortex receives signals from the brain regions described earlier and works to understand and make sense of the information. Additionally, this part of the brain fosters decision making and reacting through emotional regulation.

Somerville (2013) describes the development of the medial prefrontal cortex during adolescence and how it impacts motivation to understand others, as well as oneself. The concept of self-consciousness arises, as does the sense of peer evaluation.

Those with anxiety disorders have been shown to have decreased activity in the prefrontal cortex, which cyclically results in diminished ability to regulate emotions in response to the cognitive processes. Similarly, anxiety and the accompanying physical changes in the brain impact aspects of self-evaluation and elements of empathy. Decreased affective processing, in turn, puts the individual at risk of further anxiety.

Adolescence and young adulthood are times when relationships in context of the changing self are tested and formed. This is a time when there is an increased sensitivity to social pressures and the need for acceptance and belonging. Insults in the forms of trauma, physical and psychological; bullying; and embarrassment all contribute to actual brain changes that can worsen stress-related disorders and anxiety. This can lead to a blunting of the person's ability to assess the level of an incoming stressor, resulting in heightened anxiety and stress responses.

5.12 Vagus Nerve

The vagus nerve, also known as the vagal nerves, transmits information between the brain and other organs as an integral part of the parasympathetic nervous system. It controls functions such as breathing, heart rate, and digestion.

Activating the vagal nerves through breathing exercises and meditation begins the relaxation response and reduces anxiety. Using any of the breathing techniques discussed in Chapter 3, 'Balan 3-2-1 Method,' sends signals to the brain that it is OK to calm down and relax. Additionally, healthy behaviors, including exercise, appropriate dietary habits, and adequate sleep, all interact with the vagal nerve's actions.

5.13 Serotonin

Serotonin is a neurotransmitter that influences emotions such as anxiety and mood. It is hypothesized that serotonin plays a key role in the development and impact of the symptomatology of depressive disorders, anxiety disorders, personality pathology, suicidality, and posttraumatic stress disorder. One or more of these serotonin-associated mental health issues are often found at the same time in the same person.

Serotonin is responsible for encoding memories that have an emotional component to them, as well as feelings of social status and importance. Studies indicate that serotonin has an inhibitory effect on the effect of norepinephrine. In other words, serotonin has the effect of calming fear and decreasing arousal states such as anxieties and hypervigilance.

Serotonin levels impact appetite and sleep patterns, as well as aggressivity. Violence directed inwards, including self-injurious behaviors and suicidality, and violence directed outwards are all affected by serotonin levels. Impulsive behaviors and personality pathology such as borderline personality disorder are also linked to serotonin levels.

While the umbrella review by Moncrieff et al. (2022) demonstrated that there was no support for the link between low serotonin and depression, the FDA continues to recommend the approved serotonergic medications for anxiety, as discussed in Chapter 1, 'Identifying and Treating Anxiety.'

5.14 Case Example: Panic at the Theater

This is a case from many years ago, and all identifying information has been changed.

A 26-year-old male who had recently completed his postdoctoral training came into therapy complaining of anxiety that generalized to many parts of his life. He said it first started when he was in a movie theater watching an adventure thriller with his wife and several of their friends. He described the initial sensations as feeling as if something he ate might have upset his stomach, and he felt like he might have to go to the bathroom.

He reported feeling trapped in the movie theater, helpless in the darkness, stuck in the rows of seats. He mentioned feeling overwhelmed by having to pay attention to the loud action scenes and suppress his stomach pains, becoming exhausted trying to decide if he should stay or leave to use the restroom. He chose to excuse himself, used the bathroom, and returned to his seat. As soon as he went back in to watch the movie, he became increasingly overwhelmed and felt he needed to leave to use the restroom multiple times, fearing he might have diarrhea. It was after several trips that he told his wife he wanted to go home.

This started his years-long journey of dealing with serious anxiety and panic. He reported that, because he was working, he didn't have time to go to therapy and felt it was mostly a stomach-related issue. He reported cutting back on some of the foods he used to eat, thinking they might be giving him intestinal symptoms, including diarrhea. None of that worked, and his thoughts and anxieties of feeling trapped in the office, driving a car, and eating at restaurants all got worse and kept spreading to different areas of his life.

He began to decline invitations and chose not to attend different events for fear he might not be able to make it to the bathroom in time. He talked about feeling ashamed of having to make up reasons and then felt bad for missing the events.

Upon urging from his wife, he did follow up with his primary care doctor, who did a medical workup to check for any gastrointestinal issues. All tests were negative, ruling out any dietary causes of his feeling overwhelmed and having diarrhea during his anxious times.

It was at that point, on the advice of his wife and doctor, he decided to follow up with talk therapy. In treatment, he disclosed he had been increasing the amount of alcohol he was drinking to be able to tolerate feelings of extreme anxiety, panic, agoraphobia; feeling trapped outside; and fear of having diarrhea and not being able to reach a bathroom in time.

With his therapist, he discussed previous issues but came to the realization that at the time of the initial panic attack, he was in conversation with his wife about having their first child. Throughout treatment, they explored feelings of being trapped and loss of control.

Over the course of a year of therapy, the man started to reduce the amount of alcohol he was drinking and slowly increased the number of social engagements he attended. Therapy was concluded on the first birthday of his child, who was born two years after he started talk therapy.

5.15 Case Discussion

While the sense of loss of control and anxiety are closely related, the really interesting aspect of this case is that the physical symptoms of anxiety were at the root of the therapy itself. The feelings of stomach rumbling and his needs to go to the bathroom and the associated shame and guilt of having an accident influenced his emotional response.

The interpretation of what was going on in his mind, his anxieties, and how he felt them in his body coupled with his coping mechanism of escaping, avoiding, and then drinking alcohol to reduce the feelings of anxiety all compounded.

As is common with anxiety and panic disorders, this person's life revolved around the anxiety itself, reinforced by avoidance behaviors, a sense of shame, increased sensitivity to what others thought about him, and unhealthy compensatory choices.

The concerning aspects here are certainly the alcohol use and desire to seclude. The short-term biologic relief of anxiety through alcohol consumption allowed him to feel comfortable enough to leave the house but did not subsist. This person was a professional and worked during the day, which prohibited him from self-medicating and managing his career.

The protective factors for this person were a supportive connection with his spouse, his education, his career, and, most importantly, his access to health-care insurance. The reality that he could access care and that his primary care provider was able to rule out any medical issue before discussing psychological concerns was critical. This is the recommended approach with these types of biologically manifested psychosomatic complaints. The physician is tasked with ensuring they are not missing anything that could be the root cause, such as an intestinal or stomach-related disease.

Obviously, depending on the risk factors, age, and other medical issues the person is dealing with, the medical workup would be tailored accordingly. This particular individual didn't have a prior alcohol use disorder; drinking was a compensatory behavior to alleviate the anxiety. The risk was that the drinking did increase, raising alarms for developing tolerance and the subsequent need for more alcohol just to feel the same level of comfort.

Ruling out physiologic concerns, the next most important protective factor was his access to psychotherapy. The combination of access, strong support systems, and his willingness to dive deeper so they could start their family and healthily explore their own issues were what led to the resolution of the immediate anxiety and panic.

5.16 Irritable Bowel Syndrome

Irritable bowel syndrome (IBS) is a relatively common gastrointestinal disorder that is associated with several physical symptoms that directly impact a person's affect and behaviors. People with IBS typically present with abdominal pain, feel gassy and bloated, and have discomfort in their stomach and a change in their bowel habits.

As with any medical complaint that impacts the person's ability to lead their life the way they want, a proper medical workup needs to be done when faced with these symptoms. IBS is an interesting medical diagnosis as it is functional in nature, meaning there does not appear to be any associated physical problem such as inflammation, blockage, or damage to the intestines. IBS is therefore a diagnosis of exclusion once other medical causes are ruled out.

Having IBS often causes stress and anxiety, although is also known to be exacerbated by anxiety. According to the 2023 study by Tarar et al., over 38% of people with IBS had anxiety, and 27% had depression.

As discussed in the serotonin section earlier, the gastrointestinal tract has a high number of receptors that affect mood regulation. The interplay between the feeling of having to go to the bathroom and the anxiety it causes and worsens is one that has meaningful impacts on the individual.

People with IBS often complain about minor things and are hypervigilant as they feel a loss of control over their lifestyle. As dietary and other connections are determined to be triggers of the IBS, the person often alters their behaviors, resulting in further restrictions and isolation. These ritualistic avoidance behaviors provide some temporary relief, (see the section on OCD in Chapter 2, 'Identifying and Treating Anxiety'), although often exacerbate, may worsen, and lead to responses with stronger rituals.

Treatment for IBS includes dietary modifications as well as exercise recommendations. CBT and stress management are also indicated in working through thought patterns to manage the reactions to them. Mindfulness and other nonpharmacological methods of relaxation are also helpful. Medications for the anxiety component can be beneficial, especially as the person initiates the other forms of treatment, to help them work through the journey.

5.17 Writing Prompt

Within the framework of the Balan 3-2-1 Method, consider your response to the following:

Imagine you posted something online and just saw comments on your post that are not what you hoped they would be. How does this make you feel, and what are you planning on doing next?

3: With intention, set your internal and external environment.

■ The body: What mindfulness techniques are you choosing to allow your body to heal?

_____

_____

_____

■ The setting: How are you intentionally influencing your setting?

_____

_____

_____

■ The breath: Which breathing technique will you use as you prepare for this exercise?

_____

_____

_____

2: What are your thoughts and feelings in response to the writing prompt?

_____

_____

_____

_____

_____

_____

_____

_____

_____

1: What is your one intent or affirmation in the context of the writing prompt?

_____

_____

_____

5.18 Cortisol

When we experience anxiety, our adrenal glands release cortisol. As discussed earlier, the stress hormone cortisol allows for situational awareness and response. Intrinsically, we want to avoid pain and go towards pleasure. When we learn of a threat, be it a lion, a public speech, or an awkward social encounter, that caused us pain in the past, even thinking about it or seeing something that triggers that memory can elicit the pain through the complex interactions of cortisol and our behaviors.

Interestingly, the greater the stress, or anxiety, the more cortisol is released, which impacts the intensity of the memory formed. The stress response, which already includes an increased heart rate, increases cortisol as well, which further increases heart rate.

In most circumstances, when the threat that causes the anxiety is no longer present, cortisol and all other fight-or-flight responses go back to baseline levels. Prolonged exposure to stress and anxiety can cause chronic increases in cortisol, which can impact the immune system as well as mood. Cortisol affects sleep cycles, and increased amounts can affect sleep quality and duration.

These, in turn, can worsen feelings of anxiety and depression. Impacted mental health and well-being, as well as elevated levels of cortisol, can weaken the body's immune system, causing increased illnesses. Increased cortisol leads to increased blood sugar levels, which cause increases in blood pressure and heart rate, impact the digestive system, and cause difficulty swallowing.

5.19 Writing Prompt

Within the framework of the Balan 3-2-1 Method, consider your response to the following:

Today is a wonderful day. What would you like to experience today?

3: With intention, set your internal and external environment.

■ The body: What mindfulness techniques are you choosing to allow your body to heal?

_____

_____

_____

■ The setting: How are you intentionally influencing your setting?

_____

_____

_____

■ The breath: Which breathing technique will you use as you prepare for this exercise?

_____

_____

_____

2: What are your thoughts and feelings in response to the writing prompt?

_____

_____

_____

_____

_____

_____

_____

_____

1: What is your one intent or affirmation in the context of the writing prompt?

_____

_____

_____

5.20 Dopamine

Dopamine is a neurotransmitter that is associated with the reward system, motivation, and learning. It is released when a pleasurable stimulus is encountered, as well as during the anticipation leading up to the reward. As we are constantly on the lookout for ways not to die, to avoid threats, and to seek out rewards, when we come across a sight, smell, or place that is associated with pleasure, dopamine is released.

The association is quickly linked, and we naturally continue to seek out the same circumstances that made us feel good to feel that reward: the reinforcing burst of dopamine. It is also associated with attention and memory creation. Over the course of our experiences, our memories and behaviors have been shaped and reinforced through pleasure-seeking and pain-avoiding neurotransmitters.

Literature suggests that alterations in dopamine signals play a role in the development of anxiety disorders. The balance between a decreased ability to experience pleasure, as often is the case in anxiety, and an enhanced sensitivity to stress is impacted by our dopamine pathways.

5.21 Writing Prompt

Within the framework of the Balan 3-2-1 Method, consider your response to the following:

Imagine something you really want. When you think about it—getting your hands on it, eating it, or achieving it—how do you feel?

3: With intention, set your internal and external environment.

■ The body: What mindfulness techniques are you choosing to allow your body to heal?

_____

_____

_____

■ The setting: How are you intentionally influencing your setting?

_____

_____

■ The breath: Which breathing technique will you use as you prepare for this exercise?

_____

_____

_____

2: What are your thoughts and feelings in response to the writing prompt?

_____

_____

_____

_____

_____

_____

_____

_____

_____

1: What is your one intent or affirmation in the context of the writing prompt?

_____

_____

_____

_____

5.22 Oxytocin

Oxytocin is a hormone that allows for attachment, bonding, and trust. Altruistic feelings and our social trust are affected by oxytocin. A hug, skin-to-skin contact, and positive social interactions are all associated with oxytocin and the reciprocation in the relationship. Similar to our constant monitoring of our environments for threats to avoid and pleasures to obtain, we also are aware of opportunities for positive social interactions.

There have been reports in the literature suggesting a link between disordered oxy-tocin production and anxiety. The way we understand it currently is in the direction of reducing feelings of worry, anxiety, and loneliness through the connections and bonds one reinforces with oxytocin.

5.23 Writing Prompt

Within the framework of the Balan 3-2-1 Method, consider your response to the following:

Who in your life makes you feel positive just by thinking of them? Describe your thoughts and physical sensations when bringing this person to mind.

3: With intention, set your internal and external environment.

■ The body: What mindfulness techniques are you choosing to allow your body to heal?

_____

_____

_____

■ The setting: How are you intentionally influencing your setting?

_____

_____

_____

■ The breath: Which breathing technique will you use as you prepare for this exercise?

_____

_____

_____

2: What are your thoughts and feelings in response to the writing prompt?

_____

_____

_____

_____

_____

_____

_____

_____

_____

1: What is your one intent or affirmation in the context of the writing prompt?

_____

_____

_____

5.24 Causes of Anxiety

In this section, we provide a list of the many different things that can cause sensations of anxiety, panic, and stress. The list is divided by parts of the body, as well as different foods, medications, and recreational drugs that can all cause anxiety-like symptoms.

The diagnosis of anxiety and panic are made once medical and structural issues are ruled out. We discussed the bi-directional link between anxiety and physical issues during the case discussion about irritable bowel syndrome earlier.

If you have or think you may be suffering from any of the medical issues listed, please consult with your health provider or go to your nearest emergency department.

Brain and nervous system related:

- Ear infections, labyrinthitis
- Encephalopathies – infections, metabolic, toxic
- Essential tremor
- Intracranial mass lesions
- Post-concussive syndrome
- Seizure disorders
- Vertigo

Breathing and respiratory system related:

- Asthma
- Chronic obstructive pulmonary disease (COPD)

- Pneumothorax
- Pulmonary edema
- Pulmonary embolism

Blood disorders related:

- Anemias

  - B$_{12}$ deficiency
  - Iron deficiency
  - Sickle cell anemia

Cancer and tumor related:

- Carcinoid
- Insulinoma
- Pheochromocytoma

COVID related:

- Infection with SARS-CoV-2 is associated with an increase in psychiatric issues including anxiety and depressive disorders.

  - See Chapter 6, 'COVID, Fear, and Grief,' for an in-depth discussion of the bio-psychosocial factors of the pandemic that have impacted all our lives and mental well-being.

- COVID itself, independent of other variables, is associated with these mental health issues as those infected experience an increased risk.

  - The cause is described as both biologic and psychosocial.

- From a neurocognitive perspective, COVID has been linked with headaches, dizziness, agitation and confusion, memory difficulties, and changes in behavior and personality patterns, as well as other neurologic issues, including stroke and swelling in the brain. All these can, in turn, lead to symptoms of anxiety.
- In addition to the virus, the treatment options, including the potential for needing a breathing tube or being in the intensive care unit, can contribute to feelings of anxiety, worry, and terror.

Food and drink related:

- Alcohol

  - Consuming alcohol may reduce feelings of anxiety initially, but, as the alcohol leaves the system, its withdrawal from the brain and body can lead to feelings of irritability, anxiety, nervousness and shakiness.

- Alcohol use itself can be fatal in overdose, and, in severe circumstances, withdrawal from alcohol can also be fatal.

■ Artificial sweeteners
■ Caffeine

- As a stimulant, caffeine directly causes increases in heart rate and blood pressure and can very quickly cause feelings of anxiety, jitteriness, and nervousness.

■ Fast food

- The inflammation and oxidative stress caused by foods high in fats and processed foods has been linked to the development of anxiety.

■ Gluten

- True gluten sensitivities aside, there is evidence suggesting that reducing or eliminating foods containing gluten, such as breads and pastas, has been linked to a reduction in anxiety. Proposed mechanisms include the reduction in inflammation known to be caused by gluten.

■ Monosodium glutamate (MSG)
■ Processed foods

- The chemical additives used to increase flavor and extend shelf life are known to be linked to increased anxiety.
- Examples of processed food are hot dogs, fried foods, lunch meats, pastries, and candy.

■ Sugar

- Quick spikes in blood sugar can lead to subsequent drops in blood sugar. This can cause sensations of being irritable and on edge; anxiety; and feeling jittery, shaky, and nervous.
- Refined white sugars, including those found in candy, sodas, cupcakes, ice cream, and other extremely sweet foods such as breakfast cereals, can have an effect on your level of anxiety.

■ Vitamin deficiency

Heart and cardiovascular related:

■ Angina pectoris
■ Arrythmia
■ Heart failure
■ Hypertension
■ Hypovolemia

- Myocardial infarction
- Syncope
- Valvular disease
- Vascular collapse (shock)

Immune system related:

- Anaphylaxis
- Systemic lupus erythematosus (SLE)

Gastrointestinal related:

- Acid reflux, heartburn
- Constipation
- Diarrhea
- Difficulty swallowing, dysphagia
- Gas
- Irritable bowel syndrome (IBS)
- Nausea
- Vomiting

Prescription medication and drug related:

- Akathisia – as a side effect of medications such as antipsychotics
- Anticholinergics – benztropine, diphenhydramine (Benadryl), meperidine, oxybutynin, propantheline, tricyclics, trihexyphenidyl
- Bronchodilators – theophylline, sympathomimetics
- Digitalis toxicity
- Dopaminergics – amantadine, bromocriptine, levodopa, metoclopramide
- Drug withdrawal syndromes – barbiturates, benzodiazepine, serotonergic medications, narcotics, sedatives, alcohol, hypnotics
- Hallucinogens
- Hypotensive agents
- Prednisone
- Stimulants – amphetamines, cocaine, caffeine, aminophylline, methylphenidate, theophylline

    – Some ADHD medications are stimulants and can therefore cause or worsen anxiety.

- Sympathomimetics – ephedrine, epinephrine, pseudoephedrine
- Thyroid hormone replacement medications

Recreational drug related:

- Stimulants – cocaine, methamphetamine
- Alcohol – intoxication and withdrawal states

- Cannabis
- Cigarettes – nicotine is a stimulant

Metabolism related:

- Hyperadrenalism (Cushing's disease)
- Hyperkalemia
- Hyperthermia
- Hyperthyroidism
- Hypocalcemia
- Hypoglycemia
- Hyponatremia
- Hypothyroidism
- Menopause
- Porphyria (acute intermittent)

Physical disability related:

- Having a physical disability, especially earlier on in life, is a risk for developing mental health issues.
- Ambulation issues may impact the ability to socialize, join gatherings, participate in leisure activities, or travel places.
- Neurological issues may cause pain or fatigue, causing the person to miss out on opportunities with friends and family.
- If durable medical equipment is required, such as a prosthetic limb or wheelchair, the ability for the person to participate in certain activities such as hikes, swimming, or bicycling may be affected.
- Self-esteem may be impacted when seeing oneself in comparison to others. The ability to form or develop an interpersonal or sexual relationship may be hampered.
- Dependency on family and caregivers to achieve certain things or get places may affect an individual's sense of autonomy and self-image, creating additional barriers. Anxiety and depression may develop, adding on to the challenges of having a physical disability.
- A review article by Lal et al. (2022) discusses the relationship between childhood-onset physical disabilities and mental health. The disabilities reviewed included cerebral palsy, spina bifida, muscular dystrophies, and arthritis, and they document that mood-related issues as well as anxieties were among the most prevalent mental health issues these individuals suffered from. Additionally, social, and other behavioral issues as well as being a victim of stigma were discussed. These issues must be addressed so the individual can have the best possible opportunity to develop themselves and their relationships.

5.25 Sleep

The importance of restful sleep is self-evident. We can feel we are not at our best after unrestful sleep the night before or when jetlagged from a plane ride. We know that feeling tired during the day decreases our attention and productivity.

In the context of this book, the additional mental health impacts of poor sleep include developing anxiety and mood disorders. While anxiety and depression can cause sleep problems as well, they work cyclically.

Medically, sleep disturbances can lead to metabolic issues including high blood pressure, imbalances in blood sugar, and weight gain. We also include an in-depth discussion on the impact of social media on sleep, in Chapter 7, 'Un-Social Media.'

5.25.1 Sleep: Troubleshooting

In order to find out if there is a problem, we must break down all the components of the behaviors and consequences involved. As Paul McKenna states in his 2009 book on sleep, we must strive to eliminate sleep disruptors and introduce sleep enhancers.

This writing prompt will take you through each step of the sleep routine and create space for identification and reflection. The goal is to work towards your situation and environment around sleep and maintain the improvements achieved.

Please take a few moments to write your responses to the prompts in the spaces provided.

Do you have any health issues that affect your ability to fall or stay asleep?

_____

_____

_____

_____

_____

_____

_____

What are some of the issues you may have during preparation for bedtime? These may be moments or hours before sleep. Reflect on your routines and evening habits.

_____

_____

_____

_____

_____

_____

_____

In general, how many hours before bedtime do you stop eating or drinking?

_____

_____

_____

_____

_____

_____

_____

Where do you sleep?

_____

_____

_____

_____

_____

_____

_____

How is your sleep space organized? What else is in the place where you sleep?

_____

_____

_____

_____

_____

_____

What are the noise level and lighting situation in the place where you sleep?

_____

_____

_____

_____

_____

_____

_____

Do you have your cell phone or digital device with you when you get into bed? If so, what do you use it for?

_____

_____

_____

_____

_____

_____

_____

Is there anyone else in the room or the bed with you during your bedtime routine? If so, who, and how do their routine and sleep pattern affect you?

_____

_____

_____

_____

_____

_____

_____

In general, how long does it take for you to fall asleep?

_____

_____

_____

_____

_____

_____

Do you use any sleep aids, such as medications, ear plugs, eye shades, white noise machine, meditation apps, fans, or weighted blankets? Do you change the heating or cooling of the room? If so, please indicate in the space provided.

_____

_____

_____

_____

_____

_____

If you wake up during the night, why? How long does it take for you to fall back to sleep?

_____

_____

_____

_____

_____

_____

If you have difficulty falling back to sleep in the middle of the night, what are some things you have tried to help you?

_____

_____

_____

_____

_____

_____

On a typical day, when it is time for you to wake up, do you feel refreshed and energized? If not, describe your wake-up routine.

_____

_____

_____

_____

_____

_____

During the day, do you feel tired or have decreased energy levels? If so, what are some things you do to maintain your energy to get through the day?

_____

_____

_____

_____

_____

_____

5.25.2 Sleep: Tailored Recommendations

Great work completing the exercise!

You now have a current picture of what your sleep behaviors look like and are likely already making some connections as to where the main issues may be. We will now go through each prompt, with specific recommendations for optimal sleep routines.

Each of the steps is connected to the others, and, as discussed throughout this book, everything we put in our bodies, how we treat ourselves, our diet and exercise, our thoughts and habits, our rituals, and our environment all impact how we think and feel.

As there are many causes of sleep disruption, it is important to work to correct each issue. Correcting one will help, but if the others still persist, your sleep won't benefit as much as if you worked to improve them all.

You have a lot more control and power over your body and mind than you may imagine, and this exercise is already illuminating your path.

Do you have any health issues that affect your ability to fall or stay asleep?

There are several physical health issues that may impact your sleep. Some of these issues may be interconnected and even occur at the same time. These should be discussed with your medical care provider, along with appropriate sleep-related interventions.

The following are examples of common issues that can affect the sleep cycle:

- Musculoskeletal/pain-related issues

  - Arthritis

- Neurologic and movement-related issues

    - Restless leg syndrome (RLS)
    - Parkinson's disease
    - Periodic limb movement disorder (PLMD)
    - Tinnitus

- Cardiometabolic issues

    - High blood pressure
    - Heart disease
    - Being overweight

- Endocrine issues

  - Hyperthyroidism

- Respiratory issues

    - Asthma
    - Sleep apnea – this is a condition in which someone stops breathing during sleep, often due to the airway being blocked. The person wakes up with a loud snore and falls back asleep, not necessarily remembering waking up and having their

sleep disrupted. Waking up multiple times a night causes a person to be sleepy the next day. While sleep apnea is associated with being overweight, it can occur in people who are not and should be discussed with a clinician. The concern is that, unless you have someone who sleeps near you and can witness these episodes of stopping breathing and waking up snoring/choking, the only sign may be daytime sleepiness. Clinicians can do a sleep study that monitors sleep to diagnose this and provide treatment based on the cause of the apnea.

■ Psychological issues

- ADHD
- Depression
- Anxiety
- Stress

■ Substance use

- Alcohol can have serious impacts on one's ability to sleep restfully.
  - While it may initially make you feel drowsy or relaxed, consuming alcohol before going to bed reduces deep sleep.
  - Rapid eye movement (REM) sleep is the sleep stage associated with dreaming and cognition. REM sleep is reduced with alcohol use.
  - As discussed earlier, alcohol use and withdrawal states can cause anxiety and can cause you to wake up multiple times during the night.
  - Alcohol is a diuretic, meaning it makes you urinate more often. Having to wake up to use the bathroom is also disruptive to restful sleep.
  - It can also delay your ability to fall asleep.
  - Alcohol is generally toxic, is known to cause cancer, and can certainly worsen other medical issues such as sleep apnea, also affecting your sleep.

- Stimulant use before bedtime can delay the ability to fall asleep.
  - Look at the ingredients of things you are drinking or eating as some may include caffeine. Cigarettes include nicotine, a stimulant, and can also impact your sleep.
  - Stimulants can reduce your ability to have deep, restorative sleep, as well as reducing your REM sleep.
  - They can fragment your sleep and reduce the overall time you stay asleep.
  - Stimulants can also exacerbate other sleep-related issues you may be experiencing, including insomnia.

■ Gastrointestinal issues

- Heartburn, also called reflux, can be caused by many things, including eating right before bedtime, and can create painful sensations that wake one up.

■ Nocturia

- This is a general term for having to wake up multiple times at night to go to the bathroom and urinate.

– Nocturia can be caused by medications or substances taken before bedtime that increase urination, such as some blood pressure medications or alcohol.
– It can also be caused by medical issues such as bladder problems, diabetes, or heart disease.

What are some of the issues you may have during preparation for bedtime. These may be moments or hours before sleep. Reflect on your routines and evening habits.

▪ Consider only going to bed when you are tired. Initially, the goal is to begin correcting the habits and feelings of the inability to sleep.
▪ The bed should only be used for sleep and sex. We want to associate the bedtime routines only with those two. That's it. Not reading, not watching tv, and definitely not eating or drinking.

In general, how many hours before bedtime do you stop eating or drinking?

▪ Our bodies expend energy digesting food, and it is recommended to not eat anything heavy right before bedtime.
▪ The types of foods we eat during the day and certainly closer to bedtime will affect the quality and restorative nature of our sleep, as discussed in this chapter.
▪ We need to ensure that the amount we drink before bedtime does not wake us up in the middle of the night to urinate. This can be disruptive and create difficulties falling back to sleep.
▪ Drinking alcohol causes sleepiness, but as it is metabolized, it creates a rebound effect that causes increased restless energy and anxiety. Additionally, alcohol is a diuretic, causing us to urinate more and become dehydrated faster. The 'hangover' effect that is caused by alcohol metabolism can begin as we sleep, further disrupting rest and causing feelings of tiredness the following day.

Where do you sleep?

▪ Consider the location and general feelings of safety and security and how they impact your ability to fall and stay asleep.
▪ Your environment is critical in managing your internal rhythm – when the sun goes down and it becomes dark, our bodies naturally secrete more melatonin, creating the sleepy feeling that begins the cycle. Exposure to light, artificial or natural, causes the release of cortisol and the sensation of waking up.
▪ If possible, keep the area where you sleep dark. If not, consider using eye masks that block out the light.

How is your sleep space organized? What else is in the place where you sleep?

▪ Depending on your circumstance, there may not be much you can do to impact the physical area in which you sleep, although there may be opportunities to organize the room and the bed in a way that's more comfortable.

What are the noise level and lighting situation in the place where you sleep?

- While everyone is different in their tolerance of noise and disruptions during sleep, there are some triggers that are likely to wake us up. For example, even when asleep, we are attuned to our own names and will respond by becoming more alert and waking up when we hear it.
- Consider using ear plugs or eye shades to minimize disruption throughout the night.
- Some people enjoy using white noise machines that simulate the sounds of waterfalls or rain or fall asleep to the sound of a fan to mask the surrounding noise.

Do you have your cell phone or digital device with you when you get into bed? If so, what do you use it for?

- In addition to the inherent distractions that digital devices create, the light emitted from them can prevent the natural cycle of melatonin from helping you fall asleep.
- Try to keep your phone or device turned over, away from the bed, or off as you can become conditioned to checking the time or social media and energizing your mind at times when it needs to slow down.
- See Chapter 7, 'Un-Social Media,' for a detailed discussion of the impact of digital and social media use on sleep and health.

Is there anyone else in the room or the same bed with you during your bedtime routine? If so, who, and how do their routine and sleep pattern affect you?

- If you're sharing the same room or bed, having common bedtime routines is optimal to minimize noise and disruption. Decisions and discussions about bedtime hygiene and practices may be helpful.
- Issues to consider and agree upon include:

  - The size and softness/firmness of the mattress.
  - Number of pillows on the bed.
  - The temperature of the room – we recommend the bedroom be cooler at night while the bed and bedsheets remain warmer.
  - Presence or absence of a TV in the bedroom – we recommend no TV in the bedroom and few, if any digital devices.

In general, how long does it take for you to fall asleep?

- Consider how tired you are around the time you decide to get into bed.
- Having a set schedule is critical, so regardless of the day of the week, try to go to bed around the same time and wake up around the same time.
- Going to bed late or sleeping in on the weekends will throw your sleep rhythm off, affecting your tiredness level the following evening.

Do you use any sleep aids, such as medications, ear plugs, eye shades, white noise machine, meditation apps, fans, or weighted blankets? Do you change the heating or cooling of the room?

- There are a number of over-the-counter as well as prescription sleep aids, including:

  – Melatonin
  – Antihistamines
  – Prescription sleep medications such as zolpidem (generic for Ambien)

- While these have properties that can help you fall asleep by creating feelings of tiredness, they also have side effects and last different lengths of time.

  – For example, there are some medications, such as zolpidem, that have amnestic properties, meaning you might not remember that you woke up, resulting in your thinking in the morning that you slept all night.

- Always discuss any medications and sleep aids, even if over the counter, with your prescribing clinician so they may consider the causes of and treatment for your sleep-related issues.

If you wake up during the night, why? How long does it take for you to fall back to sleep?

- If you wake up at night, for whatever reason, and find yourself unable to fall back to sleep within 15 minutes, we recommend getting out of bed entirely and doing something calming until you are tired again.

  – The purpose is to stop the association of being awake with struggling to fall asleep and your bed.

If you have difficulty falling back to sleep in the middle of the night, what are things you have tried to help you?

- If you are having trouble falling back to sleep after more than 15 or 20 minutes, consider getting out of bed and doing something else.

  – You can try walking to another part of the house, sitting somewhere else and reading a book, meditating, or something else relaxing.
  – The key here is to uncouple the thoughts of 'I can't fall back asleep' with your sleeping area.
  – Likewise, the avoidance of stimulating material such as digital media or eating anything is important.

- Prescribed or over-the-counter sleep aids, as discussed earlier, have short-term benefits and will likely result in unwanted side effects that may complicate your sleep routine.

On a typical day, when it is time for you to wake up, do you feel refreshed and energized? If not, describe your wake-up routine.

- Coffee!

  – See later in this chapter for a detailed description of the pros and cons of coffee and suggestions regarding caffeine intake throughout the day.

During the day, do you feel tired or have decreased energy levels? If so, what are some things you do to maintain your energy to get through the day?

- Coffee!

  - Caffeine in the morning has been normalized and has created tolerances and addictions that affect most people.
  - Our relationship with coffee and its ability to wake us up provide a boost to attention and focus, and its social connotations make it a particularly difficult habit/addiction to let go of.
  - A person who drinks coffee regularly will find they need more caffeine over time to feel the same boost of energy and focus.
  - Too much caffeine can lead to bothersome and potentially problematic imbalances in heart rate, not to mention feelings of anxiety, jitteriness, and sleeplessness.
  - Similarly, if someone who is a regular drinker of caffeinated drinks suddenly stops drinking them for a day or two, they will feel withdrawal effects, including irritability and headaches.
  - Studies show that those using caffeine and other stimulants typically do better in exercises requiring cognitive attention and focus, such as exams. That being said, always weigh the risks and benefits of everything you do.
  - Stimulants may be an unfair advantage during exam sessions and have unfortunately been linked to an increased rate of prescribing, misuse, and overuse of them. We always must be careful of what we put in our bodies.
  - Consider limiting caffeine and other stimulants to the minimum amount necessary. If prescribed, please consult your prescriber and be extra mindful as to how they affect your day-to-day life. Even then, the idea of using the minimum amount necessary should be highlighted.
  - The half-life of caffeine is between four and six hours. That means that half the caffeine you put in your body is still around up to six hours after your last sip of coffee! While great for increasing energy when needed, we recommend that you not drink caffeinated beverages after three in the afternoon to ensure there is little caffeine in your system when it is bedtime.

- Naps

  - Unless you are a shift worker and your day/night schedule is disrupted unavoidably, we recommend avoiding naps. The goal is to get tired enough during the day to fall asleep at night.
  - Rather than napping during the day to try to help tiredness, consider waking up a half an hour earlier the next morning. Naps during the day will disrupt your natural rhythm. Even if you are sleepy, set an alarm and try to get out of bed half an hour earlier. You will become more tired throughout the day and find it less difficult falling asleep at your designated bedtime.

- Exercise

- We suggest daily exercise. This can be at whatever rate and intensity you can tolerate. If you have any medical issues or limitations, speak with your health-care provider as to specifics.
- Start with a small amount and work towards increasing your rate and intensity of exercise a little bit each day. This will be rewarding as you watch your stamina and strength increase and work towards reinforcing a habit you will soon make regular part of your day-to-day life.
- Exercise provides energy boosts, improves metabolism and digestion, and decreases inflammation in the body. Whether or not exercise is done for weight loss or control, it works to decrease fat and increase muscle. This healthy impact has positive benefits on the sleep cycle as well.
- Exercise increases heart and breathing rates, impacting the oxygen that goes to the muscles and organs.
- Exercise releases adrenaline and feelings of positive excitement and allows the body to regulate and balance. The endorphins released after physical activity make you feel good and foster relaxation.
- Even in small amounts, exercise has been linked to decreased feelings of anxiety and depression.
- As exercise typically increases energy levels, we recommend not doing any intense exercise too close to bedtime. We want our bodies and minds to be in balance, to feel tired at bedtime, and to naturally be able to close our eyes and fall asleep.

■ Food is mood.

- As discussed in this chapter, what we eat certainly impacts our mood and can also affect our ability to fall and stay asleep.
- Avoid processed and fatty foods that take longer to digest and can keep the body occupied, making it difficult to fall asleep.
- Foods that are fresh, including fruits and vegetables, as well as those lower in sugar content are easier to digest.
- Taking your time to enjoy a meal allows the stomach and brain to realize you are eating and when you feel full.
- Eating quickly may prevent your brain from understanding you have filled your stomach so soon and may cause indigestion, heartburn, and active energy being spent that detracts from the ability to fall and stay asleep.

5.26 Activities

5.26.1 Writing Prompt

Imagine an immersive activity you can participate in – something that requires most of your energy and focus and doesn't cause you stress. It may be spending time reading to your niece or feeding the ducks in the park.

Think of something that allows you to lose yourself in the activity itself, relatively free of wandering thoughts of your boss, the rent bill that is coming up, or your student loans.

Consider using the space provided to reflect on the following two-part prompt:

1. **If you have done this activity before, how did it make you feel? Describe the emotions and thoughts you experienced.**

_____

_____

_____

_____

_____

_____

_____

_____

_____

_____

2. **How can you incorporate this activity to reduce your feelings of anxiety before they arise? How can you remind yourself to do this activity?**

_____

_____

_____

_____

_____

_____

_____

_____

_____

_____

_____

_____

Examples of activities that are relatively easy to start and stop, that have minimal to no cost, and that we have used for ourselves as well as with our clients include:

- Bird watching
- Breathing exercises
- Calling a friend
- Coloring
- Cooking a meal
- Gardening
- Going for a walk
- Hobby model building
- Jewelry making
- Journaling
- Juggling
- Knitting
- Laughing! Consider joke books or comedy podcasts.
- Learning a new language
- Lego building
- Listening to a podcast
- Listening to music
- Magic tricks
- Making music
- Meditating
- Organizing your closet
- Origami
- Painting
- Playing an instrument
- Prayer
- Puzzle solving
- Reading
- Running
- Sculpting with clay
- Solitaire card or board games
- Spending time with animals
- Volunteer work
- Working out
- Writing
- Yoga

In the space provided, add your own activities that you would like to try or have tried and have worked for you.

_____

_____

_____

_____

_____

_____

_____

_____

_____

_____

5.27 Concluding Thoughts

In addition to the intrinsically relaxing properties of the activities listed earlier, we suggest you think about how you have control over your mind and body. An answer, a solution, or an easy fix from the outside world may never be available the moment you need one. As discussed in Chapter 2, 'Identifying and Treating Anxiety,' therapeutic options, including medications, have their proven benefits, but with this book, we are adding tools you can use to empower yourself from within.

Please note that we did not include activities that are so immersive that their detriments are greater than their benefits. Gambling, using substances, and digital media use such as video gaming or social media all have the ability to completely immerse the individual in the activity, so much so that they may lead to physically, socially, and financially draining addictions.

Also note that while we mentioned the activity of cooking, we did not include the consumption of junk foods. Everyone knows that foods high in sugar, fats, salts, and carbs are delicious and temporarily even reduce feelings of anxiety and sadness. The reality is that they may not provide balanced nutrition and, if used repetitively to reinforce the reduction of anxiety, are likely to have health and psychological consequences greater than those we began with (e.g., weight gain; blood sugar, blood pressure, and nutritional imbalances). We include a list of external causes of anxiety, including diet, earlier in this chapter.

As we get better in tune with our needs and understand how what we do affects the way our bodies react, we will empower our ability to reduce and ultimately prevent powerful feelings of anxiety and worry. This, in turn, teaches us that we have the ability to self-soothe and be in control and then reinforces the positive behaviors through the mitigation of the negative feelings. As discussed throughout the sections on cortisol, dopamine, and serotonin, we are very good at scanning for threats and also at seeking out rewards.

We also know that, with any activity, we either master it and it becomes mindless repetition or we become bored with it, not receiving the same amount of pleasure we did when we began. The value of trying new things and learning new skills is that even during the act of paying attention to learning something new, such as reading the instructions for how to play a new board game, we are devoting attention to the activity that cannot at the same time be spent on anxiety. We are simultaneously creating a circumstance incompatible with worry and staving off the feeling of being bored.

Performing an activity you have control over that reduces your feelings of being under threat will condition you to repeat it. The earlier we begin these types of actions to address our feelings of anxiety and worry, the more impactful they will be. Our brains require fewer repetitions to form habits when we are younger. Regardless of age, however, the more we repeat healthy activities, the more they will become habits and parts of our day-to-day routine of self-care.

THE ORDEAL III

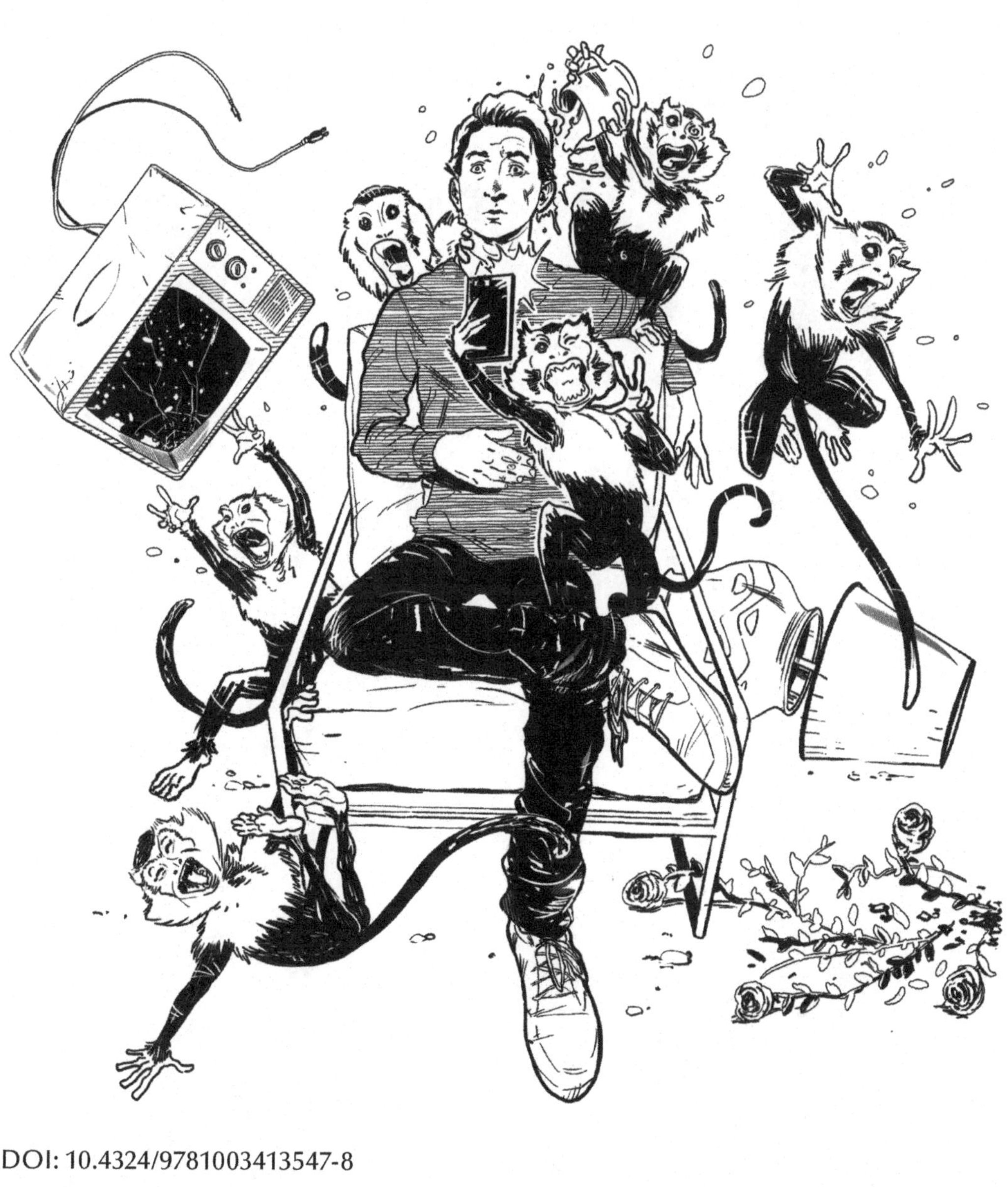

DOI: 10.4324/9781003413547-8

Chapter 6

COVID, Fear, and Grief

6.1 Introduction

The COVID-19 pandemic and the associated stigma, economic and social implications have all contributed significantly to an increase in demand for mental health care. Youth and other vulnerable populations have been disproportionately impacted by psychological distress (Varma et al. 2021).

The rates of anxiety disorders, already skyrocketing pre-pandemic, took an even more dramatic turn for the worse. As health-care providers and members of the community, we have seen the effect of the increased demand for mental health care.

During the height of the pandemic—the first two years—we experienced the impact of the increased hospitalizations associated with mental health issues including depression and anxiety. People continue to have a heightened response to this ongoing, long-term disaster.

The issues relating to acute stress, depression, anxiety, and the increases in substance use and associated behavioral impacts including self-injurious acts and intimate partner violence have been referred to as the 'epidemic' within this pandemic.

The amount of evidence in the literature regarding the impact of COVID on young adults continues to grow exponentially. We should all 'understand more, so that we may fear less,' as Marie Curie so wisely said.

> Nothing in life is to be feared, it is only to be understood.
> Now is the time to understand more, so that we may fear less.
> —Marie Curie

6.2 Primed for Panic

Compared to prior epidemics such as severe acute respiratory syndrome (SARS) in 2003, the COVID pandemic has affected the world at the height of available communication technologies. We are at a point when even if we try to avoid the news or a post, the 'info-demic' is inescapable and ubiquitous.

The negative effects of repeated morbid information perversely incentivized to generate clicks and revenue has exacerbated the anxiety and fear of the population. News media and social media have some benefits, providing updates regarding safety recommendations, but they more often maintain and spread the feeling of perpetual threat.

During the first year of the pandemic, more was unknown, and fear and panic were commonplace. The worry and desire to stay healthy dictated decisions. Throughout the last three-plus years of the pandemic, the virus itself and responses by global and local authorities progressed and evolved.

The unpredictable nature of the pandemic, coupled with the inability to have any control over mandates, laws, closures, and punishments fed into a collective sense of acute stress. As discussed in our previous book *Re-Write: A Trauma Workbook of Creative Writing and Recovery in Our New Normal* (2023), this has led to posttraumatic stress disorders as well as explosive levels of anxiety disorders.

As we enter what is being called the post-pandemic era, we continue to see numerous variants of the virus impacting our day-to-day lives. The news can be useful to monitor these developments and to educate oneself and family to take the best possible care and do one's best to manage risk. The reality is that no one is good at calculating risk with seemingly infinite variables.

In addition to valuable information, the infodemic, as the World Health Organization (WHO) calls it, has led to an increase in incorrect information, scapegoating, and misinformation online.

At the beginning of 2023, the World Economic Forum (WEF) chairman a declared that it would be an unprecedented year of multiple crises. The combined economic, environmental, social, and geopolitical crises converged into the 'Year of the Polycrisis.'

Now the virus is ubiquitous, it is endemic, there appears to be no eradication of it in sight, and according to the WEF, we are all stuck in a crisis mindset. We must make choices on how we will manage all this information, how we feel, and the manner in which we will continue our lives.

6.3 Impacts

To appreciate the devastation caused by the pandemic, we need to understand the impacts of the virus from a biological damage perspective, the medical interventions administered to treat the illness, and the socioeconomic mechanisms put into place to reduce the spread.

Biologically, the SARS-CoV-2 virus causes inflammation throughout the body, as well as injury to parts of the brain (Stein et al. 2022). Recent studies suggest the virus damages the amygdala and hippocampus, which impact emotional and cognitive processing, resulting in the development of anxiety and stress-related disorders.

We now know that the hypothalamic-pituitary-adrenal (HPA) axis is also negatively impacted by the virus, which can lead to depression, anxiety, and suicidality. Inflammation and injury to parts of the brain, as well as hormone levels, including growth hormone and cortisol, have dramatic impacts long term for survivors. See Chapter 5, 'Brain, Body, and Behaviors,' for a detailed discussion of parts of the brain and how they interact and impact our day-to-day choices and behaviors.

Being exposed to the virus and the brain and bodily damage it causes is one thing. We continue to understand the biological impact more and more, in an attempt to tease apart what long COVID is as a cluster of symptoms. The treatment of the illness, especially in severe cases, is another aspect of our pandemic journey. For example, there is a study by Dubey et al. (2022) suggesting that infection during pregnancy may be a risk factor for neurodevelopmental disorders.

Any hospitalization is associated with stress, especially when it is caused by a lethal virus. Being in a hospital increases the risk of random diseases that can be caught there – from other patients and from care providers spreading germs from one room to another. These hospital-acquired infections such as pneumonia or infectious diarrhea, in addition to the SARS-CoV-2 virus, have caused increased stress and anxiety.

The sickest patients, who required intensive care unit stays as well as breathing tubes, had an even greater risk of developing cognitive issues such as delirium, anxiety, depression, and posttraumatic stress disorders.

Prior to the pandemic, these issues were known to cause immediate and long-term neurological and psychiatric issues. The addition of the pandemic in the context of global terror has added to these negative outcomes.

For example, studies show that allowing loved ones to visit a patient during intensive care stays is associated with positive clinical outcomes such as reduced anxiety, delirium (Granberg et al. 1999), and length of stay (Agård and Lomborg 2011).

Throughout this book, we discuss informed consent and working with a care team, including family and loved ones, to enhance health. During times of isolation and restrictions, very sick patients have difficulty understanding and making educated choices about their health and treatment options. People with breathing difficulties, such as those caused by this virus, experienced even greater feelings of anxiety.

We discuss the impact fear has on decision making and our cognitive processes and truly appreciate the horror of the unfortunate circumstances people find themselves in. The longer-term mental health impact of these restrictions and lack of family support during such critical times remains to be seen. Something like simply not allowing visitors to reduce the spread of the virus has impacted countless people in ways we will continue to learn over the years.

Throughout this section, we discuss the impacts of societal and behavioral interventions, such as the lockdowns, social isolation, mandates, and school and business closures and the resulting compensatory socioeconomic behaviors.

As the ability to be physically with loved ones and colleagues decreased, screen time increased. Information regarding the virus itself was sought, then attention to lockdowns and ever-changing policies and restrictions became more intense.

Each person in every country across the world diverted their time and energy to social media and the consolidated messaging around fear. We will discuss increased screen time and social isolation and their effects on stress, resulting in significant increases in anxiety disorders, including specific and social phobias; stress reactions; and mood disorders.

While attempting to reduce the impact of the virus, people of all ages were subject to isolation, loneliness, mask-wearing, social distancing and school and work closures. These all had an effect on young adults and their education, safety, and mental health. According to a study by Moulin et al. (2022), being younger, experiencing intimate partner violence, and having mental and physical health issues were risk factors for worsening mental health outcomes.

The uncertainty around the school year and how and when exams would be given, as well as the overnight switch to online virtual learning, had a deleterious impact on students and young people. Concerns regarding graduation and obtaining internships were placed on hold during the lockdowns, and questions of basic safety increased anxiety. Perceived stress and the resulting mental health issues, according to van Loon et al. (2022), are linked to pre-pandemic vulnerabilities, including higher levels of stress as well as patterns of maladaptive coping.

As discussed in *Re-Write: A Trauma Workbook of Creative Writing and Recovery in Our New Normal*, by Balan and Balan (2023), the impact of the pandemic and associated lockdowns, school and work closures, quarantines, social distancing measures, policies regarding hygiene, screening, and financial stressors all exacerbated mental health conditions.

> **In every crisis, doubt or confusion, take the higher path – the path of compassion, courage, understanding and love.**
> –Amit Ray, *Nonviolence: The Transforming Power*

6.4 Viral Anxiety and Social Distancing Phobia

The social distancing and hygiene rules recommended at the onset of the pandemic, coupled with the worry and fear of catching the illness itself, have exacerbated the anxiety caused by the virus as well as the phobia termed 'social distancing phobia.'

The amount of attention the concept of social distancing received and the numerous times everyone repeated it and thought of it created the perfect foundation for a social distancing phobia to emerge.

The compensatory fear reactions – emotional and behavioral – are characterized as disproportionate by Mahamid et al. (2021), resulting in the various psychiatric issues described.

People with lower socioeconomic statuses, as well as those with poor coping mechanisms and intolerance of uncertainty, have been shown to be at increased risk of developing symptoms of anxiety and depression.

The terror instilled in the public worldwide and frequently echoed in every school, business, bus, plane, and restaurant was more than enough to solidify this phobia that, up until the pandemic, never existed.

Symptoms of social distancing phobia include extreme stress and feeling nervous in public places as well as when around other people. Studies describe the fear of being infected despite having no symptoms and the stigma associated with potentially being infected and getting others sick.

According to a study by Cho et al. (2022), social distancing phobia is correlated with:

- Age: elderly and at-risk people were recommended to social distance earlier and more often and, therefore, felt the effects of loneliness more intensely. The reality that age and chronic medical conditions place people at higher risk of worse outcomes from the virus adds to the potential development of this phobia.
- Viral anxiety, rumination, and fear of COVID are measured on the Stress and Anxiety to Viral Epidemics-6 items (SAVE-6) scale, as discussed in an article by Chung et al. (2021).
- Depression.
- Intolerance of uncertainty, described as the excessive inability to tolerate the fact that something negative or, more importantly, unexpected may occur.

It is intuitive that people anxious in general have been and continue to be more conscious of social distancing recommendations. Those with a higher intolerance of uncertainty do so in ways that interfere pathologically with their day-to-day lives and negatively impact their mental health.

During the first two years of the pandemic, the stigma of the illness and the fear of getting infected or infecting others, even without symptoms, led many people to isolate themselves. This isolation, either mandated as lockdowns or quarantines or self-imposed, added to the anxiety and fear and had negative impacts on their day-to-day lives.

Additionally, studies contain descriptions of concerns about getting food and basic supplies and shortages and supply chain issues that exacerbate the anxiety related to the virus itself.

Work productivity, attendance at school, and presence at work all suffered, as described in this chapter. This has had a negative impact on organizations and the financial stability of individuals and families. Cyclically, these then lead to deepening anxiety, fear, and hopelessness about the future.

We present this updated list, with current evidence that specifically includes what we have learned over the past three-plus years, of the mental and behavioral impacts of the pandemic on young adults.

- Anxiety disorders increased.

    - See Chapter 2, 'Identifying and Treating Anxiety,' for in-depth discussions of the increased rates of various anxiety disorders.
    - According to a study by Callender et al. (2022), those individuals who had a prior history of experiencing a disaster, such as a hurricane, a fire, or a flooding event, had an even higher (cumulative) risk of more severe anxiety from the pandemic.
    - Hypochondria and specific phobias increased, including germ phobias, public transportation anxieties, agoraphobia, and claustrophobia.
    - Anxieties relating to being away from work then having to return to the office. Remote working was a rarity before, then, during the pandemic, it was suggested to be the best thing ever. Now, post pandemic, people are being forced to return to campuses and offices, resulting in different types of stress and worry.

- Obsessive-compulsive disorder increased.

    - With the increased, very rational fear of contamination, rumination regarding disease state increased. Compensatory compulsions such as hand washing, sanitizing, and routine testing for the disease all increased (Tanir et al. 2020).
    - Maintaining sanitary hands, doorknobs, and groceries was recommended and reinforced, which, as can be imagined, worsened those already predisposed to anxiety as well as obsessive and compulsive tendencies.

- Stress-related disorders, including posttraumatic stress disorders, increased.

    - A review by Elharake et al. (2022) reports that up to 67% of the participants had PTSD symptoms during the pandemic.

- Stress-related disorders increased as individuals bore witness to the trauma and additional stressors associated with the virus.
- Societal, community-level, and collective trauma also increased.

■ Alcohol use increased.

- Studies indicate a 30% increase in alcohol use during the pandemic.
- With an increase in alcohol use, unhealthy drinking behaviors increased, risky behaviors increased, and, unfortunately, alcohol-related physical illnesses, such as liver disease, increased.
- People who were abstinent relapsed, and a reported one in three adults used alcohol during the workday.
- A study by Murthy and Narasimha (2021) discusses the significant impact of the pandemic on increased alcohol use, an increase in alcohol-related emergencies, changes in use patterns, and even an increased risk of contracting COVID.

■ Nicotine use and smoking increased.

- Studies report an increase in the amount people smoked, as well as a relapse during the pandemic of people who had previously quit smoking.
- Pokhrel et al. (2023) report that young adults who experience higher COVID-related stress are at increased risk of cigarette and e-cigarette use.

■ Opioid and other drug use increased.

- Unintentional overdoses and deaths related to opioid use increased tragically during the pandemic. Per the CDC, US national overdose mortality increased from 21 per 100,000 in 2019 to 30 per 100,000 in 2021 (Moghtaderi et al. 2023).
- Relapses in drug use have reportedly increased (Keith et al. 2023).
- Cannabis use increased, as defined by sales compared to before the pandemic.
- Overall emergency department visits due to substance use increased.

■ Behavioral addictions increased.

- Online gambling (Quinn et al. 2022) and gaming addictions significantly increased as a result of several factors, including social isolation, boredom, and increased time at home.
- Young adults, a vulnerable population, saw an even higher rate of increase of behavioral addictions.
- In the fall and winter months of 2023, we saw an increase in the number of cases of the virus being detected. Our patterns of constantly checking media, news, and social media to obtain information are worsened by repeated exposure to panic-inducing and retraumatizing headlines.

■ Burnout increased.

- In 2021, over 47 million people left their jobs voluntarily, according to the United States Bureau of Statistics.

- The BBC reports that rates continue to climb worldwide. According to the US think tank Future Forum, in February 2023, 42% of workers (its highest figure since May 2021) experienced burnout.
- The increased feelings of sadness, worry, exhaustion, depersonalization, stress, and suicidal thinking are even more concerning in the young adult population.

■ Health-care provider burnout increased.

- An article by Kapil et al. (2022) discusses the negative long-term mental health impact on health-care workers throughout the pandemic. It was the first study to examine the risk of mental health issues in health-care providers over multiple phases of the pandemic.
- Among our health-care friends and colleagues, we have witnessed serious burnout at levels we have never seen before.
- Studies also show the disproportionately higher rates of burnout among healthcare providers. As we write this book on anxiety, during the third year of the pandemic, we are living through a time when patient-facing clinicians are experiencing rates of anxiety, depression, sleep problems, substance use problems, emotional exhaustion, burnout, and suicidality higher than ever before.
- This has already resulted in decreased clinician productivity and providers dropping down to part-time work, quitting, resigning, and taking early retirement. So many of our colleagues are opting for early retirement as they describe a loss of passion and an inability to see why they are doing what they do.
- As retaining health-care staff continues to be an issue, recruiting has become an increased challenge. Due to supply-demand mismatch, clinicians are able to command higher salaries in temporary positions. This puts an enormous strain on hospital systems to continuously credential and train new providers, not to mention the increased financial burden.

■ Child abuse and neglect increased.

- A significant increase of physical abuse of children has been reported, compared to before the pandemic, and is associated with the increase in intimate partner violence described in this section.
- A study by Rawal et al. (2022) discusses the impact school closures had on youth and how they placed them in unhealthy and unsafe living environments.
- The World Health Organization (WHO) and UNICEF reported in 2022 that global vaccination coverage decreased, with over 25 million babies not receiving lifesaving immunizations against illnesses such as diphtheria, measles, tetanus, and pertussis. It was suggested that this was due to supply chain disruptions.
- Child protective services and agencies responsible for providing regulatory and legal protection for vulnerable populations were suspended or severely understaffed, resulting in this very important safety net not being available.

■ Eating disorders increased.

- Studies indicate an increase in disordered eating, including overeating.
- Quality of life was reduced, impacting eating patterns and worsening anxiety and depressive disorders.

- A study by Muth et al. (2022) discusses the relationship between eating behaviors and eating disorder symptomatology during the pandemic.
- Eating disorder symptoms for those with anorexia nervosa increased, as evidenced by a significant increase in medical and psychiatric inpatient hospital admission rates.

■ Education was negatively impacted.

- School closures created historic learning setbacks for children and widened socioeconomic disparities.
  - In 2022, the Educational Opportunity Project at Stanford University found that poverty compounded the negative effects of the pandemic.
- Extended remote learning harmed students.
- Mathematics scores plummeted.
- Reading scores showed sweeping declines.
- Overall scholastic achievement lost decades of progress; children were left behind, and those with the least to lose lost the most.
- Discussing 'learning loss' was controversial at the height of the pandemic, although with reports coming out more frequently, the impacts are painfully real.
- Children who missed months and years of adequate schooling and socializing may never be able to recover or catch up to their age equivalents.

■ Family life was affected.

- Daily routines were lost.
- Healthy modeling behaviors were affected as everyone was under similar stress from the virus and the fear of the unknown, resulting in the decreased capacity of elders and caregivers to provide guidance and support as before.
- Family members who may not have been the most supportive or empathic towards one another or, worse, were downright abusive were forced to stay indoors together for weeks and months with no reprieve.
- Communication breakdowns occurred.
- People weren't able to visit their loved ones and family members who lived outside the household, resulting in worsening anxiety, worry, and grief.
- Transitions between school, work, and leisure all blended.
- Stress increased, resulting in fractured connections amongst family members.
- Due to increased rates of anxiety and depression among caregivers (Farooqui et al. 2021), the mental health of families also suffered.
- When a loved one died, infection prevention precautions prohibited burials and attendance at funerals, resulting in complex stress and grief reactions. See the section on grief in the time of COVID.

■ Fear in general increased.

- Contracting the virus and becoming sick became the focal point of worry and terror for everyone around the world.
- Fear of dying, dying alone, or causing someone else to get sick and die has permeated everyone's minds.
- See the section on viral anxiety.

■ *Gaslighting* became the word of the year in 2022.

- Our book *Re-Write* was already in press with Taylor & Francis when we found out that the word *gaslighting* had been recognized as the word of the year. We have an entire chapter on gaslighting and betrayal traumas in *Re-Write*, which provides insight into what was happening during the year we wrote it. As we complete *Confidently Chill*, we are choosing to talk about the anxiogenic sequalae of what we have all lived through for years.
- Contradictory information from trusted agencies and media outlets that contained half-truths and direct misinformation was easily confused with accurate, up-to-date science. As people began to realize that trusting any organization entirely was not in their best interest, collective gaslighting deepened its roots.

■ Guilt and worry about being guilty of something became our reality.

- The concept of pre-symptomatic spread and asymptomatic spread of the virus became part of our lives, contributing to the pre-guilt of the unknowable.
- The desire to mitigate illness and obsessive rumination on possibly infecting someone without knowing caused even more guilt. Potentially infecting Grandma and being the cause of a loved one's death permeated the consciousness, specifically in schools, skyrocketing anxiety and pre-guilt.
- Finding out that someone became sick with the virus added to that worry for self-preservation reasons, as well as for possibly having infected them oneself.

■ Helplessness and hopelessness increased.

- As the sense of loss of control of our day-to-day lives became a reality, we looked to sources of comfort and answers.
- In an attempt to calculate the risks of the few choices we were presented with, people adopted new forms of structure.

■ Intimate partner violence (IPV) increased.

- There has been a significant increase in violence between partners, at home, and against children.
- Research findings suggest that all types of violence against girls and women significantly increased (Moulin et al. 2022).
- Studies indicate a 50 to 70% increase in intimate partner fatalities since 2020, the first year of the pandemic.

■ LGBTQIA+ communities were disproportionately impacted.

- While anxiety and depressive symptoms have increased significantly throughout the years of the pandemic, the disparities in access to care and stigma have disproportionately affected the LGBTQIA+ community.
- Studies indicate that LGBTQIA+ individuals experienced increased anxiety, compared to cisgender, straight individuals, during the pandemic. Of note, there

has also been a reported overall decrease in suicide attempts and in victimization, specifically among students, during the pandemic.

- The impact of lockdowns and having to stay at home has been a positive experience for some, as they report being away from bullies at school or in the workplace (Gill and McQuillan 2022). Comparatively, LGBTQIA+ youth experience higher degrees of bullying, harassment, stigma, discrimination, and victimization than cisgender, straight youth. The distance from schools during the pandemic served as a relative relief from those stressors.
- On the other hand, being forced to stay at home with family members who are not supportive or, worse, are actively hostile, abusive, and aggressive acted to worsen the feelings of anxiety, depression, and suicidal ideation for some.

■ Loneliness and isolation increased.

- Loneliness increased, initially dictated by social isolation mandates, and continued as fear of contracting or spreading the illness increased.
- Isolation itself worsens mental and physical health.
- A study by Gabarrell-Pascuet et al. (2023) discusses the association between age and preexisting mental health issues and the correlation between psychosocial well-being and feeling lonely. According to this study, age was negatively related to mental health symptoms and loneliness.
- In 2023, the US Surgeon General raised the alarm about the impact of loneliness and isolation in the context of the pandemic. They even provided a call to action and a framework to advance social connection.

■ Life satisfaction – our subjective sense of well-being – decreased.

- Studies and surveys have shown that general satisfaction and enjoyment of life decreased compared to pre-pandemic levels.
- Young adults spent less time outside during the pandemic, played fewer sports, and had fewer opportunities to be with their friends and colleagues.
- Communities were disrupted as congregating was banned due to necessary viral mitigation policies.
- Isolating and solitary, sedentary practices were encouraged, affecting these decreases in overall happiness and quality of life.
- As discussed in Chapter 2, 'Identifying and Treating Anxiety' (specifically the section on bio-psychosocial determinants), those in lower socioeconomic status groups were affected disproportionately.
- A study by Lee et al. (2022) discusses how the quality of life of those with attention deficit-hyperactivity disorder was more negatively impacted during the pandemic than those without it.

■ Life expectancy decreased.

- According to studies, including one by Schwandt et al. (2022), life expectancy decreased during the years 2020 and 2021 compared to pre-pandemic levels.

■ Maternal outcomes worsened.

   – Maternal and fetal (baby-related) outcomes worsened during the pandemic, and
      we saw wide-ranging levels of disparities in access to care and outcomes across each
      country. The concerns mothers and families had and continue to have about either
      contracting the virus themselves or their babies falling ill skyrocketed. The changes
      in hospital admissions and visitor policies, including the decrease in available sup-
      port structures for new families, all worsened anxiety, stress, and fear.
   – A study by Viaux-Savelon et al. (2022) discusses the negative impact of lock-
      downs, including development of postpartum depression and anxiety disorders
      in mother-child interactions. The authors also reviewed the impact of the lack of
      a partner during delivery and the association between increased risk of anxiety
      and depression.
   – Ruyak et al. (2023) describes an associated increase rate of alcohol and other
      drug use in pregnant and postpartum women.

■ Psychosomatic complaints manifested.

   – The number of somatic complaints, described in some studies as 'somatic syn-
      drome,' increased.
   – Experiential as well as literature evidence supports there having been an increase
      in primary care visits during the pandemic. Many of them have been directly
      linked with anxiety and fear related to the virus itself and associated consequences.
   – Upwards of 90% of primary care doctor visits are reported to be related to stress
      and other mental health concerns.

■ Physical routine changes led to mental health issues.

   – Sedentary, solitary, isolating habits were reinforced.
   – Young adults engaged in fewer outdoor activities, as did older adults.
      • Physical and mental fatigue increased, including caregiver and compassion
         fatigue.
   – People were limited in the amount they were allowed to walk, resulting in more
      sitting and more sedentary activities.
   – Decreased access to natural daylight during lockdowns impacted mental and
      physical health and well-being.
   – A study by Gotlib et al. (2023) looked at the effects of the pandemic on brain
      maturation in adolescents and concluded that the pandemic appears to have led
      to accelerated brain aging in adolescents. They also discuss the challenges these
      types of interruptions bring to longitudinal studies of normative development.
   – Technology use increased, resulting in:
      • Back and neck pain.
      • Sedentary lifestyles, bringing on or exacerbating medical conditions due to
         inactivity, such as heart disease, blood sugar imbalances, and diabetes.
      • Addictive behaviors, resulting in anxiety, attention difficulties, depression,
         bullying and being a victim of bullying, self-injury, and suicide.

- As of the writing of this book, there are lawsuits against several of the major social media companies alleging that their apps resulted in mental health harms to children using them.
  - Our transitions throughout our day changed. See the section discussing transitions specifically.

■ Sleep disorders have proliferated.

  - Upwards of 55% of those in the review by Panchal et al. (2021) reported a prevalence of sleep disorders.
  - The negative impacts on sleep schedules, falling asleep, staying asleep, and early awakening have all been documented.
  - Decrease in restorative sleep has resulted in tiredness during the daytime, further exacerbating absenteeism, presenteeism, and decreased productivity.
  - Sleep is also discussed in detail in Chapter 5, 'Brain, Body, and Behaviors.'

■ Social media use increased.

  - From studies that came out in the later years of the pandemic, we now have a better sense of how much the use of social media has increased. Specifically, the impact on young adults and their rate of use has increased.
  - Increased use of social media by everyone, young adults in particular, inherently brought with it the statistical odds of increasing inappropriate language and posts.
  - This brought with it the anxiety of either extreme social conformity to salvage what few social interactions were left during lockdowns or being cancelled. Critical thinking and the ability to voice opinions and ask questions were threatened as mistrust and fear mounted.
  - This has led to increases in anxiety, substance use, and other mental health issues, as discussed throughout this book.
  - Use of social media has been reported as a risk factor in and of itself for worsening mental and physical health, especially during the pandemic. With this as a risk factor, and as its use increased, use of social media accelerated the spiral of worsening well-being.
  - It also has been associated with concerns including cyber bullying and being taken advantage of. See Chapter 7, 'Un-Social Media.'
  - Similarly, it worsened the physical health and well-being of young adults and those most susceptible to its addictive nature.
  - Lastly, more time away from academics and the workplace led to decreased performance in school and lost productivity at work, ultimately culminating in dropouts and termination.

■ Suicide rates increased.

  - Suicide is a leading cause of death among young people.
  - According to a May 2023 article by the National Institute of Mental Health (NIMH) and Bridge et al. (2023), who analyzed national suicide data from the Centers for Disease Control and Prevention (CDC), youth suicide rates increased during the pandemic.

▪ Trust decreased as mistrust increased.

- Humanity absorbed a mindset of being sick until proven healthy. The intense fear instilled by agencies making sure everyone knew their daily sickness status shifted the paradigm of how we previously lived our lives.
- Friends and family no longer viewed each another as a source of warmth and love but, rather, saw each other as potential sources of disease and death.
- Wearing a mask to mitigate the spread of the virus was mandated and then became a beacon of hope.
- Masking and not masking became symbols of mutual mistrust and eroded societal and communal norms.
- The mistrust increased anxiety as people felt the need to police one another to protect themselves. The desire for safety, security, and a sense of control likely had the opposite effect.
- Contact tracing saw governmental tracking of citizens in an attempt to reduce the spread, which solidified the mistrust of the individual by the collective and one another.
- Asymptomatic testing to be able to participate in any part of society, including being able to go to work or school, significantly increased anxiety.
- Routine sniffles and allergies were enough to be declined admission to school or work, very different from the pre-pandemic times, when a note was required from a licensed doctor for an excused absence.
- The pendulum swung so far that we are now seeing the serious collective repercussions of all this built-up anxiety.
- Schools became a place of testing, fear, anxiety; more testing; and more fear.
- Unfortunately, many of the new normal measures require access to financial and health-care resources as well as literacy to comply with the mandates and increased challenges of day-to-day life.
  • This, without question, highlighted the already-problematic inequity in society, specifically in the United States.
  • Minorities and those with lower socioeconomic statuses were disproportionately affected.
  • Anxiety, depression, lack of access, job loss, food and housing insecurity, and an all-around general decrease in health and increased rate of disease and death were greater in those communities.
  • Discrimination and inequity inherently generate anxiety, fear, and ignorance, and the widening gap made anxiety worse for everyone.
- The general, collective feeling of discomfort, exclusion, and constant anxiety exacerbated the repetitive trauma of the lockdowns.

▪ Violence increased significantly.

- Over the years of the pandemic, existential angst has increased. There have been uncertainty, economic instability, and civil unrest in the United States and wars around the world.
- Substance use has increased, as have untreated medical conditions, contributing to a sense of hopelessness and aggressivity in some.

Issues relating to mental health and other bio-psychosocial areas have an especially greater impact when experienced earlier on in life. The long-term health consequences of the aforementioned repercussions are yet to be seen, although in what is now the fourth year of the pandemic, we are already seeing the short-term consequences, and they are concerning.

6.5 Writing Prompt

Within the framework of the Balan 3-2-1 Method, consider your response to the following:

How has the pandemic impacted your understanding of your own mortality?

3: With intention, set your internal and external environment.

■ The body: What mindfulness techniques are you choosing to allow your body to heal?

_____

_____

_____

■ The setting: How are you intentionally influencing your setting?

_____

_____

_____

■ The breath: Which breathing technique will you use as you prepare for this exercise?

_____

_____

_____

2: What are your thoughts and feelings in response to the writing prompt?

_____

_____

_____

_____

_____

_____

_____

_____

_____

_____

_____

1: What is your one intent or affirmation in the context of the writing prompt?

_____

_____

_____

We hope that by bringing awareness to these thoughts and feelings of our own mortality and the finiteness of everything and everyone around us will allow us to put things in perspective. Throughout the pandemic, there has been an awakening among employed young adults as to their values and what they will and will not tolerate, especially in the workplace.

Imagine if we could broaden this perspective, make decisions, and give the appropriate amount of thought and emotion to the things we need to do. We would likely take things less seriously and realize there is a lot we can control and influence.

6.6 Transitions in Our Daily Cycles

Another tremendous change during the pandemic that altered our lives forever has been the disruption of our daily transitions. Transitions are the time between ending one thing and starting something different. We likely take transitions for granted as they are built-in downtimes when we don't notice we've slowed down or stopped doing something and are mentally preparing to do something else.

Beginning in 2020, our transitions—our commute to work, to school, to stores, to loved ones, to restaurants, and then back to our routines—all changed. Even a small amount of time allows the mind to clear, reduces the excitatory phase, and lets the mind and body feel ready to start something else. Each part of our daily cycle can cause us to feel anxious about starting something new, especially if it's something we haven't done before.

Reflect on your daily cycle and each aspect of the day that might cause you anxiety and how they changed during the pandemic. Having to work from home, attend school from home, and modify our travel behaviors, as well as having to be in close quarters with people we may not have spent much time with, created different ways of communicating and blurred so many boundaries.

The transition of commuting—a daily routine such as getting on the subway or a bus or driving or walking to work or school—while it may be stressful and tiring, also allows the body and mind to acknowledge that something is ending and a new thing is beginning. When the entire world, except for essential workers, was told to stay at home, the transition from outside living to inside living disappeared.

Those fortunate enough to have multiple rooms or different areas in their houses that they could work from or walk in between had less difficulty, as did people who had access to the outdoors. For those who were less fortunate and were stuck with many family members in proximity, those transitions were affected even more.

6.7 Writing Prompt

Consider your daily cycle and any aspects of it that might cause you anxiety, specifically around transitions.

- Start from the moment you wake up: brushing your teeth, eating breakfast, going to school or work.
- Think about the transition of the commute to school or work, picking up or dropping off your children.
- Consider the time you have at work and the meal that you might have at school as well as your transition back home.
- Think about your self-care routine, if you go to the gym before or after work, and any socializing you do, such as going to a restaurant or bar.
- Reflect on your transition back home, preparing for dinner, and catching up with family and friends.
- Consider your winding down phase as your bedtime routine begins and then going to sleep.
- Think about your weekend routine, such as reaching out to family and loved ones. Think about the errands you might need to complete, such as yard care, and any religious or social events you have, such as church or sports practice.

Use the space provided to document and allow yourself to revisit these times and events during your daily cycle.

_____

_____

_____

_____

_____

_____

_____

_____

_____

_____

_____

_____

_____

_____

_____

_____

_____

_____

_____

_____

As you've probably noticed, your new normal includes changes in your routine and your transitions. You have the ability to re-write the story about your transitions as well as your reactions to them.

6.8 Grief in the Time of COVID

Since we last wrote about trauma in *Re-Write* (2023) and the development of grief, stress-related disorders, and posttraumatic stress disorder due to the pandemic, we have even more data that corroborates the initial findings.

The complex relationship between grief and COVID, the pandemic, and our new normal continue to be topics rarely discussed publicly. The stigma and shame associated with our reactions to the past three-plus years have made it so people want to go on with their lives without processing the immense loss and terror we all experienced.

Many millions of people lost family members, loved ones, and colleagues during the pandemic. Visiting people in one's own country, let alone other countries, was nearly impossible. Helping care for a sick and dying loved one became fraught with obstacles and problems, leading to complicated grief that may never be processed. One study by Szuhany et al. (2021), for example, describes the potential increase of prolonged grief disorder due to the pandemic.

Losses were experienced in many domains of our lives, including the loss of roles, jobs, transitions, freedoms, health-care access, recreational opportunities, spiritual gatherings, and most importantly, any sense of stability or hope. Some lost businesses, homes, and even the ability to put food on the table. Safety nets, nonprofits, and other community resources were also impacted, leaving the most in need all alone.

The changing messaging, difficulty separating true information from fake news, and financial insecurity the pandemic brought all continue to add to the challenges in dealing with this grief. We discuss the serious impact it had on the school system later as we brace ourselves for the known problems it already is uncovering.

6.9 Academic Outcomes

Studies from around the world for the years since the initial lockdowns began are showing they caused severe and long-lasting consequences for mental health. According to an article by Dalpati et al. (2022), young adults and students suffered significantly in the context of school closures and limited outdoor activities and socialization during the pandemic.

Anxiety symptoms continue to be the most frequently reported issue. Prevalence of anxiety was as high as 74% according to reviews during the second year of the pandemic (Panchal et al. 2021).

The imposition of public health policies mandating social distancing guidelines, then vaccination and booster regimens, coupled with the uncertainty surrounding the virus, resonated with the public, resulting in a dramatic increase in mental health issues and decrease in quality of life.

Heeren et al. (2021) discuss excessive worry as a central feature of the first year of lockdowns. The study discusses the relationship between difficulty controlling worry and symptoms such as feeling restless, trouble relaxing, and feeling afraid that something awful might happen.

6.10 Educational Outcomes

We know that mental health–related problems including anxiety, depression, and ADHD early in childhood have a direct impact on the health and well-being of the individual. These can range from short-term to long-term effects. A study by Hoffmann et al. (2021) goes into a detailed discussion of the impact of child psychiatric outcomes on future educational outcomes.

The academic effects of these early childhood issues include:

- Ability to concentrate and stay on task at school.
- Lateness to class
- Attendance in general
- Completion of exams
- Stagnant literacy scores

- Stagnant mathematics scores
- Decline of scholastic aptitude
- Acting out and other behavioral issues at school
- Being a victim of bullying
- Being a perpetrator of bullying
- Delayed emotional intelligence and social interactions
- Not being taken seriously by teachers
- Teachers and school administrators not being as compassionate
- Attributing their actions to laziness or disrespect rather than a mental health concern
- Disciplinary and other measures taken by school administrators.
- Delay or absence of promotion to higher levels of education
- Repeating the grade
- Getting suspended from school due to behavioral issues
- Getting expelled from school
- Dropping out of school

These concerns then tend to lead to the following:

- Difficulty finding a job
- Difficulty applying for a job
- Delay or absence of starting a career
- Challenges in social lives
- Financial difficulty
- Poverty
- Food insecurity
- Housing insecurity
- Stagnant or declining socioeconomic status
- Decreased opportunities in their lives

These may lead to further impact on the person's mental health, including:

- Sense of sadness
- Feelings of inadequacy
- Sense of hopelessness
- Worsening anxiety
- Worsening depression
- Substance use and misuse
- Onset of other behavioral addictions such as gambling

Like other themes discussed in this book, we are strong advocates of early identification and appropriate intervention. Specific to the academic issues and resulting short- and long-term impacts, we recommend early identification of possible mental health issues that may arise in the student.

Optimal systems would be those that have clear, open, and frequent communication between the school, the family, and the treating health-care providers. If the child is not in treatment, a goal would be to facilitate their starting treatment as soon as possible.

While the child and family are learning about their issues and treatment options, the school administration, ideally, would be preparing additional support structures for the child.

Possibilities include additional classes and/or tutors to augment the current teaching. If there is a delay and catch-up is required, specific tracks and opportunities can be provided.

We witnessed what occurred during the pandemic, school closures, and the varying responses of the schools. In theory, what we mentioned regarding additional tracks and boosting academic opportunities for identified children should already be in place and happening. It is not. It was not a routine part of the lockdown strategy, and only those fortunate enough to have parents who are diligent advocates are attended to.

Policies in educational settings should be extremely mindful of these effects, and try to mitigate or reduce them as close to zero as possible. The preference would be to work towards preventing them from happening all together.

In an article written by Woessmann in 2016, the author emphasizes the economic case for education. They discuss the importance of educational outcomes to ensure employment later on and the resulting economic growth and prosperity of future generations.

6.11 Faculty Well-Being

The majority of the focus of the studies and experiences discussed have been on the student and family. An often-overlooked yet similarly important piece of the puzzle of school closings and lockdowns is the impact on faculty, teachers, and school administrators. Close friends and colleagues of ours who are on the faculty of medical schools and universities described the struggle and creativity required to switch from the way they were teaching one day to an entirely online mode the next.

A study by Schwab et al. (2022) discusses a systematic comparison of faculty well-being and need satisfaction before and during the pandemic. The authors discuss the satisfaction of basic needs for relatedness and autonomy and how they were negatively impacted during the lockdowns and the switch to a virtual teaching environment.

Up until the pandemic, faculty had a routine way of providing in-person face-to-face teaching, mentoring, and interactions. The abrupt removal of that option forced them to think of ways to provide similar levels of education, either live, synchronously, or offline, through self-guided homework. Class sizes that were limited to the number of students that could fit in one room became a non-issue with remote learning, as anyone from anywhere could attend at any time.

The faculty who embraced this as an opportunity to be creative and provide value at broader scales were less fragile. Those who had difficulty adapting to the new normal suffered in their well-being, and many faculty and staff were downsized and let go.

Not all students who chose to attend online classes, especially while there were widely variable attendance requirements during the first year or two of the pandemic, turned on their video cameras or microphones. This made repairing an already-severed connection even less viable. In addition to overcoming the hurdles of technology and new teaching styles, faculty found themselves figuring out inventive ways to keep the attention of these online students.

6.12 Risk Factors

The following risk factors have been identified in studies, including one by Young et al. (2022), as being associated with an increased risk of developing or worsening mental health outcomes during the pandemic.

■ Prior mental health diagnosis

  – History of obsessive-compulsive disorder (OCD)
  – History of attention deficit hyperactivity disorder (ADHD)
  – History of anxiety disorders
  – Presence of personality disorders
  – History of autism spectrum disorder
    • Evidence of comorbidities of autism spectrum disorders and anxiety and depression are known.
    • Studies report that the increase in anxiety and depression in people with autism spectrum disorders was higher during the first years of the pandemic than for those without autism spectrum disorders.

■ Family history of mental illness
■ Virus-related issues

  – Family member or a loved one who became ill with the virus
  – Fear of infection

■ Increased screen time, including increased digital media use

  – See Chapter 7, 'Un-Social Media,' for an in-depth discussion of the negative physical and mental health outcomes of social and digital media use.
  – Increased cell phone usage
  – Increased internet use
  – Online learning scenarios – the correlation has been observed to be worse outcomes with increased use. Interestingly, being a student, regardless of the modality of education, is also described as an increased risk factor for developing anxiety and depression.
  – High levels of social media use
  – Smartphone and internet addictions
  – Increased access to media and being overexposed
  – Access to excessive information

■ Increased time at home
■ Lack of daily routine
■ Poor food and nutrition intake

  – History of eating disorders

■ Gender and age

  – According to studies, female gender was associated as a risk for developing mental health issues, including anxiety and depression.
  – Younger age was associated with higher levels of anxiety, depression and PTSD.

■ Social determinants of health-related risks, according to the World Health Organization:

- Financial strains
- Socioeconomic adversity
- Decreased parental education
- Minority communities
- New unemployment

- Poor sleep patterns
- Poor self-control
- Social stigma
- Interrupted child protective regulatory services, such as Child Protective Services (CPS) and other child abuse reporting agencies

6.13 Protective Factors

Throughout the pandemic, the following factors have been noted to be protective factors against serious anxiety and depression:

- Being able to share the fears of the pandemic, viral anxiety, and one's social distancing phobias
- Better knowledge of and better information about the pandemic
- Decreased screen time
- Encouraging children and young adults to go to sleep on time
- Family communication
- Feeling as if one belongs – to a family, friend or peer group, or social network
- Having siblings
- Higher levels of education
- Higher levels of income
- Having hobbies
- Hope
- Increased levels of parent-child communication
- Informed knowledge about the virus, including protective measures
- Leisure activities
- Life satisfaction
- Listening to music
- Meaning of life – while we saw a significant increase in existential crises manifesting during the pandemic, those who identified as having a meaning and purpose in their lives were better equipped to manage the uncertainties and fears during the pandemic.
- Exercise
- Parental responsiveness
- Play activities
- Positive emotional regulation skills
- Praying
- Relationships
- Resilience – an article by Taylor et al. (2022) describes the positive relationship between resilience, self-reliance, and mental health outcomes, including those across the neurodiversity spectrum. See Chapter 8, 'Confidence and Recovery,' for more information on resilience and its impact on mental health.

- Yoga – according to a study by Sinanovic et al. (2022), yoga practitioners showed a significantly lower average severity of stress and symptoms of anxiety and depression.

6.14 Recommendations

Governments, health organizations, and, most importantly, mental health systems should learn from the challenges we faced during the pandemic and adapt to ensure care is provided in a COVID/trauma-informed manner.

Due to the protracted course of the pandemic and continual threats of resurgences, it is imperative that we provide access and opportunity and improve in the following domains:

Access

- Ensure appropriate access to services to ensure early diagnosis and treatment.
- Increase access to evidence-based self-help tools and apps, and, combined with the aforementioned learnings, ensure that people are using digital solutions only as needed.

Community

- Work towards reducing the stigma of mental health issues and reaching out to get help for mental health and wellness.
- Work towards healing and improving relationships – at home between couples and families, as well as within our communities.
- Increase safety-net organizations available for youth and young adult mental health and well-being.

Equity

- Ensure equitable care practices, cultural humility, and flexibility.
- Increase funding for mental health services, specifically for youth and young adults, with emphasis on social and culturally appropriate, equitable care.
- Provide culturally competent and culturally humble care resources.
- Improve equitable access to mental and physical health care.
- Improve social determinants of health, such as addressing food and housing insecurities, as well as concerns regarding employment.
- Increase research for mental health for children, adolescents, and young adults in a culturally sensitive, equitable manner.

Mental and Physical Health

- Provide integrated care that includes mental health with physical health, including in family practice and pediatric care settings.
- Provide clinically relevant screening for concerns including postpartum depression, anxiety, depression, burnout, and other stress-related disorders.

- Increase mental health access, including modalities such as tele–mental health options to ensure those in rural areas have equitable access to care.
- Provide meaningful support for those professions associated with higher risks of anxiety, depression, and posttraumatic stress, including school faculty, health-care providers, and first responders.
- For issues amenable to group therapy, increase training for that type of modality to provide access and appropriate care to those in need.
- Improve family mental and physical health, access to care, and reimbursement rates to incentivize clinicians to pay attention and treat people.

Education

- Ensure accurate messaging and information is available, especially to vulnerable populations, who may be unable to discriminate between appropriate and harmful information.
- Provide resources and education to develop and enhance resilience for individuals and communities.
- Increase education programs relating to mental health for families and schools.
- Increase research into the long-term effects of COVID-related issues on population mental health.

Sleep

- Provide education regarding the need for adequate sleep duration and quality, based on age and specific needs. As discussed earlier, sleep is a leading protective factor for many issues, and the lack of restorative sleep leads to many mental health issues.

Safety

- Increase access and resources for child protective agencies, like community safety net programs, that are also available for urgent and unsafe circumstances.
- As intimate partner violence has increased, it is critical to ensure organizations that help those in need are funded and staffed appropriately.

Screen Time

- Improve public health messaging and education regarding the ill effects of screen time and internet and cell phone addictions.
- Provide education on alternative, preventative, and protective factors.
- Revisit official medical guidelines as to what pediatricians recommend for children and screens.

Spirituality

- Increase spirituality-based options for those interested. Cultural and other belief-based rituals have been shown to increase meaning in daily life, to provide a sense of community and security, and to help develop a purpose in life.

Substance Use

■ Address substance use–related issues. From harm reduction methodologies to active treatment, we must ensure people have access to treatment and care. Prevention-based education and resource allocation must be developed.

Self-Care

■ Provide accurate and actionable information to ensure people can practice self-care and live healthy lifestyles, including proper diet and exercise.

Exercise

■ Improve exercise and recommend increased physical activity, especially for youth and young adults. The earlier people get into the routine of self-care, the more habitual it becomes and the greater the life-long benefits.

Nutrition

■ Improve the nutrition of youth and young adults by addressing the availability and affordability of healthy foods, coupled with improving education around the value of healthy eating.

Resources

■ Increase accessible, equitable resources for children, adolescents, and young adults.
■ Ensure that communities know their available mental health and other critical resources, including crisis hot lines, shelters, and safety net organizations.

Chapter 7

Un-Social Media

7.1 Introduction

This chapter discusses the increased trends in digital media use and the mental and physical health impacts on individuals and communities. We discuss in detail the influence of the recent pandemic and related lockdowns and the significant increase in exposure to screen time and social media use among students and young adults.

The main takeaway is that the excessive consumption of digital and social media during isolation and lockdowns further exacerbated the pre-pandemic rise in anxiety and depressive disorders.

Woven throughout this chapter are useful prompts to provide time to reflect and absorb the information included, solidify the thoughts elicited, and foster the development of ideas you may wish to share with loved ones or your health-care provider.

We provide a review of the literature on each negative health and psychological impact that increased use of social media has on vulnerable populations. There is a section specific to cyber bullying and victimization as that too has increased recently and must be addressed.

We conclude the chapter with distinct and actionable recommendations for individuals, families, clinicians, school administrators, teachers, doctors, nurses, policy makers, and regulators.

> **When a person can't find a deep sense of meaning, they distract themselves with pleasure.**
>
> —Viktor Frankl

7.2 Always Online

The use of digital media has increased significantly over the years. Young adults and adolescents use social media and mobile phones at the highest rates. We live in a world where up to 95% of adolescents have access to and use mobile devices. Thankfully, the research and literature regarding the associated maladaptive behavioral patterns have also improved.

DOI: 10.4324/9781003413547-10

The online world is very different from the real world. The limitless possibilities offer people experiences at the edges of their imagination. Adolescents and young adults strive for acceptance and belonging through their interactions online and spend increasingly more time on their social appearance. Peer relationships and exploring social, romantic, and other connections are meaningful and healthy ways to use digital platforms.

Social media can be a great tool when consumed and engaged with in moderation. A real-world example is while writing this book, in February 2023, there was a very large earthquake in the south of Turkey. We have many friends and relatives in Istanbul who have relatives impacted by the earthquake. Many thousands of people died, and rescue efforts were enhanced by the connectivity that social media provides. This is, without question, an extremely positive aspect of being able to connect and share information and resources such as monetary aid with those who are in need.

Another example is being able to video chat online with loved ones not permitted to travel outside their countries or enter the United States during the first years of the pandemic, which was tremendously valuable.

A study by Akhther and Sopory (2022) describes the role of social media in facilitating coping and sharing experiences and mental health–related issues with others during the pandemic. There is a limit, however, to the value of self-disclosure in unburdening oneself on social media. The line distinguishing moderation and excessive use is defined by the individual. Resulting negative impacts on the user and family system may appear insidiously as addictive patterns set their roots.

The pandemic shifted and changed every part of our lives and significantly altered our relationship with the internet. School and business closures, as well as the recommendations for social distancing, contributed to an increased online presence for all ages.

Studies report that during the pandemic, over 95% of adolescents and young adults spent nine or more hours each day in front of a screen, with most of them using screens until they fell asleep (Wehbe et al. 2022).

These extremely long hours online then cemented these habits, resulting in addictive-like behaviors that are very difficult to overcome, especially when there is little or no advocacy to reduce them. On the contrary, the ease of entry, seductive nature, and clearly designed neuro-manipulation, not to mention the multiple billions of dollars of profit in this space, make this effort seem impossible.

Needs can be met online that may be difficult or impossible to meet in real life. Apart from the essential workers and jobs that require direct physical contact, many people and events have switched to the comforts and economic ease of virtual gatherings. Introverts have benefited from decreased pressure to be social under the guise of staying healthy, and anxious individuals have become glued to the news cycles for their minute-by-minute fear drip to further validate their need to stay online.

The infodemic, as described by the World Health Organization (WHO), is an increased amount of information—some appropriate, some filled with malicious incorrect information—that has made it difficult for people to assess which source to trust.

When people have difficulty knowing which sources are trustworthy and which are not, they have a tendency to increase their digital and social media consumption in an attempt to allay their concerns, fears, and worries.

Increased time online, on social media, and playing video games correlates with increased risk of developing habitual use, leading to addictive behaviors. There is a consistent, linear association between digital media use and negative mental health outcomes (Primack et al. 2022).

When participating online on social media and various platforms, the risk of cyber victimization also increases. Available research suggests that one in every three adolescents and young adults is victimized by their peers!

A study by Espinoza (2022) discusses the impact of witnessing cyber victimization and the effect it has on levels of anxiety. Previous studies have demonstrated that witnessing bullying in real life increases one's anxiety levels and feelings of depression as well as physical health issues.

As mentioned, internet as well as social media use increased significantly during the pandemic. When our means of socialization rapidly became narrowed to an online-only universe, the impact of internet use became more prominent. While there have been some benefits to being increasingly connected, with minor improvements and access to some areas of work- and health-related activities, there have been significant downsides as well.

In the not-too-distant past, technology companies as well as the WHO tried to advise families, schools, and students to limit the use of digital devices, especially in school settings.

The increased amount of time spent online during the pandemic also appears to have increased racism and xenophobia, according to reports. Online coordinated bullying and discriminatory and illegal activities have increased, resulting in worsening anxiety and acute and posttraumatic stress.

Researchers and clinicians already had access to evidence of increased social media use and associated anxiety and depression during prior health outbreaks, including bovine spongiform encephalopathy, SARS, the 2009 H1N1 flu, Ebola, the avian flu, ZIKA, and MERS.

Those who can incorporate learnings from the past into their current lives and work to build healthy habits have a greater chance of overcoming these types of challenges.

> **What if changing the world was just about being here, by showing up no matter how many times we get told we don't belong, by staying true even when we're shamed into being false, by being true to ourselves even when we're told we're too different.**
> **—Rami Malek (Mr. Robot),** *Hello, Elliot* **(TV episode, 2019)**

There is a clear link between social media use and serious negative impacts on cognition and mental health—so much so that the American Academy of Pediatrics has supported committees and councils on communication and media and published numerous reports detailing the detriments.

While there have been positive impacts of being online, especially helping distract from the extreme fear of the pandemic or relieving one's mood, because of continued social distancing requirements and most schools and workplaces adopting online options, people have been spending more time online.

Technology companies have done a fantastic job at creating an irrationally premature fear in parents, suggesting that even young children need to learn coding and have increased exposure to online activities to be competitive.

We have seen this in our family friends, who have insisted on enrolling their children in coding classes as early as age five. Initially we even tried this with our son, but seeing how much time he was spending online and the gamification of that constant online presence, we rethought the approach.

Simultaneously amusing and alarming, since we began writing this book (early 2023) to the time we're preparing to submit it to our publisher (early 2024), the increase in AI capabilities has already made (rudimentary) coding skills obsolete!

Social media companies are aware of the impact of their technology and, unbeknownst to the average user, have on many occasions manipulated social feeds and posts to influence affect. For example, when sadder posts that are displayed, the user posts fewer happy posts. We are aware of current lawsuits against these companies that allege their family members were negatively impacted by such manipulated information.

The American Academy of Pediatrics reported in a paper by Chassiakos et al. (2016) that 'parents can be reassured that their children will learn to use digital media quickly.' The authors warn against too-early and prolonged online exposure.

Some articles are easier to read and digest by non-clinicians while others remain buried in medical academia. We hope to list these as clearly as possible, in an evidence-based manner, for no other reason than to shed light on the concerns, validate individuals and families who may be noticing concerns or trends, and prevent as many of the negative effects as possible.

Every family and every individual is different. We all have our sets of protective factors and risk factors that push us towards and pull us away from the harms of digital media consumption. The type of social media and purposes for which one uses them differ.

How social media use impacts the mental health and well-being of any individual is complex, as discussed in an article by Awao et al. (2022). Specifics that relate to the individual, their mental health needs, and support structure are all nuanced, and therefore the information provided in this chapter must not be taken as absolutes that occur every time.

The evidence-supported information provided is intended to show what is currently known about people in general so you can be better informed in making balanced decisions going forward.

Social media overuse and digital misuse have been linked to the following:

▪ Increase in anxiety disorders:

- See Chapter 2, 'Identifying and Treating Anxiety,' for in-depth information regarding anxiety disorders, diagnosis, and treatment.
- In the context of digital and social media platforms, addictive and pathological use is significantly predictive of anxiety disorders.
- Study after study demonstrate a clear causal link between increased screen time and increased anxiety. Azhari et al. (2022) discusses issues that increase anxiety, including the number of times someone posts online in a given period, as well as the number of social media platforms the person is on.
- According to a study by Shabahang et al. (2024), anxiety may lead to oversharing of personal, private information online and, cyclically, may lead to worsening anxiety. Additionally, attention seeking as well as social media–related addictions are related to oversharing and high-frequency disclosures. See later in this chapter for dangerous use and other consequences of inappropriate information sharing online.
- Those with anxiety and depression, according to studies, are more likely to use social media to seek information and share experiences and are also at an increased risk of deepening their anxieties and depression.

■ The development and exacerbation of addictive behaviors.

– Similar to the patterns of substance use addictions, there is a clearly observable pattern of symptoms, including:
  • Thoughts of and desires to be online.
  • Feelings of craving and wanting to check the latest notifications or join a chat thread.
  • Preoccupation, including spending more time thinking about the social media app, one's next post, or a comment in response to a previous post.
  • Increased anxiety and tension when unable to access one's phone or be online.
  • Constantly thinking and ruminating about the most recent post or reactions to a comment; thinking about what one will do next online.
  • The variable rewards of post notifications may be momentarily satisfying but deepen the craving for more.
  • Loss of control and the inability to stop using social media despite one's desire and plans to limit use. This can be viewed as a parallel to altered decision-making processes, similarly seen in substance use addictive behaviors.
  • Continued use despite potential or real negative effects. These may include increased time spent online to the detriment of one's health, schooling, or work. They may also include negative peer interactions, chastising, or even being cancelled at school or in one's community.
  • Development of tolerance to social media use over time. This refers to not obtaining as much pleasure from use, requiring increased use to feel the same levels of satisfaction/happiness or alleviation of symptoms of anxiety.
  • Decreased sense of gratification from being online.
  • Overall increased use over time, with minimal returns on emotional investment.
  • Increase in financial spending, purchasing subscriptions or apps that link to or are associated with other apps, as well as on advertising.
  • A feeling of withdrawal when not online or checking one's cell phone.
  • Loss of interest in doing other things.
  • Neglecting other priorities and responsibilities to be online and spend more time on social media.
  • An associated negative impact on social relationships, in person or online
  • Potential for or actual relapse in using despite decisions to cut down or stop.
– Numerous studies, including one by Kovačić Petrović et al. (2022), discuss the increased addictive behavior during the pandemic and its association with other mental health issues.

■ Altered dopamine and reward pathways:

– One example is the gamification of apps and combining them with the real world.
  • There are cell phone games that suggest walking around real-world environments to find and collect different rewards.
  • This reinforces the loop of continuously checking the app, obviously spending more money on in-app purchases and providing more personal information to the app companies.
– Augmented-reality apps that display different graphics overlayed with the real world can create distortions of real life.

- Day-to-day interactions and surroundings become less interesting without full or augmented immersion in digital media.
- The excessive need for stimulation, excitement, and validation and the desire to be rewarded with attention are other cyclical issues for some individuals that increase their social media use.
    • This can result in conditioned patterns, not only altering the brain's reward pathway but also creating problematic use, anxieties, and depression.
- Doom scrolling, described as the ongoing tendency to keep looking at posts and news feeds despite feeling negatively about their content, has been linked to the addictive pattern of behaviors described earlier, as well as worsening anxieties and depression.

7.3 Writing Prompt

Consider using the space provided to reflect on the following prompts:

How many times in a two-hour period do you think you check your cell phone?

_____

_____

_____

We recommend you track how many times you check your cell phone in the next two hours. Consider writing them down in the space provided, including the length of time you use the phone each time.

_____

_____

_____

_____

_____

Now compare this log to your response to the first prompt, noting any disparities.

■ Attention difficulties:

- Deficits in attention are connected with poor performance in school and at work.
- These are also connected with and may result from sleep disturbances related to social media use, exacerbating the cycle.
- Concentration difficulties may also arise.
- Information processing difficulties and corresponding memory challenges may emerge.

- Attention difficulties may result in an increase in attention deficit-hyperactivity disorders (ADHD).
- In addition to issues relating to multitasking and distracted attention, there is a correlated deficit in retention of information as well.
- According to studies, information learned through interacting with another person is retained longer and more completely than that learned digitally online.

■ Aggressivity and other behavioral problems:

- Acting out, combined with decreased emotional regulation skills, may result in outward physicality.
- Aggressive and violent physical behaviors may emerge.
- In addition to aggressive behaviors displayed outwardly, studies suggest that increased digital media use and exposure are correlated with a desensitization to pain, violence, and suffering (Mathiak and Weber 2006).
- Exposure to violent digital content increases the tendency of the user towards aggressivity and thoughts and feelings of anger, as well as impacting the person's arousal levels. These are known to contribute to difficulty concentrating and sleeping and, most concerningly, acting out in aggressive ways online and in real life.
- Trying to copy things seen on social media can cause the individual to (accidentally or on purpose) seriously harm or kill themselves or someone else.
- If a parent or caregiver is overusing cell phones and other digital media, time available for interactions with the family is decreased. This can lead to parent-child interaction issues, as well as mental health concerns in the parent that subsequently may cause or trigger additional behavioral issues with the child.

■ Body image and body esteem–related issues:

- A narrative review by Mougharbel and Goldfield (2020) discusses the link between challenges with worsening body image and associated screen time and exposure to social media.
- Increased social media time increases body image issues when users are exposed to idealized body representations.
- Negative self-evaluation affects body image, life satisfaction, and ability to regulate emotions and interact with others socially.
- Appearance ideals are routinely a component of online posts and what users compare themselves with and aspire to be like, which distorts their beliefs.
- Social appearance anxiety, how it develops through the 'influencers' on social media, and its impact on mental and physical health are discussed in an article by Caner et al. (2022).
- See the section in this chapter on eating-related problems.
- Unhealthy relationships with smart watches and fitness trackers are also linked to negative thought patterns, shame, guilt, and anxiety.
  • Disordered behaviors that stem from continued monitoring of body metrics include restricted eating patterns and overexercising.
  • Sharing workout statistics with friends and competing for various digital awards can also come with negative consequences, including worry and depression.

- On a positive note, a study by Thai et al. (2024) found that reducing social media use improves appearance and weight esteem.
  - Within as little as a few weeks of reducing time spent online, the researchers found that the teenagers and undergraduates experienced significant improvements in their body image.

■ Conditioning:

- The more someone goes to the internet to escape or cope with negative feelings, the more they become conditioned to seek comfort online (Wegmann et al. 2015).
- The cell phone, the social media platform, the posts, and the searches all become conditioned stimuli to a perceived sense of calm when, in reality, the cycle feeds itself with worsening feelings.
- This pattern of reinforcing avoidance behaviors to keep from feeling anxious or depressed pulls the user deeper online, away from real-life situations.

■ Cyber bullying:

- Resulting in anxiety, depression, and suicidality.
- See section in this chapter that discusses bullying in detail.

■ Dangerous use:

- Being distracted while using cell phones has been an increasingly problematic social hazard.
- Inappropriately using cell phones—checking social media while driving or walking on busy streets—has led to numerous car accidents and pedestrian deaths.
- The National Safety Council analysis of National Highway Traffic Safety Administration (NHTSA) data reported that, in 2020 alone, 3,142 people died in distraction-related crashes!
- There may be potentially dangerous cell phone/Wi-Fi/Bluetooth interactions when laptops or phones are used in areas they are not supposed to be used in, such as on planes.
- Sexting and other sexually inappropriate, compromising uses are additional examples. See later in this chapter for more details.
- Cyber bullying, as the victim and even as the aggressor, is another problematic consequences of increased social media use, especially in vulnerable populations.

■ Decreased creativity:

- Consumption of media, browsing, and passive entertainment have all been linked to a decrease in ability to think independently, as well as a decrease in creativity.
- Areas that are impacted include artistic and musical creativity, as well as cognitive flexibility, reasoning, and deductive skills.
- Studies also show a correlation between increased internet and social media use and a decrease in cognitive and mental flexibility. When things are presented

digitally for consumption, rather than options to create, the mind suffers from a lack of a need to push itself.
- Problem-solving deficits arise, as do the emotional aspects of being able to see things from another person's point of view. Studies have shown a negative impact on empathy as well.

■ Decreased independent thinking:

- The ability to read long texts, grapple with complex thoughts, and understand multiple perspectives and points of view are all decreased with social media use.
- Questioning and reasoning are largely impacted by short bite-size clips designed to decrease attention and occupy the user's attention and time.
- This leads to a decreased ability to make decisions, either for oneself or under pressure in social situations.
- One's ability to think and articulate concepts such as personal identity becomes diminished as confusion and humiliation become features rather than accidental bugs of a system designed to squash individuality and self-expression.
- The desire for social conformity encourages increased anxiety, reinforces toxic social conditions, and grinds away at the person's ability to think critically for fear of judgment and ostracization. This demand for conformity is cyclically reinforced by the desire to avoid being humiliated or cancelled.

7.4 Writing Prompt

Consider using the space provided to reflect on the following prompts:

How confident do you feel that you can sort out real information from false, misleading information?

_____

_____

_____

_____

How do you know this?

_____

_____

_____

_____

■ Decrease in physical self-care and exercise:

- With more time spent online, connected to a cell phone, or concentrating on posts and messages, there is inevitably less time to do other things, including exercise.
- Combined with the unhealthy eating patterns described later, these issues point in the direction of declining mental and physical health.

■ Decrease in self-esteem:

- Self-esteem is another cyclical risk factor for and the cause of increased digital and social media use.
- Social comparisons (comparing oneself to those online one finds to be superior in beauty or financial status) often lead to cognitive distortions, decreasing self-esteem and sense of worth.
- Research by Jarman et al. (2021) discusses the perception of the user, how they feel they compare to those they view online, and their own negative evaluations of themselves.
- Feelings of envy associated with being exposed to ideal representations of body images and false/exaggerated lifestyles may also lead to self-esteem issues.

■ Decrease in life satisfaction:

- A study by González-Nuevo et al. (2022) discusses the link between social media use, high levels of anxiety, and low life satisfaction.
- This is described in the connection of the addictive consequences of social and digital media use, as well as the negative social comparisons when interacting online.

■ Decreased performance on cognitive tasks:

- Depending on age, things such as perceiving three dimensions in real life can be impacted when a very young child receives their information from a two-dimensional screen.
- Interactions such as speaking, enunciation, and complex patterns of thinking are all impacted when large amounts of a child's communication are experienced through digital media, including television.

■ Decreased interest in real-life situations:

- There has been a correlated worsening of and difficulty maintaining relationships in the real world.
- People report feeling more comfortable with a cell phone than face-to-face with a person.
- Challenges solving problems during interpersonal interactions with others may arise.
- In general, as seen post pandemic lockdowns, there may also be difficulty interacting socially when so many of one's relationships are developed online.
- Concerningly, there is also an associated decreased ability to develop healthy bonding with children, peers, and colleagues.

- Digital overdose:

  - The concept of diminishing returns with social media use, resulting in physical and mental health consequences, is described throughout this section.

- Disrupted school and academic performance:

  - Increased social media use, especially in vulnerable populations, has been associated with increased difficulties in school.
  - Not surprisingly, these issues relate to attention, retention, and not spending appropriate time on school and academic-based activities.

- Disrupted work performance:

  - Attention, achievement, and efficiency are all impacted by increased social and digital media use.
  - This is specifically conspicuous when a person is digitally preoccupied to the exclusion of their work and career.

- Distortion of reality:

  - Considering the increasingly open-minded, tolerant spaces becoming available, there continue to be high risks of exposure to gender, sexual, racial, and ethnic stereotypes online.
  - These concepts can further confuse or exacerbate complex thoughts and emotions of belonging, peace with oneself, life satisfaction, and mental health and well-being.

- Unhealthy eating:

  - Issues from neglecting balanced diets to the development of true eating disorders have all been linked to screen time, digital media use, and social media activities.
  - Emotional eating is discussed in an article by Caner et al. (2022) in the context of social appearance anxiety and how it is linked with social media use. The authors discuss the users' perception of their family and income level as they relate to themselves and how this may impact their anxiety and compensatory eating patterns.
  - Studies have made it clear that companies significantly increased their marketing and advertising campaigns directed towards children and young adults during the pandemic.
  - Similar to the marketing of alcohol and other substances that are ever present online, calorie-rich, nutritionally poor foods are also heavily marketed online (Tan et al. 2018).
  - Junk food and fast foods are mega businesses.
    - They are easily accessible and provide temporary comfort but have disproportionately negative longer-term effects with continued consumption.
    - Both foods high in real, natural forms of sugar and foods with artificial sweeteners are known to have negative effects on the mind and body.

- In addition to endocrine issues such as imbalanced sugar levels, diabetes-related concerns, and sleep disorders, the spikes and falls of blood sugar can lead to anxiety and depression.
- Consumption of artificial sweeteners as well as the artificial coloring used in junk foods and sodas is directly linked with the exacerbation of anxiety disorders.

- Unhealthy eating behaviors lead to weight gain and obesity. Alarm bells were sounding even before the pandemic regarding significant increases in rates of 'very high body weights' (formally described as morbid obesity).
- Use of digital media, screen time, and social media are known to be correlated with an increase in eating despite not feeling hungry. The mismatch of increased calorie intake and decreased physical expenditure of energy results in a net increase in weight.
- Studies show that people engaging with social media at higher rates have higher body mass indexes (BMI). Victimization and social isolation are risk factors for eating-related disorders, and the link between social media use and the factors mentioned earlier contributes to the increase in weight gain and other eating problems.
- When you combine increasingly sedentary behaviors and decreased physical activities (either available or engaged in) with the stress and anxiety of the pandemic, the increased advertising of junk food to younger people, the habits and linkages of junk food and temporary gains, the reinforcing feedback loop, and the near absence of proponents trying to minimize this harm, you see the unfolding of these concerns.
- Evidence suggests that social media use is the first independent risk factor for obesity for children in elementary school (Khajeheian et al. 2018) and the second independent risk factor for obesity for students in high school. The more time spent on social media, studies suggest, the greater the weight gain of the individual.
- Disordered eating is certainly not unidirectional towards overeating. There is a link between social media use and calorie restriction as seen in anorexia, as well as eating and purging behaviors as seen in bulimia. Impossibly unbalanced physical images and portrayals of beauty standards impact everyone, especially the vulnerable and impressionable.
- Through researching this book, we came across and learned of pro–eating disorder forums and websites.
  - Pro-anorexia forums, in which individuals are encouraged to adopt unhealthy eating behaviors, exist.
  - These are reinforced and perpetuated through messages of thinness, body perfectionism, and self-esteem.
  - Unmitigated online presence, especially for the younger and otherwise more vulnerable people, presents grounds for these forums to exist and advance harmful agendas disguised as acceptance and positivity.
- Unregulated information regarding nutritional contents of foods also impacts those who try to do their own research and may fall prey to incorrect and even malicious information. Throughout the years, we have been exposed to one diet fad after another, many of them ineffective and some of them genuinely harmful

to people's health. As of the writing of this book, there is a diabetes medication being suggested by influencers online to induce rapid weight loss. There have even been reports of shortages of this specific medication, indicating a rapid uptake and use for intentions other than those recommended. This also has the additional negative effect of the drug not being available for people who truly need it for their clinical issues.

■ Emotional dysregulation:

- People with difficulty regulating their emotions have a tendency to escape online, and being online and using social media are also correlated with dysregulated emotions.
- The conditioning of avoiding feelings of anxiety and sadness by being online and the eroding coping skills when spending more time online all feed into one another.

■ Fear:

- Fear can manifest as a consequence of the contents of online media itself.
- Stress and trauma symptoms can develop from witnessing and being exposed to content viewed online and via other digital media.
- The lack of ability to easily filter by age appropriateness and access to all ranges of suitable and inappropriate content such as violence, graphic images, pornography, and drug and alcohol messaging can create increased stress.
- Fear of missing out (FOMO) is described later in this chapter.
- Another type of fear described in the literature is the fear of being inadequately connected (Hoge et al. 2017). Studies discuss the feeling or fear of being ostracized if an individual does not receive a response text or post online within a short time period. According to these studies, anxiety was increasingly correlated with the greater the number of posts and texts sent.

■ Feeling judged:

- An article by Billieux et al. (2015) discusses the 'excessive reassurance pathway,' a pathway by which people engage in increased digital media and cell phone use in order to obtain reassurance from others online and the need to maintain relationships.

7.5 Writing Prompt

Consider using the space provided to reflect on the following prompts:

How do you feel when you see someone's clothes, their body, or the experiences they share online?
The value of this writing prompt is to have you consider scenarios and how they make you think and feel.

When I see someone's . . .
(Example: Beach pics online)

I feel . . .
(Example: inadequate)

_____	_____
_____	_____
_____	_____
_____	_____
_____	_____
_____	_____
_____	_____
_____	_____

■ Feeling shame:

- The multifactorial and personal responses people have to exposure to body ideals, flaunting of wealth and status, and curated relationships and experiences have all been shown to lead to embarrassment, envy, and shame.

■ Gaming and gambling:

- Social media and other components of online interactions are also linked to the gamification of relationships, as well as an increase in the onset and exacerbation of gambling.
- Online gaming serves as a chemical substitute that is unable to replace true connection, altering the reward pathway and creating unrealistic expectations of receiving pleasure and reward.
- The prevalence of online gambling among adolescents and young adults has increased significantly. Examples include the following:
  • Sports gambling
  • Blind 'loot' boxes in video games
  • Add-ons and downloadable content, as well as variably reinforced unlockable virtual objects in games played with friends, all strengthen and solidify the reward pathway, addictive behaviors, and the spending of increased time and money online.

- Increase in depression:

  - Studies suggest that each hour online increases the risk of the development and worsening of depressive disorders.
  - Increased social and digital media use is a significant predictor of mood disorders and resulting consequences, including:
    - Dysthymia
    - Depression
    - Self-injurious thoughts and behaviors and even death by suicide

- Increases in emergency department visits:

  - Numerous studies, including one by Chiu et al. (2020), report the link between social media use and resulting ED visits for anxiety, depression, and addiction.

- Increase in impulsivity:

  - A study by Lewin et al. (2023) discusses their review of over 20 separate studies on problematic social media use and the clear positive associations with impulsivity.
  - In addition to general impulsivity, facets of impulsivity including attentional impulsivity and impulsive choice are also impacted.

- Increase in loneliness:

  - Frequent users of digital and social media experience greater levels of loneliness, and those who describe themselves as lonely use social media more often to decrease these feelings. This contributes to the cycle, resulting in the worsening of mood and physical health.
  - In May 2023, the United States Surgeon's general advisory raised the alarm about the devastating impact of loneliness and isolation. This advisory and the framework they presented for remediation were in the context of the pandemic and even described loneliness as an epidemic.
  - A study by Balcombe and De Leo (2023) reports a link between frequently watching online videos with increased levels of loneliness, anxiety, and depression, especially among young adults.

> **It's not denial. I'm just selective about the reality I accept.**
> **– Bill Watterson, author of *Calvin and Hobbes***

7.6 Writing Prompt

Consider using the space provided to reflect on the following prompts:

What are the reasons you use social media? Consider the entire range from reading news articles to connecting with friends.

_____

_____

_____

In what ways does using social media help you cope and relax?

_____

_____

_____

_____

In what ways have you noticed that social media use has increased your stress?

_____

_____

_____

_____

- Increase in stress:

  - Worsening symptoms of depression, anxiety, and stress have all been linked with frequent social media use.
  - Resulting FOMO, dissatisfaction, feelings of inadequacy, and isolation are all additional causes correlated with stress.

- Increase in vulnerability to online predatory behaviors:

  - Digital information lasts forever. People appear to forget that a direct message or post may realistically never be completely erased. Personal identifying data, including photographs, regardless of how 'safe and secure' an app claims to be, are and will always be retrievable.
  - Exploitation, including the potential for identity theft, taking things out of context, bribery and blackmail, are very real problems we all face online.
  - Inappropriate and coerced sexual behaviors are increasingly common online, where studies suggest high numbers of young adults having engaged in sexting (Gregg et al. 2018), as well as other sharing of explicit photos and information.
  - Depending on the vulnerability of the person, age, and developmental stage, these interactions often lead to increased stress, anxiety, PTSD, depression, substance use, sexualized behaviors, and suicidal thoughts and attempts.

■ Low social support:

- More time spent online means less time spent in real life with other people, interacting and practicing social skills. This can lead to social anxieties and depression.
- Decreased social interactions and ability to regulate emotions and solve problems lead to decreased connections and weakened friendship bonds.
- A study by Zhao et al. (2023) reports suppressed brain activity during online video chats compared to real life. The authors discuss the importance of reciprocal exchanges of social cues between people in person and their decrease or absence while online.

■ Mass social media–induced illness:

- Prior neuropsychiatric issues and current mental health stressors, as well as personality and other vulnerabilities to being influenced by suggestive material, are all hypothesized as predisposing one to mass social media–induced illness.
- A study by Fremer et al. (2022), for example, describes an outbreak of mass social media–induced illness that presented with motor and vocal tics – essentially Tourette-like symptoms. This was traced to someone on a social media platform who presented their issues with vocal and motor tics, and subsequently, dozens of people began displaying such behaviors.
- These types of mass outbreaks are known to be associated with emotional arousal as well as identification with the person and content observed (Bartholomew et al. 2012).

■ Negative social comparison:

- Attractive, wealthy, adventurous models and actors online bear no relation to the average person's reality, creating a comparison that often leads to dissatisfaction, sadness, and emptiness.
- Harmful social comparison damages mental health and leaks into many other areas of one's life, according to a robust paper by Braghieri et al. (2022).
- A study by Joseph et al. (2022) looked specifically at mothers viewing content about motherhood online and the negative impact it had on their hormone and stress levels. The authors discuss the feelings stemming from self-evaluations and comparisons and the activation of the HPA axis, resulting in measurable changes in cortisol levels.

■ Overstimulation:

- There are now countless ways to connect with someone online. Texts, video apps, social media posts, direct messages, emailing, and old-fashioned calling someone by phone are all adding to a world where attention spans have decreased. The desire to always be aware of the various ways someone can get in touch with you is overwhelming.
- Simply the potential for missing a text or chat message brings anxiety about missing out on an opportunity.

- Even in workplace situations, we find ourselves with so many ways that a colleague or supervisor can contact us that just to keep up, we must always be checking for notifications, dings, and chimes. We have personal phones and work phones, personal tablets and work tablets, personal laptops and work laptops. We've set up different chimes for different contacts so as not to miss an 'important' message. Phones even have the ability to customize the vibration pattern, so you don't miss a text while in silent mode.
- Multitasking in general is overstimulating and actually decreases productivity due to the amount of energy spent trying to keep up. Multitasking is associated with poor attention, poor academic performance, poor work performance and productivity, and a decreased sense of well-being.

■ Peer pressure:

- Studies indicate that social media posts that have more 'likes' and 'hearts' tend to influence individuals to click the like button as well.
- Social comparison, the need for belonging, and social acceptance are all subconsciously connected to this form of peer pressure.

■ Peer victimization:

- Between 5 and 10% of students aged 11 to 17 are victims of cyber bullying.

■ Preferring being online to face-to-face interactions:

- Social anxiety, fear, and worry may lead to social media use behaviors, and those then reinforce the anxious behaviors by removal of the stressor of relating in person.
- In-person interactions suffer due to online mannerisms and preferences, further pushing the individual to stay online as opposed to having real-life interactions.
- Negative self-evaluation can lead to fears of being evaluated and judged by others the way the person judges themselves, further pulling them away from others in real life.
- Avoidant personalities as well as introverts may find online interactions less stressful to begin with, although, like any compensatory behavior, this leads to exacerbation of the avoidant issues and deepens the introversion.
- Fear of embarrassment and fear of failure may lead one to stay online more, although the conditioning responses described earlier also create situations in which practicing these behaviors and emotions is decreasingly available.

■ Racial discrimination:

- In addition to the factors described earlier, including cyber bullying, victimization, being judged, and exposure to various aggressions, studies describe the impact of racial discrimination as it relates to social and digital media use.
- A study by Layug et al. (2022) discusses in detail the impact of social media use and racial discrimination. This study focuses on social media use during the pandemic and the traumatic stress of racism, hate, cruelty, and xenophobia against

the Asian community. The authors describe the impact on individual online racial discrimination, which is targeted against a specific person, and vicarious online racial discrimination, which is the secondhand exposure to discrimination directed at the person's community.
- Anxiety, depression, secondary traumatic stress, and increased alcohol use are linked to being a victim of racial discrimination.

■ Secondary traumatic stress:

- This is emotional stress that an individual experiences when reading about the trauma someone else experiences.
- This has increased during the pandemic and contributes negatively to anxiety, depression, and feelings of hopelessness.

■ Sex-related issues:

- Sexting is correlated with anxiety and depression, as well as increased sexual behaviors, substance use, and self-injurious behaviors.
- Increased sexual activity has been associated with social media use. Gazendam et al. (2020) describe the connection between disrupted family structure, lower socioeconomic status, poor body image, social media use, and increased rates of early sexual activity.
- Risky sexual behavior includes being put in compromising situations, blackmail, and revenge scenarios.
- Decreased privacy, exploitation of information, and sexually charged cyber victimization also result.
- Being exposed to unsolicited sexual and other inappropriate images is not only a problem in general but also puts younger individuals at risk of coming across explicit material they may not understand, causing confusion and stress.
- Intentional exposure to and consumption of pornographic material online causes harm to developing empathic, romantic relationships in real life. Aggressive and violent material causes psychological harm to the vulnerable viewer, creating rifts in perceived expectations online and what occurs among people face to face.
- There are correlations with an increase in unprotected sex, putting the individual at risk of unplanned pregnancy as well as sexually transmitted infections.
- Sexual activity with strangers may increase.
- Online grooming is a form of cybervictimization that involves one person building a relationship with another, typically an older person with someone younger, that becomes sexualized. The risks and concerns are similar in these scenarios to those described in the bullying section.

■ Substance use disorders:

- In addition to the known coping, compensatory mechanisms that alcohol and other drugs provide to temporarily calm, numb, or decrease feelings of anxiety and sadness, increased online presence exposes students and young adults to an increased number of advertisements for alcohol and other currently legal and available substances of abuse. Marketing works, and these types of targeted marketing work phenomenally well – to the point that we witnessed a significant, alarming increase in alcohol use during the pandemic.

- Ironically, these digital ads consumed by lonesome individuals often depict and sell the fantasy of togetherness and consumption of alcohol to fit in and enjoy time together.
- The mid- and long-term effects of increased habitual alcohol and other drug use are seen in the forms of increased liver and other organ damage.
- Tobacco-, cigarette-, and vaping-related marketing is also prevalent online, and exposure to these products is directly correlated with first-time as well as increased use, resulting in chemical addictions and the serious cardiopulmonary problems associated with smoking.
- In addition to drug use, according to the study by Vieira et al. (2022), excessive use of social media is also associated with smoking.

■ Unrealistic expectations:

- Interactions online are rarely the same as they are in real life.
- Exposure to aggression and behaviors that are hidden behind anonymous users disrupt the vulnerable person's appreciation of how the world works, creating mistrust, fear, and worsening anxiety.
- Seeing things online being reinforced through views or likes may reinforce the activities depicted being socially acceptable.

■ Worsening health outcomes:

- Neglecting personal hygiene due to attention being spent exclusively on digital and social media can worsen health outcomes.
- An article by Guthold et al. (2020) reports that throughout the world, upwards of 80% of adolescents and young adults lack appropriate levels of physical activity.
- We know sedentary behaviors worsen cardiovascular issues such as heart rate and blood pressure.
- Decreased physical activity is linked to weight gain, which can affect blood sugar levels and exacerbate or even initiate problems such as diabetes.
- Head and neck strains are common in cell phone as well as desktop computer users, which can result in headaches. A study by Wehbe et al. (2022) discusses the effects of screen time during the pandemic and its impact on physical symptoms, including headaches. The authors detail the types of headaches, which include tension-type headaches and migraines, exacerbated by excess screen time. The increase in headaches is correlated with issues at school, missed days, and decreased performance.
- Musculoskeletal disorders, including poor posture, and repetitive stress injuries such as carpal tunnel syndrome occur.
- Visual problems have been linked with increased digital media and social media use, specifically with cell phones. The range of problems documented in the

literature includes eye strain and worsening vision such, myopia, dry eyes, and macular degeneration.

- Studies even link these behaviors to increase in cavities due to the neglect of oral hygiene.

■ Worsening sleep hygiene:

- Increased online and social media use has been linked to problems including sleep onset and other circadian rhythm disorders. Studies suggest that girls are at higher risk than boys of developing sleep problems.
- Depending on the developmental age of the individual, a fairly agreed-upon number of hours is recommended/required for a brain to continue developing healthily.
- When cell phones and tablets are brought to the bedside, bedtimes are extended and delayed, and the arousal provided by the content, as well as the physical stimulation by the bright (blue) lights, contribute to worsening sleep outcomes. The blue light is known to suppress the melatonin the body normally produces, which naturally regulates the sleep cycle.
- Interestingly, a study by Thornton et al. (2014) discusses that even the 'mere presence of a cell phone may be distracting,' resulting in decreased attention, poor task performance, and other unintended consequences.
- The development and worsening of difficulties falling and subsequently staying asleep. A study by Al Kazhali et al. (2021) describes the impact of increased social media use, bad sleep quality, and intermittent/anxious sleep patterns.
- The quality and duration of sleep are affected, resulting in daytime sleepiness, problems with attention mentioned earlier, and other physiologic issues such as decreased exercise the following day, increased headaches, and mental health issues, including increased sensitivity to anxiety (Minghelli 2022).
- Articles by Chassiakos et al. (2016) and Hoge et al. (2017) review and provide supporting evidence for the connection between digital media use and sleep disorders such as insomnia.
- Addictions, obsessions, and other compulsive behaviors impact waking up throughout the night to check social media posts, early morning awakenings to participate online, and subsequent difficulty falling back to sleep due to cognitive overstimulation. Those who are increasingly addicted to their social media platforms and posts wake up during the night to check their posts for reactions and comments, further disrupting their ability to attain restorative sleep.

We lead our lives so poorly because we arrive in the present always unprepared, incapable, and too distracted for everything.
—Rainer Maria Rilke, *Letters on Life*

7.7 Red Flags

Risks of problematic social media use differ based on the individual's use pattern, prior circumstances, and support structure.

There are a number of relevant red flags to look out for as a parent, loved one, or clinician that suggest an intervention may be necessary.

Things to look out for include:

- Duration of use and changes in patterns of usage.

    - The greater length of time and the higher the frequency, the more concerning.

- Exposure to posts that may be related to self-harm or suicide.
- Changes in patterns of posts and interactions online.
- Changes in style of posts, potentially indicating worsening mood or onset of a thought disorder.

7.8 Risks of Social Media Addiction

The following list includes personality traits, relational patterns, and circumstantial factors that are known to increase the risk of social media and digital use addiction, as well as available support structures.

- Boredom:

    - Distractions from boredom can be easily found online, especially on social media. The desire for an immediate dopamine rush of escapism and voyeuristic indulgences on others' profiles is satisfied.
    - As discussed earlier, our collective decrease in ability to sustain concentration, attention, and even patience is further reinforced by the instant gratification that being on social media provides.
    - Social media and curated feeds provide unlimited delicious content, designed to provide an endless supply of tasty treats. People don't even have the opportunity to be bored in the face of such appealing entertainment!

- Fear of missing out (FOMO):

    - Excessive internet and cell phone use has been linked to FOMO, the concept that life and enjoyment will pass you by if you are not constantly connected to your social network online.
    - FOMO is depicted in mental health literature as the strongest predictor of risk of increased social media use.
    - FOMO has been linked as an associated risk factor to developing social media addictions, and recent evidence suggests that the pandemic strengthened and worsened this relationship.

- Interestingly, as seen in cases of compensatory compulsive behaviors, FOMO itself may temporarily reduce symptoms of anxiety while online, although it has been documented to increase anxiety as well.
- FOMO increases social media use, which, in turn, increases FOMO itself.
- The pandemic, mandated lockdowns, and the switch to an increasingly online world for work and school shoved everyone into the loop ready for FOMO. People trying to escape their fears and worries went online, which worsened their emotional state. Temporary relief was short lived, resulting in a repetitive, compulsive need to monitor and interact online.
- While there may have been some benefits in staying connected by the only means available during lockdowns, the downsides quickly emerged, and the association with FOMO, especially how it affected vulnerable populations, including young adults, became apparent.

■ Loneliness:

- The desire to reach out, connect, and be part of a group, especially when these are lacking in real life with peers or at home with family, increases the risk of addictive social media use.
- Unmet social needs contribute to loneliness, which may lead to increased social media use and addictive patterns.
- Ironically, despite having many connections online, individuals continue to report feeling lonely, forming a cyclic loop of dissatisfaction, anxieties, and sadness.

■ Low family communication:

- An article by Favotto et al. (2019) discusses the link between quality of communication between the family and the individual and the increased use of digital and social media.

■ Socio-cultural factors:

- People often model what they witness: what they see growing up at home and around them in peer groups. Increased use of social media around them will influence them and may cause increased use.

■ Maladaptive cognition:

- This can include the need for competence, as well as a history of having a negative self-concept.

■ Social anxiety:

- Difficulty fostering and maintaining real-world, face-to-face relationships may lead to a shift to compensatory online behaviors.

■ Gender:

- While there are no definitively known gender-related risks, studies report that females have higher incidences of social anxiety, as well as higher levels of mobile phone addiction (Tu et al. 2022).

■ Pandemic-related life concerns:

- People with increased concerns during the pandemic had increased social media consumption (Daimer et al. 2022).

■ Vulnerability:

- This can be conceptualized in terms of developmental neurocognitive abilities, as well as young age in general, contributing to susceptibility to online messaging and addictive tactics.

■ There are personality-related factors that may influence an individual to use social media more and develop more addictive habits.

- According to an article by Andreassen (2015), some explanations for increased social media use include the personality traits of narcissism, extroversion, and neuroticism.
- Extroversion involves increased levels of energy and sociability.
- Neuroticism is related to feelings such as anxiety and being self-conscious, which, according to an article by Primack et al. (2022), may impact how people interact on social media.

7.9 Cyber Bullying

Before the pandemic, clinicians, families, and schools were working together to prevent, identify, and treat the effects of bullying and its online counterpart, cyber bullying. A large volume of research demonstrates the development of anxiety disorders, including acute and posttraumatic stress disorders, panic disorders, social phobias, and other stress-related disorders.

The cycle of being a victim of bullying as well as being a victimizer are analogous both online and in real life (Mateu et al. 2020). The impact on the mental and physical health of the individual, families, and support networks are similarly problematic.

Research suggests an interesting cyclic nature of victims of cyber bullying. Those with a higher predisposition for risk-taking behaviors tend to find themselves in higher-risk situations that may result in their being a victim. The victimization then leads to additional stress-related responses, leading the user to be online in further risky situations.

Cyber bullying can complicate matters by allowing the victimizer to use avatars, usernames, and de-identifiers to anonymously bother, belittle, and harass. The individual is often alone, with minimal witnesses or distractors. For younger, more vulnerable people, their parents or caregivers may not be around or may assume the school is providing oversight, resulting in greater exposure to bullying.

According to Espelage et al. (2018), maladaptive peer interactions that include bullying occur when one person or group of people intentionally does unpleasant things to another. These may be in the form of physical hostility or aggression, as well as the online version of negative, hostile communication and threatening behaviors.

The pandemic and lockdowns shifted the real-world bullies into the online world, resulting in the need to be increasingly conscientious of cybervictimization. The real-world benefits of being able to physically separate from the aggressor no longer exist online, with limitless access to interact and harass. The increased time spent online has reduced barriers for the bully to connect with the victim, and, unfortunately, there has been a dramatic increase in reported cyber bullying.

Examples of bullying include:

■ Causing suffering
■ Chasing
■ Doing unpleasant things
■ Excluding
■ Humiliating
■ Ignoring
■ Isolating
■ Manipulating relationships
■ Overt acts of physical aggression such as:

  – Assaulting
  – Breaking
  – Hurting
  – Pushing

■ Saying unpleasant things
■ Spreading rumors
■ Stealing
■ Teasing
■ Using mean nicknames

7.10 Ongoing Consequences

Short-term effects of bullying include:

■ Depression

  – Studies indicate that victims of bullying are twice as likely to develop depression.

■ Increase in anxiety disorders

  – Significant association between being a victim of bullying and development of anxiety (Schacter et al. 2022)
    • Panic attacks
    • Acute traumatic and other stress-related disorders

- • Social anxiety
- • Increased startle response
- • Anxiety about being victimized again

- ■ Decreased self-esteem
- ■ Decreased social self-efficacy
- ■ Suicidal ideation and attempts

  – Victims of bullying are twice as likely to develop depression, and studies indicate a strong correlation with suicidal ideation and attempts (Hinduja and Patchin 2018).

- ■ Alcohol and substance use
- ■ Psychological distress

  – Hypervigilance, as well as expecting this type of harm to repeat and continue
  – Fear
  – Internalizing of the negative words and actions

- ■ Reputational damage
- ■ Further isolation and feelings of loneliness

  – Research suggests that victims of bullying, especially younger children and adolescents, often do not share with their parents or other adults their experiences. This makes it more difficult for families to identify and intervene early on. In turn, this has the potential to aggravate the feelings of isolation, anxiety, and depression that arise from being a victim.

- ■ Social manipulation, including altered subjective social status
- ■ Impairment of processing of social interactions

According to a research article by Takizawa et al. (2014), long-term risks of childhood bullying include:

- ■ Altered threat sensitivity
- ■ Challenges in social interactions
- ■ Health issues
- ■ Impact on relationships
- ■ Impact on socioeconomic status
- ■ Lower life satisfaction
- ■ Negative economic outcomes
- ■ Poor health – these consequences last longer and can be more difficult to treat
- ■ Poor perceived quality of life
- ■ Poor cognitive functioning
- ■ Posttraumatic stress disorder

We know that individuals who have been victims of bullying have up to a 70% increased likelihood of developing anxiety disorders that continue throughout their later years. These mental health issues that begin in younger life cause more problems in the person's day-to-day life, last longer, and are typically more difficult to treat.

While prevention from bullying in any form is critical, early identification and treatment of those involved are also very important. A study by Hutson and Melnyk (2022) describes a therapeutic intervention that involves skill building, psychoeducation, and cognitive behavioral interventions that involve the individual and family that has shown a reduction in mental and physical health symptoms.

7.11 Identity

How do you know who you are? Is it in relation to your past self or those around you? We discuss individual values, goals, and systems and, in this section, focus on individual identity.

How do you identify? Who do you identify as? Is your identity solely based on how you appear, or are there more complex interactions between the way you think, feel, and consider yourself in a social structure?

Identity is the way you perceive yourself and is made up of your beliefs, experiences, innate traits and qualities, and interests. The roles we have certainly influence our identities, such as our academic or professional identity. One may have a spiritual or religious identity, a sexual identity, and a national identity.

Within the realm of one's internal sense of gender, there arises a gender identity that may be separate and distinct from one's sexual identity and orientation.

Cultural identity can include traditions and language spoken, as well as ethnicity and heritage. How one connects with their family and larger social groups and community can also be part of their generational and social identities.

7.12 Writing Prompts

Consider using the space provided to reflect on the following prompts:

When did you know you were you?

_____

_____

_____

_____

_____

_____

Who and what have influenced your identity?

_____

_____

_____

_____

_____

_____

What are your current roles?

_____

_____

_____

_____

_____

What do you do to escape your reality?

_____

_____

_____

_____

_____

What would it take to change you?

_____

_____

_____

_____

_____

What do you do to gratify yourself?

_____

_____

_____

_____

_____

_____

When I discover who I am, I'll be free.

– Ralph Ellison, *Invisible Man*

Our chosen roles and past experiences have significant impacts on our identity. It is important to have a strong sense of identity to allow for:

■ Confidence:

  – Having a generally defined sense of identity will allow you to feel more comfortable about what you can do and where your boundaries are.
  – Having confidence relates to decreased feelings of stress and worry, which can help with coping during times of vulnerability and ambiguity.

■ Belonging:

  – Understanding your position within a community and within your family helps form your identity.
  – Cultural and national belonging are important aspects that develop throughout one's life.
  – Appreciating one's identity in the context of belonging further allows one to be motivated to be a part of one's community and social support networks.

■ Understanding of self:

  – As you begin to explore and internalize your values, goals, interests, and desires, you become increasingly aware of your shortcomings and, more importantly, your strengths.
  – Authenticity is interconnected with confidence and self-understanding.
  – Self-understanding leads to improved decision-making ability, specifically decisions that are congruent with one's identity.

■ Resilience:

- Increasing self-awareness, confidence, and belonging all correlate with the ability to remain persistent and resilient.
- Resilience is particularly important during times of uncertainty, doubt, and stress. Having a clearer sense of identity allows one to maintain their true north with purpose and direction.

7.13 Reading Minds

Are you a mind reader?

It is unlikely that you are.

Can you tell what people are thinking, experiencing, or feeling based on what they look like in a photo?

Probably not.

Does it make a difference if you are standing right next to them?

Also unlikely.

How about when someone tells you how they feel? Do you really know what they are truly thinking?

Still unlikely.

Our minds are extremely good at filling in blanks, extrapolating from cues and signals, and incorporating the information based on our own thoughts and feelings.

For example, there are psychological testing cue cards that have nondescript sets of images, such as a person doing an activity and another person around them. The clinician may show this to their patients and ask them to describe what is happening in the picture and how each of the people is thinking and reacting. Obviously, this has nothing to do with the photo itself and everything to do with the patient and what is going on in their mind.

Another interesting thing to think about is our dreams. When you dream, there is no script; there is no one else. It is you and your imagination. When you see a friend or touch a loved one in a dream, they are all manifestations entirely created by yourself. In a sense, you play the role of every character in your dreams, and you are the script writer and director of everything that occurs. The fascination of exploring dreams, in therapy or through writing exercises, is all about learning more about yourself.

It is natural for us to be ego- and self-centric. As infants, our mode of survival is to believe the world revolves around us, and we demand safety, food, and love. As we grow older and have a better grasp on language and the subtleties of interpersonal relationships, we remain self-centric, although with additional layers to mask it. During periods of stress, anxiety, fear, and uncertainty, our protective barriers erode, revealing our continued primal need to protect the self.

When someone attributes their own thoughts and feelings to someone else, it is called projecting. It is described as a defense mechanism we aren't immediately aware we are using. Essentially, projecting is a form of our own minds trying to protect ourselves from uncomfortable thoughts and feelings. As discussed earlier, this may be a subconscious way to shield ourselves from insecurities and anxieties. Through self-exploration, therapy, and developing one's sense of identity, it may become easier to identify these protective defenses and to allow for alleviation of anxieties.

7.14 Writing Prompts

In what areas of your life do you feel like your perception is limited to one perspective?

_____

_____

_____

_____

_____

_____

What helps you listen to someone else's point of view?

_____

_____

_____

_____

_____

How can you practice opening your mind and seeing different perspectives?

_____

_____

_____

_____

_____

If you widened your perception in a certain area you feel stuck in, what would you see?

_____

_____

_____

_____

_____

_____

7.15 Recommendations

The continued uncertainties regarding the sequalae of the pandemic, the evolution of the variants, public/private responses, and their impacts on our lives make it so we must take specific additional actions.

Here are some of our recommendations regarding screen time, education, use of social media, and preventing and addressing mental health issues that continue to arise.

- We recommend increased availability of information for families and users of social media platforms, as well as digital media consumers in general, regarding the potential for the ill effects described.
- Practical short-term suggestions also include trying to make social media apps and devices as unappealing as possible.

    - Consider having an area of your home or workspace that is free of social media. Perhaps try putting your phone down in a set space when you are studying or sleeping to create a physical barrier.
    - Conversely, you can set a space exclusively for social media use and only use your device/app in that area.
    - While it may not be realistic to remove the app from your device altogether, reducing the attention it demands may help.
    - Consider setting the phone in grayscale to minimize the bright colors and tactics used to keep your attention.
    - Turn off push notifications or place the device in 'do not disturb' mode so there isn't a constant diversion of focus and concentration.
    - Set time limits on the device to alert you to your total usage minutes, as well as to restrict specific app use to certain designated times.

- We recommend further policy and regulations be developed regarding online privacy as well as safety, especially for the most vulnerable.
- Pediatricians and other health-care providers, for the most part, are aware of the issues relating to social media, although screen time recommendations have varied and, unfortunately, have been abandoned during the pandemic-related lockdowns because there are 'no alternatives.'

    - We remember that, in the before times, our pediatrician said that even up to an hour a day of screen time was too much for our son, who was seven years old at the time.
    - According to a report by Listernick and Badawy (2021), close to 50% of adolescents spent a mean of five hours a day on social media, with 12% spending more than ten hours. Every day.
    - While our pediatrician friends certainly do not endorse that much screen and social media time, not enough is being done to limit use.
    - Children, young adults, and everyone else can benefit from a reminder by a trusted health-care professional of the risks and harms known and encouragement of a balanced, healthier lifestyle.

- If a true addiction and problematic use pattern have been identified, there are a number of options for treatment. They range from self-help, including the exercises in this book, to increase mindfulness and create healthy patterns, to cognitive behavioral therapy, as well as medication options.

■ At school or work, specific policies and expectations should be set in place to promote health and discourage the known negative effects of social media and excessive digital consumption.

  – Along with the professional recommendations by health-care providers, schools should also be clearly educated, informed, and on the lookout for the signs and symptoms of social media misuse described in this chapter.
  – The goal is to prevent as many of these things from starting as possible and to bring them to the attention of the student and their family so they can get intervention as soon as possible.

■ Based on the studies and findings of the research articles described in this chapter, as well as our clinical experience in acute and outpatient settings, we recommend that cyber bullying and victimization be top of mind for clinicians and schools.

  – Imagine if pediatricians; mental-health providers; family practice doctors; nurses; clinicians in the emergency department; and teams, including social workers, as well as parents, schoolteachers, and guidance counselors all identified social media use and risk of bullying as risk factors for mental health issues.
    • Students and young adults would be identified, and appropriate interventions could be offered on time.
    • The massive amount of physical, mental, and emotional health and financial consequences could be mitigated.

■ Risk factors of developing short- and long-term consequences of bullying should be a part of the ongoing assessments and incorporated into the decision to intervene with an individual and their family.
■ Schools can and should be the organizations outside the home that support and educate children on social media use and either provide or connect children with the equivalent of coaches or consultants for online media use in general. In addition to aspects of online privacy and being aware, to the extent possible, of predatory behaviors, the value of buffering the students' self-esteem and helping them navigate the pressures online would be immeasurable.
■ For as long as the effects of the COVID pandemic continues, as well as in preparation for future similar disasters, we must ensure that we are all informed of the potential and real downsides of social media and exposure to information that may be misleading and harmful.
■ We recommend increased digital literacy and awareness campaigns in schools and even in places of work and other community areas.

  – The goal is to do one's best to be able to sort appropriate, healthy information from that which may be unreliable or cause harm, intentionally or otherwise.
  – Media care plans can include elements such as setting boundaries for the amount of time spent online, recommending more outdoor activities, and education regarding age-appropriate online content.

■ According to a study by Lambert et al. (2022), stopping social media use for even as short as a week yields demonstrable, significant improvements in well-being, depression, and symptoms of anxiety.

- While quitting entirely may be nearly impossible in the real world, where demands to be constantly online are very high, knowing that the evidence supports the restorative effect of a break from social media and digital media use is hopeful and can be incorporated into care plans.

■ We envision case management, or the equivalent of care coordination, to be able to shepherd and support individuals so they can have the best possible chance.

- These coaches could help with education regarding nutrition and the value of physical exercise. Physical activity is known to help with resilience and to reduce the effects of social media–induced stress and anxieties.
- They can help with advertisement blockers to minimize targeted ads for junk food, and alcohol, and other drugs.
- They can provide education and framework and allow for questions and discussions in nonjudgmental forums relating to what a person is exposed to, the reasons behind it, and their reactions to it.

■ We encourage those reading this book to work towards developing their resilience for family members and loved ones to foster and deepen social relationships.

- A study by Gong et al. (2022) discussed the protective factor of resilience and social support as they had a significant positive impact on reducing things like fear of missing out during the pandemic lockdown years, as well as reducing the impact of problematic digital and social media use.

THE ROAD BACK IV

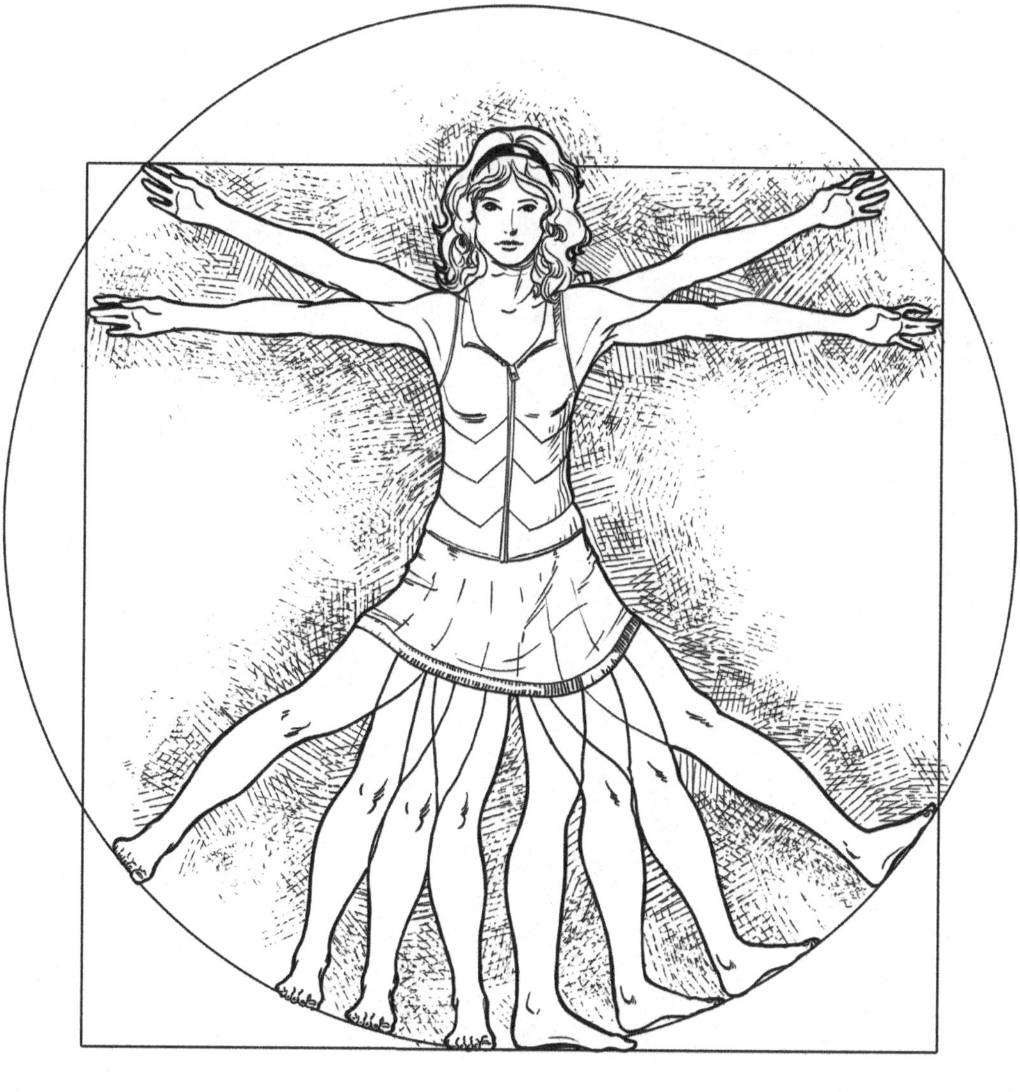

DOI: 10.4324/9781003413547-11

Chapter 8

Confidence and Recovery

8.1 Introduction

Fear is an unpleasant emotion that arises from a possible threat or a real circumstance, such as a shark attack or a fire. Fear itself functions as a mechanism for the brain and body to alert us and keep us safe. If we suspect someone may be dangerous or perceive our environment as unsafe, the accompanying feelings of fear allow for analyzing and making a decision to protect ourselves.

Anxiety, on the other hand, is a feeling about something that may or may not pose a threat or something in the future with an unclear outcome. It is a series of feelings that may include worry, fear, unease, jitters, apprehension, and nervousness.

> **Fear can hold you prisoner. Hope can set you free.**
>
> —Stephen King

8.2 That Anxious Feeling

The brain and body connection is ever so obvious in anxiety-related conditions. The physical sensations and feelings throughout our bodies can be described in different ways. Throughout this book, we continue to focus on giving feelings a name, identifying them, and describing them. Having words available to connect with feelings is important as the label will allow the sensation itself to be isolated.

Think about the feeling and what descriptive words are associated with it. Are they open-ended, active feelings? Closed-ended, passive feelings? Connecting them with their cause and the interpretation and energy we spend on them will allow for healing and recovery.

DOI: 10.4324/9781003413547-12

8.3 Writing Prompts

In the context of anxiety, fear, and worry, we include some examples of bodily sensations by body part here. Consider adding your own descriptors and feelings you may have in the space provided.

- Our HEADS may feel:

    - Light, achy, dizzy, spinning, heavy, foggy, like it's hard to concentrate, disconnected, tight, throbbing
    - Add your own: _____

- Our EYES can get:

    - Dry, blurry, out of focus, tired
    - Add your own: _____

- Our EARS are sometimes:

    - Ringing, muffled, throbbing, pounding
    - Add your own: _____

- Our NOSES can feel:

    - Dry, runny, clogged
    - Add your own: _____

- Our MOUTHS and TEETH may become:

    - Clenched, dry, tingly, itchy, feel like you have difficulty speaking, or want to yawn
    - Add your own: _____

- Our NECKS can be:

    - Tight, stiff, painful
    - Add your own: _____

- Our THROATS may feel:

    - Like we're choking, like they're closing up, scratchy, dry, feel as if there is a lump in our throat
    - Add your own: _____

- Our SHOULDERS can become:

    - Tight, achy, tired, painful, tense
    - Add your own: _____

■ Our CHESTS may feel:

- Tight, painful, tense, heavy, fluttering, pounding, like our hearts are racing, a sense of impending doom, constricted
- Add your own: _____

■ Our LUNGS can feel:

- Difficulty breathing, like our breaths are shallow, like we're hyperventilating, shaky, feel as if we need to cough, dry
- Add your own: _____

■ Our STOMACHS and INTESTINES may feel:

- The need to use the restroom, grumbling, nauseous, achy, gassy, fluttery
- Add your own: _____

■ Our ARMS and LEGS sometimes feel:

- Tingly, restless, jittery, heavy, numb
- Add your own: _____

8.4 Consequences of Anxiety

As discussed throughout this book, untreated anxiety can impact many aspects of one's ability to do the things they want. Experiencing anxiety and reflecting on these responses can also bring up complicated emotions such as shame and guilt.

8.5 Writing Prompt

What are some consequences of your emotions you have noticed? What have you avoided? What have you changed?

_____

_____

_____

_____

_____

_____

8.6 Writing Prompts

To become an expert at understanding ourselves, we must learn to identify and name our emotions. We have expanded the list from our last book, *Re-Write* (2023), to include the broadest range of anxiety and related emotions. The updated list is provided.

Consider thinking about your own emotional experiences. What is your range of emotions?

Put a check mark next to the emotions and feelings you have felt in your lifetime. Consider using the space by each word to add personal sensations and memories attached to these emotions, feelings, and states of being.

- Acceptance _____
- Adoration _____
- Aesthetic appreciation _____
- Affection _____
- Afraid _____
- Aggressive _____
- Agitated _____
- Agony _____
- Alarmed _____
- Alienated _____
- Amusement _____
- Anger _____
- Angst _____
- Annoyed _____
- Anticipating _____
- Anxiety _____
- Apprehension _____
- Arrogant _____
- Attraction _____
- Aversion _____
- Awe _____
- Awkwardness _____
- Baffled _____
- Bemused _____
- Better _____
- Bitter _____
- Blissful _____
- Boisterous _____
- Boredom _____
- Burned out _____
- Calm _____
- Caring _____
- Cheated _____
- Cheerful _____
- Comfortable _____
- Compassionate _____

- Confident
- Confusion
- Connected
- Content
- Coping
- Courageous
- Cowardly
- Craving
- Curious
- Cynicism
- Defeated
- Deflated
- Delighted
- Depression
- Desire
- Desperate
- Detached
- Determined
- Devastated
- Disappointment
- Discomfort
- Discouraged
- Disgusted
- Dislike
- Disoriented
- Disturbed
- Distracted
- Doubtful
- Dread
- Eager
- Ecstasy
- Edginess
- Embarrassment
- Empathy
- Enjoyment
- Envy
- Euphoria
- Excitement
- Exhaustion
- Exposed
- Fascinated
- Fear
- Friendly
- Fright
- Frustrated
- Fury
- Gaslit

- Glad _____
- Gloomy _____
- Gratitude _____
- Grief _____
- Grumpy _____
- Guilty _____
- Happiness _____
- Harmony _____
- Hatred _____
- Heartache _____
- Heartbroken _____
- Helplessness _____
- Homesick _____
- Hopelessness _____
- Horny _____
- Horrified _____
- Hostile _____
- Humble _____
- Humiliated _____
- Hungry _____
- Hurt _____
- Hypochondria _____
- Hysteria _____
- Impatient _____
- Indifferent _____
- Infuriated _____
- Insecure _____
- Insulted _____
- Interested _____
- Irritated _____
- Isolated _____
- Jealousy _____
- Jitters _____
- Joy _____
- Kind _____
- Lazy _____
- Limited _____
- Loathing _____
- Lonely _____
- Lost _____
- Love _____
- Loyal _____
- Lust _____
- Mad _____
- Meaningful _____
- Melancholy _____
- Miserable _____

- Modest _____
- Moody _____
- Morbid _____
- Mourning _____
- Nauseated _____
- Negative _____
- Neglect _____
- Nervous _____
- Nirvana _____
- Nostalgic _____
- Numb _____
- Obsession _____
- Offended _____
- Optimistic _____
- Outrage _____
- Overstimulated _____
- Overwhelmed _____
- Pain _____
- Panic _____
- Paranoid _____
- Peaceful _____
- Perverse _____
- Pessimistic _____
- Phobia _____
- Pity _____
- Pleased _____
- Positive _____
- Pride _____
- Puzzled _____
- Questioning _____
- Rage _____
- Regret _____
- Relaxed _____
- Relief _____
- Reluctant _____
- Remorseful _____
- Resentful _____
- Revulsion _____
- Romantic _____
- Ruthless _____
- Sadness _____
- Safe _____
- Satiated _____
- Satisfied _____
- Scared _____
- Secure _____
- Sedated _____

- Self-aware _____
- Self-caring _____
- Self-compassion _____
- Self-pity _____
- Self-respecting _____
- Serenity _____
- Sexual desire _____
- Shame _____
- Shocked _____
- Shy _____
- Smug _____
- Sorrow _____
- Stressed _____
- Stuck _____
- Sublime _____
- Suffering _____
- Surprised _____
- Suspicious _____
- Sympathy _____
- Tension _____
- Terrified _____
- Terror _____
- Thankful _____
- Thirsty _____
- Thrilled _____
- Timid _____
- Tolerance _____
- Traumatized _____
- Trepidation _____
- Troubled _____
- Trust _____
- Uncertainty _____
- Uncomfortable _____
- Undermined _____
- Unsettled _____
- Upset _____
- Vanity _____
- Vengeful _____
- Vicious _____
- Vindictive _____
- Vulnerable _____
- Wariness _____
- Warm _____
- Weak _____
- Withdrawn _____
- Worried _____

- Wrath   _____
- Yearning   _____
- Zealous   _____
- Zen   _____

Use the space provided to add any additional emotions, feelings, and states of being that you've experienced, and include the bodily sensations and memories attached to them.

8.7 Connecting the Dots

We have discussed the connection between mind, body, and behavior, and through the previous exercise of putting names to our emotions, feelings, and experiences, we can now create these personal connections for ourselves.

This next writing prompt involves thinking about a physical sensation, such as 'waves of dull pain,' that you may have experienced. Next think of where these sensations occurred, such as 'in my gut or stomach.' Lastly, reflect on how your mind interprets these physical sensations as a thought or emotion, such as 'grief and sadness.'

Even if you don't immediately complete this exercise, read through the examples provided and consider them as you go through your day-to-day experiences. If you are working with a clinician, you can also share your responses with them.

Are your emotions a product of your physical sensations? Or are your perceived physical symptoms due to your thoughts and feelings? The interplay between them is fascinating, and having a better understanding of the *why* will help you appreciate how to proceed.

> **Take the risk of thinking for yourself, much more happiness, truth, beauty, and wisdom will come to you that way.**
>
> **—Christopher Hitchens**

8.8 Writing Prompt

Consider the following template to complete this exercise:

Example 1:

When I feel *waves of dull pain* (physical sensation) in my *gut and stomach* (body part), I feel *grief and sadness* (emotion/feeling/associated thoughts).

Example 2:

When I feel *tightness* (physical sensation) in my *right shoulder* (body part), I feel *anxious* (emotion/feeling/associated thoughts).

Personal experiences:

1. When I feel _____(physical sensation)
   in my _____(body part),
   I feel _____(emotion/feeling/thoughts).
2. When I feel _____(physical sensation)
   in my_____(body part),
   I feel _____(emotion/feeling/thoughts).
3. When I feel _____(physical sensation)
   in my _____(body part),
   I feel _____(emotion/feeling/thoughts).
4. When I feel _____(physical sensation)
   in my_____(body part),
   I feel _____(emotion/feeling/thoughts).
5. When I feel _____(physical sensation)
   in my_____ (body part),
   I feel_____(emotion/feeling/thoughts).
6. When I feel _____(physical sensation)
   in my_____(body part),
   I feel _____(emotion/feeling/thoughts).

8.9 Writing Prompt

Within the framework of the Balan 3-2-1 Method, consider your response to the following:

If your anxiety dissolved in your sleep, what kind of a day would you wake up to?

3: With intention, set your internal and external environment.

■ The body: What mindfulness techniques are you choosing to allow your body to heal?

_____

_____

_____

■ The setting: How are you intentionally influencing your setting?

_____

_____

_____

■ The breath: Which breathing technique will you use as you prepare for this exercise?

_____

_____

_____

2: What are your thoughts and feelings in response to the writing prompt?

_____

_____

_____

_____

_____

_____

_____

_____

1: What is your one intent or affirmation in the context of the writing prompt?

_____

_____

_____

8.10 Gratitude

The state of being thankful and appreciative is the foundation of the concept of gratitude. It is an emotion as well as a cognitive process. Gratitude involves recognizing and acknowledging the positive qualities in ourselves, recognizing the good in others, and appreciating the world around us.

There are numerous psychological and physical health benefits to expressing gratitude, in addition to the interpersonal and social benefits.

Clinical Benefits of Gratitude:

Improves mental health:

- Enhances well-being
- Improves mood
- Decreases symptoms of anxiety
- Decreases symptoms of depression
- Helps cope with trauma and find meaning

Improves emotional resilience:

- Increases optimism
- Promotes posttraumatic growth
- Improves cognitive processing

Improves physical health:

- Increases level of physical activity
- Improves sleep
- Improves dietary choices and habits
- Helps lower blood pressure
- Improves the immune system
- Increases adherence to prescribed medication regimen
- Decreases inflammation
- Decreases HbA1c, associated with blood sugar levels and diabetes
- Assists in treatment of substance use disorders

Improves self-esteem:

- Decreases negative thinking
- Helps you recognize your strengths and positive qualities
- Improves self-worth

Improves quality of life and satisfaction:

- Improves insight
- Helps you appreciate what you have
- Fosters focus on the positive in the present and plans going forward
- Decreases and buffers against burnout
- Models and attracts more gratitude

Reduces materialism:

- Improves ability to rethink priorities
- Shifts focus from possessions to experiences and connections
- Improves productivity

Improves pro-social behaviors:

- Improves conflict resolution skills
- Improves creativity
- Fosters a sense of connection and reciprocity
- Increases acts of kindness and generosity
- Increases sharing with others

Improves relationships:

- Increases patience
- Strengthens social bonds
- Increases humility
- Increases empathy

8.11 Expressing Gratitude

Several examples of how to express gratitude and make it a habit to recognize and appreciate things you may have overlooked in the past are included next.

1. **Say 'Thank You!'**
   It's easy, costs nothing, demonstrates you appreciate the other person, increases connection, and reinforces positive behaviors. Genuine appreciation is always the best. People can tell the difference between a sincere thank you and one that is forced. The more you practice saying 'thank you' or writing it in an email or text, the more it will become a habit.

2. **Self-Appreciation**
   Think about your own strengths, attributes, and qualities you appreciate. You can make a list or simply acknowledge them during your day-to-day experiences. Some people are better at this than others as they may have had caregivers who helped them identify their attributes.
   There are so many things to be grateful for, such as your physical and mental health, the people in your life, your ability to care for yourself, and reading self-help books to improve yourself. As you are able to appreciate your own achievements and personal growth, think of how you can celebrate yourself. While this may seem silly, it actually will improve gratitude for yourself and positively impact your self-worth.

3. **Appreciate Others**
   If someone has supported you or helped you, recognize it and express your gratitude. Even if they didn't do anything specific, their mere presence may be supportive or inspiring. In addition to saying 'thank you,' consider telling them why and how you are grateful for them.
   We often think of people we love but rarely tell them how grateful we are to have them in our lives. This is your opportunity to change that and create a new habit of reaching out and telling your loved ones that you appreciate them.

4. **Appreciate Moments**

"Stop and smell the roses" is something people don't say much anymore. Embedded in the mindfulness aspect of this saying, as well as the dictate to being present, is the encouragement of the capacity to appreciate the moment.

Whether we are grateful for the sun's warmth or the engaging book we're reading in the comfort of our bed, there are numerous opportunities to cherish every day.

8.12 Gratitude Exercises

1. **Create a gratitude tree.**

A gratitude tree can be an artistic expression of the things you are grateful for. This can be made using various materials or mediums such as drawing, collage, mosaic, or computer graphics. You can have different trees about different aspects of your life and keep growing them as the things you appreciate in your life increase.

2. **Do volunteer work.**

Giving back to your community and those who are less fortunate increases your sense of fulfillment and your appreciation of the resources and support you have in your life. Consider volunteering at a soup kitchen, your community place of worship, or your local library or joining a nonprofit/charity group.

3. **Keep a gratitude journal.**

Keeping a gratitude journal can be a calming experience and encourage positivity. Writing down the highlights of your life, new experiences, small wins, and moments of connection can feel grounding and healing.

4. **Write letters of gratitude.**

Taking the time to express your gratitude will be invaluable to the other person and, additionally, will positively impact your own altruistic motivations.

There are many people we don't even personally know or who are no longer alive who may have had great impacts on our lives. Consider writing a letter to a thought leader, an author who inspires you, or your ancestors.

5. **Practice mindful meditation or yoga.**

Mindful meditation and yoga are practices that increase awareness and encourage a calm mindset and staying in the present moment. There are many apps and online communities that can provide guidance on this journey.

6. **Read inspiring memoirs.**

Reading stories of people who have gone through adversity can be motivating, humbling, and inspiring.

7. **Create a gratitude altar.**

Consider creating a little altar with objects that represent things that bring peace to you. These could be photos of loved ones, seashells from a vacation, a trophy won at a competition, or anything that reminds you of your achievements, your positive qualities, good times, or your loved ones.

Thinking of happy memories will trigger a good mood. A gratitude altar can be elaborate with multiple sentimental objects, or it can be as simple as a photo on a fridge or a note on a mirror.

8. **Create a gratitude jar.**
   Write down things you are grateful for and collect them in a container or jar. At times when you need motivation or inspiration, you can pull out these little notes to remind yourself of the things you are grateful for.
9. **Show gratitude through artistic expression.**
   Using arts and crafts to express gratitude in tangible ways can be a healing experience.

No matter how you decide to incorporate gratitude practices in your life, you will experience the benefits in your overall mental and physical health. Being in a state of gratitude is incompatible with being simultaneously in a state of despair. When we practice gratitude in a structured way, it gives us the experience of being in an appreciative state, and the more we do it, the more automatic it becomes. Since gratitude practices include positivity and kindness, they will also improve your social relationships.

Introducing a new way of relating to the world may take time and feel frustrating at times, but even the smallest change will set the foundation for it to become more automatic. It is important to be compassionate and allow yourself to experiment with different gratitude practices to see which ones work best for you.

8.13 Writing Prompt

Within the framework of the Balan 3-2-1 Method, consider your response to the following:

What are you grateful for?

3: With intention, set your internal and external environment.

- The body: What mindfulness techniques are you choosing to allow your body to heal?

_____

_____

_____

- The setting: How are you intentionally influencing your setting?

_____

_____

_____

■ The breath: Which breathing technique will you use as you prepare for this exercise?

_____

_____

_____

2: What are your thoughts and feelings in response to the writing prompt?

_____

_____

_____

_____

_____

_____

_____

1: What is your one intent or affirmation in the context of the writing prompt?

_____

_____

_____

8.14 Writing Prompt

Incorporating your response to the previous prompt, consider using the space provided to brainstorm one or two ways you will begin expressing gratitude.

_____

_____

_____

_____

_____

_____

_____

_____

_____

_____

_____

_____

8.15 Outdoor Activities

The benefits of being in nature, having access to green spaces, blue spaces, and open air, have been evident for many years. The pandemic and associated lockdowns further cemented the reality that we are all connected to nature and thrive when in connection with the earth and the elements.

When we interact with nature, there are several mental and physical health benefits. There are often social and community-level benefits as well.

Being locked indoors, with a reduced ability to exercise or have access to sunlight and other natural spaces such as parks and beaches, increased the comorbidities of the virus itself.

Thankfully, research aligns with our very obvious experience that spending time outdoors improves our health and well-being and specifically decreases anxiety levels (Wicks et al. 2022). We have included a brief list of outdoor activities you can try alone or with a friend.

Outdoor Activities:

- Acting and outdoor theater
- Archery
- Art outdoors
- Backpacking
- Bicycling
- Bird watching (Stobbe et al. 2022)
- Boating
- Bug hunting
- Camping
- Cataloging plants
- Chalk drawing
- Climbing a tree
- Collecting rocks
- Commuting to school or work by walking, scooter, or bicycle

- Dancing to music
- Exercising outdoors
- Flying a kite
- Fruit or berry picking
- Gardening
- Geocaching
- Going fishing
- Going to a park
- Golfing
- Having a barbecue
- Having a picnic
- Having a race
- Hide and seek
- Hiking
- Hopscotch
- Horseback riding
- Hunting
- Ice skating
- Jet skiing
- Jogging
- Jumping rope
- Kayaking
- Leaf collecting
- Making an obstacle course
- Nature photography
- Outdoor reading
- Planting a tree
- Playing frisbee or catch
- Playing limbo
- Playing music outdoors
- Playing sports, such as tennis, soccer, or basketball
- Rock climbing
- Running
- Scavenger hunting
- Skateboarding
- Skipping stones on the water
- Sledding
- Snowball fighting
- Spending time at the beach
- Star gazing
- Surfing
- Swimming in a pool or at the beach
- Trampoline
- Vegetable gardening
- Walking in the forest
- Walking or playing with pets

- Watching the clouds
- Watching the sunset or sunrise
- Water balloon fight
- Yoga outdoors

Studies have confirmed a correlation between something as simple as looking at pictures of nature and a positive effect.

8.16 Gardening

A life is like a garden.
Perfect moments can be had, but not preserved, except in memory.
—Leonard Nimoy

There is an increasing amount of research that shows the positive mental and physical health benefits of gardening (Wood et al. 2022). Whether for low-impact exercise, to grow one's own food, or for general reduction of anxiety and stress, the value of gardening has been well documented.

Several studies came out during the pandemic that showed the positive effects of gardening for those fortunate to be able to garden. Families and individuals were able to change their practices and devote more time to gardening during the pandemic, especially since folks were told to minimize nonessential work and travel. Those people have been found to have increased resilience and a decreased sense of angst.

According to a study by Gerdes et al. (2022), people who garden eight or more hours over two weeks have lower levels of anxiety. The physical act of gardening, being active and attentive, has been shown to improve feelings of fear and guilt and decrease stress levels. Gardening has also been shown to decrease feelings of sadness and depression.

Connecting with mother nature develops patience and helps you get in touch with the cycle of life. Planting a seed and watching it grow can be very satisfying. You can keep a gardening journal and track what you plant, how you take care of it, and its growth.

Additional health benefits of gardening include improving cognitive function, attention, and memory. The physical activity associated with gardening, being outdoors, planning, and performing tasks purposefully is beneficial to the mind, body, and spirit.

Clinical Benefits of Being Outdoors

Improves mental health:
- Decreases stress levels
- Improves attention span
- Helps one feel more relaxed
- Increases resilience
- Reduces boredom
- Decreases feelings of anxiety

- Decreases sadness and depression
- Increases feelings of happiness
- Decreases feelings of tiredness, fatigue

Improves physical health:
- Decreases cortisol levels
- Improves blood pressure
- Improves blood oxygenation
- Increases vitamin D intake
- Increases physical activity and health
- Improves musculoskeletal health
- Improves sleep

Improves connections:
- Improves relationships
- Increases sense of belonging and oneness with nature and the earth
- Increases sense of communal responsibility and accountability to nature and the earth

The impact of being outdoors in nature is dose dependent, meaning the more time one is able to spend outside, the more positive benefits one acquires. Being active outside works as a hobby as well as a coping mechanism that decreases stress and increases resilience.

8.17 Emotional Regulation

Emotional regulation is the ability to defuse and moderate one's intense emotions. It is an active decision that requires continuous energy and awareness to strategize the best methods. Through practice, one can learn to regulate the intensity of emotional reactions. When emotional regulation fails, we may end up saying things we later regret, closing doors to opportunities that may benefit us and hurt people we love.

According to studies, those with a healthy ability to regulate their emotions and responses to certain stimuli are in a better position to be resilient and overcome obstacles.

Emotion regulation can happen either before you experience the emotion or after. For example, if you are in danger but you freeze, you might need to coach yourself to heighten your emotions so you can respond to danger, or you might turn your emotions down if you are getting overactivated. An example may be if you see a car on fire and you freeze, or your brother says something to embarrass you in front of your new girlfriend. With the fire, you may need to hype yourself up to do something, whereas with your brother, you might need to tone your anger down by removing yourself from the situation or reframing and thinking of the meaning of his actions.

Thinking about the circumstance, being aware of how you are responding internally, and then adjusting how you will react outwardly can be practiced and improved. Being conscious of the way you are feeling is an important first step in putting it in context.

Reframing a negative emotion and working to solve a problem are valuable under stress. The key to reframing a negative emotion is to be able to identify and name it first and then allowing yourself to experience it since pushing down or suppressing the emotion is less healthy and can lead to undesired longer-term psychological harm.

Emotions such as anger, jealousy and resentment are stigmatized in many societies, thus making the vocalization of them socially unacceptable. People often are inclined to suppress these emotions in order to prevent rejection or isolation; however, they are human emotions that can be controlled and expressed in healthy ways and don't need to be pathologized.

Techniques such as bringing awareness to body and breath, shifting attention from what is causing negative emotions, reframing emotional situations, rethinking or challenging the situation, practicing positive self-talk, identifying triggers, and using grounding techniques and mindfulness strategies are effective ways of emotion regulation.

Regulation is achieved through becoming aware of our emotions and understanding the situation and our interpretation of it, our emotional response to it, and our reaction to it. When someone cuts us off, the interpretation of that situation might be that we are disrespected, the emotional response could be anger, and the emotional reaction might be to curse them out.

Developing healthy emotional regulation habits will prevent meltdowns and hurtful reactions and foster healthy relationships. Emotional regulation has been shown to increase resilience and, as discussed in other parts of the book, acts as a protective factor against developing severe anxieties or depression.

8.18 Mindful Listening Exercises

The following prompts have been developed to encourage introspection and increase awareness of our surroundings. Use the space provided to reflect on the following writing prompts.

When I hear people arguing, I feel:

_____

_____

_____

When I hear someone snoring, I feel:

_____

_____

_____

When I hear a baby giggle, I feel:

_____

_____

_____

When I hear my favorite TV show theme song, I feel:

_____

_____

_____

When I hear a door slam, I feel:

_____

_____

_____

When I hear a sports game, I feel:

_____

_____

_____

When I hear sirens, I feel:

_____

_____

_____

When I hear a text beep or ring tone, I feel:

_____

_____

_____

8.19 Healing Power of Music

Music is a language. Even if it is playing your old childhood xylophone or maracas, music has great healing benefits and will allow for you to access emotions that are not available to you verbally.

You can use digital mixing tools to create songs that express your inner world. It is not about being a master musician or the song sounding 'good.' Creating music is about expression and releasing. Over time, it can also turn into a hobby you enjoy and share with others.

Consider incorporating music in your life with the following examples:

■ Sing or write your own song
■ Create a playlist for different moods.

- For example, if you are feeling sad, create a playlist that reflects that. We heard an artist talk about having a 'rain' playlist for songs they liked listening to in the rain.
- You can create a playlist for your crush or a best friend.
- If you are feeling energized and optimistic, make a playlist that reflects that.

8.20 Catastrophizing to Confidence

Anxiety can cause us to feel as if something terrible and uncontrollable is going to happen, as if our mind's worst-case scenario may come true. The concept of catastrophizing is an interesting thought problem in that it prevents us from being able to enjoy things. Our minds end up preemptively stopping us from enjoying the process of an experience, creating reluctance to try something new.

This may be due, in part, to previous negative experiences or may simply come out of nowhere. Either way, it is something that needs to be addressed so we can go from being inhibited to feeling calm and in control of our lives.

One way of reducing fear of and anxiety about uncertainty and the unknown is through education and knowledge. Some people are hypersensitive to their bodily sensations and associate innocuous feelings with the potential for serious illness.

Someone with serious anxiety and sensitivity towards somatic sensations might think something like a scratchy throat could be cancer. This might then lead the person to go online to read about the symptoms of throat cancer or look up causes of throat scratchiness, which invariably will also include terrible illnesses. If they are not a medically trained professional or doesn't have access to health-care providers, their anxiety may increase exponentially.

Hypochondria is an anxiety disorder characterized by excessive worry about having a serious medical condition. This form of catastrophizing bodily sensations can lead to ongoing, persistent worries about one's health, increased doctor visits, and increased laboratory testing and procedures, with minimal relief despite expert reassurance. Severe forms can impact the individual's day-to-day life, affecting other areas of their ability to function.

Throughout this book, we discuss methods of using this energy constructively and ways to reduce feeling overwhelmed. Give yourself the time and compassion you would give a friend. One way to do this is to look at your current responsibilities and to-dos, your midterm goals, and the amount of time and energy you have available.

We recommend creating a schedule of your day/week/month. You can use the calendar on your phone or print one out for free. In our family, we keep a paper monthly calendar on the fridge and write out things we need to do, such as dentist appointments, soccer carpool schedules, and travel plans. Throughout the month, we add scheduled dinners, podcast appearances, or meetings we need to attend. Every one of us can quickly see our plans and deduce the time commitment embedded in each.

This practice reduces surprises and pushes us to plan ahead. By doing so, we don't wait until the last minute and can be prepared for commute times, purchasing birthday gifts, or making reservations. Planning ahead frees up time to do the things we enjoy, such as writing, spending time together, and volunteering in our community.

These plans for things 'to do' also allow for a sense of calm and quiet to plan for things 'to feel.' If you have anxiety, for example, you can plan your energy for the day around your physical to-dos to reduce and even prevent your anxiety. Taking a couple of minutes extra to get to your destination, choosing healthier meals, and going to bed earlier the night before are examples of ways to increase your success.

8.21 Grounding Techniques

Examples of grounding strategies you can try including the following:

- Splash cold water on your face
- Clap your hands
- Sing a song you love in your head
- Take a drink of water
- Clench your fists and release them a few times
- Remember the people you love
- Think of your favorite place
- Notice things in the room
- Notice the temperature and sounds around you
- Touch things
- Carry something small in your pocket that soothes you and helps you release stress: a keychain that symbolizes or reminds you of your family, a fun vacation, or your friends; a crystal; a seashell; a stress ball; a slinky; a stuffed animal

8.22 Body-Scanning Exercise

This exercise is about paying attention to your body. Understanding how your emotions feel in your body will make it easier to accept the way you feel and calm yourself.

- Lie on your back, let your arms drop to your sides, close your eyes, and breathe deeply.
- If you want to put something under your neck or knees, do so.
- Notice the floor, the carpet, the bed, or the yoga mat supporting you.
- Notice your heels, the back of your legs, your spine, your back, and your neck.
- Move to your face: notice your chin and your eyelids.
- Notice your heart rate.

There is no right way or wrong way of doing this exercise, so if your mind wanders off, gently invite your attention back to your body.

- Observe any sensation such as coolness, or warmth.
- Send a message of gratitude to your body before you slowly start moving your toes.
- Stretch your arms and legs and slowly bring yourself up to a seating position.

8.23 Writing Prompts

How did it feel to focus your attention on your body? Was it difficult or easy?

_____

_____

_____

_____

_____

_____

What did you notice? Was there tension or soreness in certain areas?

_____

_____

_____

_____

_____

_____

How did you feel after the body scan? Did you feel energized, relaxed, or tired?

_____

_____

_____

_____

_____

_____

8.24 Track Your Feelings

Use the following prompts to identify and name your feelings.

Where do I feel things in my body?

_____

_____

_____

Body scanning: What is my face doing? Am I clenching my jaw? Is my neck stiff?

_____

_____

_____

What are my triggers?

_____

_____

_____

What have I tried to cope?

_____

_____

_____

What else can I try?

_____

_____

_____

8.25 Track Your Emotions

You can use these writing prompts to help understand and follow your emotions.

What did I feel? For example, sad, stressed, or angry.

_____

_____

_____

What happened before?

_____

_____

_____

When did it happen?

_____

_____

_____

Who did it happen with?

_____

_____

_____

What triggers were there?

_____

_____

_____

Where did it happen?

_____

_____

_____

What did I do?

_____

_____

_____

What made it worse?

_____

_____

_____

What made it better?

_____

_____

_____

What happened after?

_____

_____

_____

8.25.1 Learn to Say 'No'

An important life lesson is learning how to say 'no.'

Most people do not want to be perceived as negative or turn someone down. In general, people are conflict averse and would prefer not to disappoint others.

Fear of missing out (FOMO), discussed in Chapter 7, 'Un-Social Media,' can make it challenging to decline an invitation and may even bring up preemptive feelings of guilt as the desire to gain approval and please others weighs heavily. Even though it's challenging, it is a critical skill to learn in order to maintain boundaries, cultivate healthy relationships, and advocate for and protect your own mental health and physical energy.

Questions you can ask yourself before saying 'no':

- Do I have the time and energy to do this?
- What will I miss if I say no?
- What will I miss if I say yes?
- Do I truly want to do this?
- What are the pros and cons?
- Am I doing this for myself or for someone else?
- Am I doing this just to please someone else?
- What would need to change for my answer to be yes?
- Am I saying no because I am afraid of missing out?

1. **Take your time to respond.**
   Almost nothing requires an immediate answer. You can ask for time to think about your response to a request or invitation. Simply say, 'I'll check my calendar and get back to you.' People will understand and even respect you for making a calculated decision. Upon checking your prior commitments and having the time to think whether you would actually like to participate or not, you will make a true decision and be able to genuinely commit.

2. **Acknowledge your boundaries.**
   By understanding your limits, through calendaring as discussed earlier or being in tune with your thoughts and energy levels, you will have an easier time saying 'no.' Being self-aware will allow you to honestly get back to the person with your response.
3. **Be respectful and clear.**
   Once you have decided to turn down the invitation, consider being polite and respectful. You can express that you 'appreciate the opportunity' and 'are unable to commit at this time due to other priorities.' If you truly do want to accept or spend time with the person and genuinely are unable to due to other priorities, consider providing alternative times or things to do together.
4. **Practice makes permanent.**
   Try practicing saying 'no' to things today. Reflect on how it makes you feel and the reactions you get from others. If you are someone who has an intense desire to please, this sudden shift may feel foreign and uncomfortable. Practice setting boundaries and then follow up with yourself to see how the time and energy you preserved benefit you later.

8.26 Fake It Till You Make It

We have discussed the value of genuine appreciation, integrity, and honest communications. What happens when these are absent? You can still work towards developing these qualities, although you may have to adopt the appearance of having them for a while.

'Faking it till you make it' isn't pretending to be someone you are not; it is about developing a mindset and actions until you truly feel that way. In the context of building confidence and decreasing anxiety, you will need to step out of your comfort zone and externally project a sense of calm.

Knowing you are 'faking it' involves the additional anxiety of being found out for who you really are: that you are fraudulent, deceptive, naïve, and even incompetent. Obviously, we do not recommend lying about a skill or performing a duty that would put you or anyone else in harm's way. We are referring to developing a sense of self-assuredness so you begin to see yourself in a way you would like others to see you as well.

Think of it as wearing a costume. This can be something as silly as a Halloween costume, pretending to be a superhero, or the 'costumes' we wear for school and work. Many places require uniforms to decrease variation, decrease expressivity, and encourage conformity. Uniforms work to identify a member of a group easily and remind the wearer to think and behave in accordance with the rules and principles of the environment.

By developing your self-image in accordance with the way you would like to be perceived, you can boost your self-esteem and overcome self-doubt and fear. Acting confidently in an anxiety-provoking situation can help you develop resilience as you succeed through challenges. Barriers once thought of as insurmountable soon become small obstacles easily overcome.

As you push yourself into scenarios you may have avoided, you begin to learn new skills and develop your character. Behaving confidently, even if initially 'fake,' fosters improved insight as well as interpersonal communication skills. Like the example of learning to take time before making the decision to say 'no,' discussed earlier, your projected confidence will be received positively by others, leading to increased respect.

8.27 Perfectionism

When it comes to anxiety in the realms of academia, sports, and work-related performance, the concept of striving for excellence and perfectionism are common factors. Perfectionism, defined by a high demand of oneself or others, is more than what may be needed for the circumstance.

Almost every source defining perfectionism proceeds to discuss the negative mental health consequences associated with it. The desire to compare oneself with others, as discussed in Chapter 7, 'Un-Social Media,' can be linked with harmful effects of social comparison while consuming digital media.

With full access to a manufactured external-facing social media presentation, there is an ever-increasing amount of pressure on teenagers and young adults to succeed and to fit in. This energy takes away from the ability to develop and be productive according to one's own goals and values.

According to studies, including an article by Tóth et al. (2022) that details maladaptive perfectionism, the negative consequences of comparison and competitive anxiety can lead to:

- Decreased focus
- Preoccupation and excessive worry
- Lower energy, causing a decreased ability to prepare
- Poor performance, due to preoccupation with anxiety, decreased energy, and inadequate training
- Self-criticism and self-blame
- Decreased frustration tolerance
- Feeling helpless

There are connections between perfectionism and 'all-or-nothing' thinking. This is a way of describing when someone takes concepts to an extreme. Examples include self-talk such as "I am the worst mathematics," or "I am the best soccer player."

The reality is that there are no absolutes: nothing is perfect, and nothing is the worst. There are always nuances and shades somewhere between the extremes. The likelihood of you being the best soccer player is very low, and it's also extremely unlikely that you are the worst soccer player in the world.

When it comes to relationships and comparisons, the concepts of a 'best friend ever' or 'worst friend ever' are similarly inaccurate. Just as achieving perfect grades all the time is unattainable, so is being the perfect employee, perfect boyfriend, perfect wife, or perfect child.

As you develop a better understanding of your own anxieties and insecurities, you will gain an improved ability to look at your relationships and how they present themselves. With increased confidence and self-compassion, you will begin to feel more comfortable in the gray zones of all-or-nothing thinking.

8.28 Creative Exercise: Glass of Water

There are several creative and useful ways to visualize and process all-or-nothing thinking. One way is to use the illustration of a glass of water. While there is some water in the glass, it could be either half full or half empty, depending on your frame of reference and how you're feeling and thinking at the time.

Consider using the glass of water to write in things in your life that cause you anxiety because you look at them as being either half full or half empty. Examples could come from various domains of your life, such as school, after-school activities, sports, friendships, romantic relationships, work, issues at home, the way you appear and present yourself, etc.

As you are either drawing things or writing notes about your anxieties and thoughts, think about how often you find yourself in one of these extremes. You can also come back to this exercise later, when you've had time to think about it so, as you complete the illustration, you'll start to gain more insight into how you look at the world.

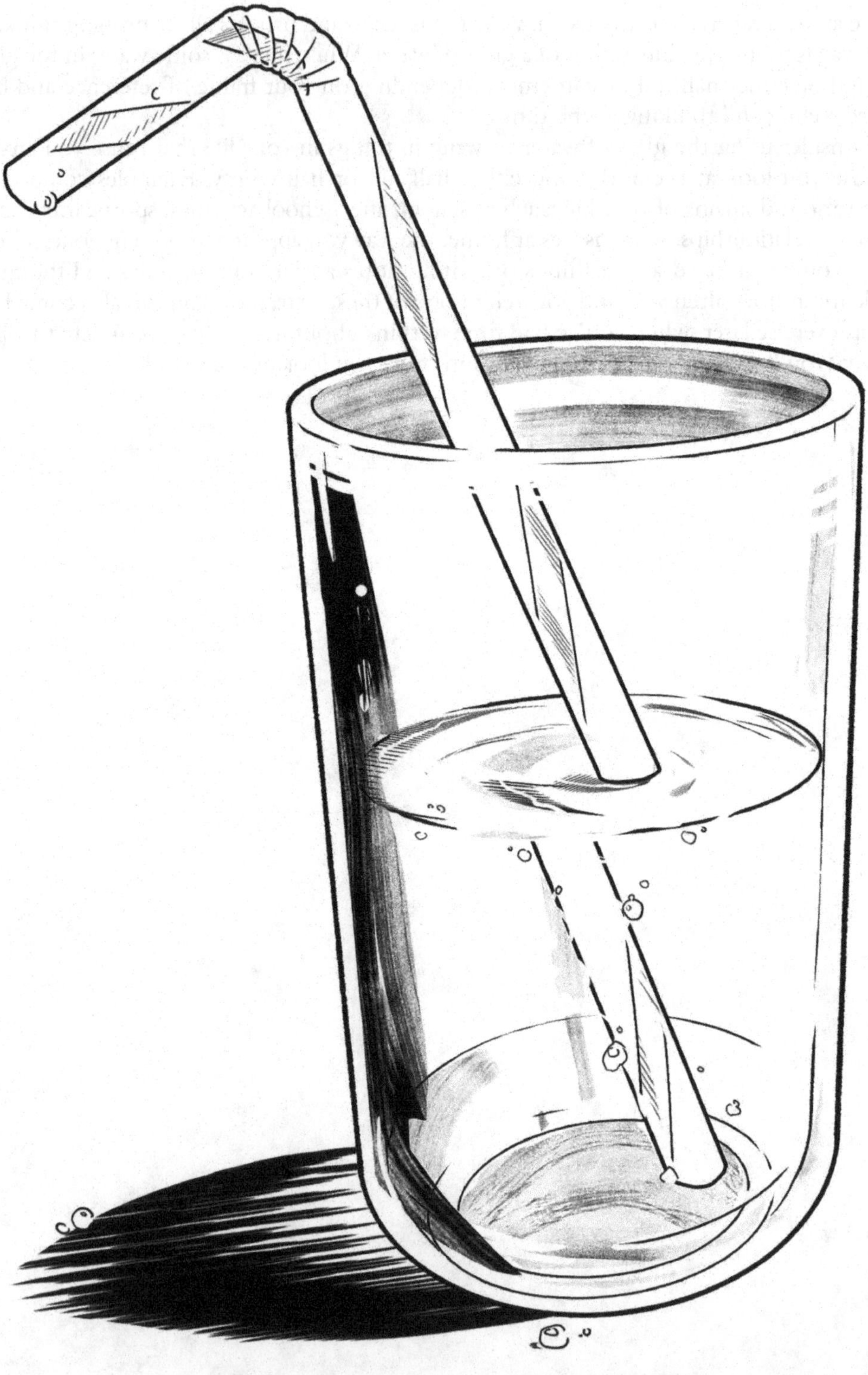

8.29 Writing Prompt

Having completed the glass of water exercise, reflect on how you are critical and tell yourself you are either the best or the worst at something.

Consider using the space provided to re-write some of these self-conceptualizations with a more realistic view of where you are in the world in comparison to others and your previous self.

_____

_____

_____

_____

_____

_____

_____

8.30 Additional Exercises

Additional exercises to soothe and divert attention while centering yourself include the following:

1. **Crossword Puzzles**

   ■ Crossword puzzles help focus, slow thinking, and allow us to think about something else.
   ■ They provide cognitive stimulation as they require problem solving, critical thinking, pattern recognition, patience, and persistence.
   ■ Perhaps the solution to the challenge you are dealing with will present itself organically.
   ■ In addition to a sense of accomplishment upon completion, crossword puzzles have also been shown to improve memory.

2. **Animals**

   'Meow' means 'woof' in cat.

   —George Carlin

   ■ Spending time with animals can be calming and helps feelings of bonding. Even interspecies connections will provide the experience of unconditional love and security.

- Animal therapy and emotional support animals aside, even looking at or appreciating a neighbor's pet has calming effects.
- There is a growing body of research, including a systematic review by Brooks et al. (2018), linking the therapeutic aspects of pets and reducing anxiety and depression, as well as improving focus, self-esteem, empathy, and accountability.

3. Art

- Painting, drawing, coloring.
- You can experiment with different materials, and if you like to draw, you can tell stories of things that have happened in your life or things you wish had happened.
- You don't necessarily have to be skilled in drawing; you can also make abstract paintings that express your emotions and how you feel about certain things.
- You can create comic strips detailing events that occurred and how they could have been different.
- Consider coloring in this cat mandala. This is a variation of a character and a symbol used in the graphic novel companion to this book, titled *Kader's Quest*. See Appendix section, 'But Wait, There's More.'

4. Collage

- Make a collage of things that are important to you or that help you feel calm.
- Collect images from photos, magazines, stickers, or books. You can also use other items, such as feathers, beads, or shells.
- Find a base you would like to collage. This can be a posterboard or cardboard.
- Choose glue or tape to stick the images and items onto the base.
- Some people prefer collaging based on a theme, such as gratitude or future plans; others prefer to have a collage of things they enjoy looking at and remembering. Either way, you are doing this exercise for yourself, and there are no wrong choices or mistakes.

5. Stress Ball

- Create your own stress ball.
- Physically squeezing something will allow for energy release and can help with regulating emotions.
  - The easiest is to fill a small balloon with rice.
  - A somewhat messier version is to fill a balloon with flour or cornstarch and add some warm water to it.

6. Clay

- Create your own clay.
  - You will need two cups of flour, a cup of salt, and a cup of water.
  - Mix the flour and the salt in a bowl, then gradually add water and stir until you get the consistency you like.
  - Kneading the clay for a couple of minutes will make it more elastic and smoother.

7. Journaling

- Journaling can include the creative writing exercises included in this book, as well as free-form writing on your own.
- Consider choosing one or more of the following prompts to begin creative exploration as you journal:

What are you most proud of?

_____

_____

_____

_____

_____

_____

_____

_____

_____

Who are you grateful for?

_____

_____

_____

_____

_____

_____

_____

_____

_____

What does tomorrow look like?

_____

_____

_____

_____

_____

_____

_____

_____

_____

8. Letter Writing

- Letter writing is a good way to express anger and hurt or apologize and take accountability for your actions.It is a great way to connect with people who won't listen and to prevent yourself from getting worked up.
- You can write whatever comes to your mind. Citing incidents and detailing everything that happened on the page may help you organize your thoughts and process your feelings.
- You can choose to give the letter to the person, write an edited, more filtered version, or keep the letter to yourself. You can even destroy it altogether.

Who are you writing this letter to?

_____

_____

_____

_____

What would you like to say in your letter?

_____

_____

_____

_____

_____

_____

_____

_____

_____

_____

_____

_____

_____

_____

_____

_____

How does writing this letter make you feel?

_____

_____

_____

_____

_____

_____

_____

_____

_____

Next, we suggest writing a letter to yourself – actually, two separate letters.

Write a letter to your younger self about your current self. What would you want to tell that kid?

_____

_____

_____

_____

_____

_____

_____

_____

_____

_____

_____

_____

_____

_____

_____

_____

Write a letter to your future self.

_____

_____

_____

_____

_____

_____

_____

_____

_____

_____

_____

_____

_____

_____

_____

9. A Box

- You can use an old shoebox or a wooden crate from a store.
- Consider painting or decorating it with construction paper, old magazines, or newspapers or gluing things onto it.
- Use this box to collect little items and scraps that are meaningful to you. They can be things that remind you of people who love you, important milestones, places you enjoy, things that motivate you and keep you focused, and your dreams.

10. Storytelling

- Writing stories can be a great outlet or distraction and can be used to process things that happen.
- Create characters and settings that are related or unrelated to your life.
- You can fictionalize certain changes in your life by exaggerating or using sci-fi or things that wouldn't happen in real life.
- You can use this to release your anger and frustration.

  - For instance, if you are dealing with a bully or your sister is annoying you, you can write a story magnifying certain instances by making emotions louder and add a happy ending.

8.31 Storytelling: Re-Write Your Narrative

Storytelling has always been how people coped with life. Even during caveman times, humans told stories about life to create meaning and understand their relationship with nature and with themselves. People would pass information to each other, protect one another, and connect through this extremely powerful tool.

There's always a hunger, even though the format has changed from caves and talking around campfires to movies and video games. It's always the story and human aspects that people are searching for. There's always a need and a craving for that.

Combine mythological heroes with bright primary colors and you have multimedia comic book franchises that have now been thriving for a century!

Even if it's an alien or an android beeping and booping, it's the people who are connecting to the characters of the journey, their relationships, grief, ambition, and love. People always connect to the human experience and the emotion.

Carl Jung talks about elementary ideas including archetypes of the unconscious and experiences that come from the nervous system and are then assimilated in terms of these archetypes. He also talks about myths and the interrelationships of culture and the environment and how these ancient myths have been designed to harmonize the mind and the body. These old stories still live within us.

Think about the basic narrative of a young boy, born and raised to be obedient, who then must grow into adolescence and start to differentiate himself into independence and autonomy. The challenges of transitioning from childhood to maturity are then met in the next phase of life as the hero progresses to the winter of their years and eventually passes away. These myths and stories help us understand, cope with, and accept the ways of nature rather than pathologically holding on.

Joseph Campbell talks about this hero's journey when he examines the emerging patterns of the hero leaving home in search of something and then returning after having gone through a series of trials and tribulations.

Almost all the great stories we know employ this universality – from Gilgamesh to Indiana Jones. There are patterns of diving deep into the unconsciousness and this requirement of a death of the previous self and the subsequent rebirth of a renewed and different version of oneself.

Think about Persephone, her abduction to the underworld by Hades, and her return, signaling a renewal and growth. These stories also include an artifact the hero brings back with them, This may be in the form of a magical chalice, a sword, or wisdom itself.

But this triumph and rebirth can only occur after the hero slays the dragon, which, in fantasy stories like *Lord of the Rings* or the ancient tale of Fafnir, represents greed and one's ego.

Campbell described dragons as guarding heaps of gold and virgins in their caves. The dragon can't make use of them – he greedily guards them with no true need or ability to experience them. In this hero's journey, the story talks about the psychology of the dragon and the binding of oneself in one's own ego, trapped in a cage of their own doing.

Think of how many times you have felt stuck in your career or your relationships. How many different stories are you in? How many roles do you have?

The point of therapy – the pursuit of self-actualization and understanding – is to open up, break free of that cage, and slay that dragon so one can have greater experiences and improve their relationships.

Rewriting your narrative allows you to explore your unconsciousness and go down deep through your journey to find the dragon within you – the ego that's holding you back from things you fantasize being able to do.

A large component of what is missing is being able to follow our own happiness. Many people are afraid to do that. Lori Gottlieb says that even productive, happy change is a loss – a loss of one's comfortable prior narrative.

How wild is it that we would rather be in predictable pain than take steps into the journey of the unknown forest of our unconsciousness?

There are many different tools people use to make sense of their experiences – the value of one person writing their own story, for example. In Jennette McCurdy's recent best-selling memoir, *I'm Glad My Mom Died*, she states that the more the painful it was to tell her story, the more important it was for her to do it.

The public's response to her book was not merely a voyeuristic peek into her suffering but a roadmap for healing and resilience for many others as well. This is what is crucial in the human psyche; we always need to be in connection with one another.

When you think about Maslow's hierarchy of needs, once you are secure with things like physical safety, warmth, food, and obviously Wi-Fi – the basic needs – at the top of that need pyramid is self-actualization: the purpose and meaning of our lives.

When we have an awareness and feel like we are contributing to change, our stories have the power to inspire others to tell their stories and shed light on their difficulties.

Growth that occurs at the individual level has a way of spreading to the community.

In the back of our minds, we all acknowledge that there are many things we are losing touch with in our societies with the demands of Western life, our busy day jobs, the shortcuts of how we get our food, and technology that seemingly makes life easier. The loss of these fundamental connections leads to a sense of disempowerment and, ultimately, hopelessness.

Through storytelling, we can achieve empowerment. As we understand how certain narratives were downloaded by society onto us – the social norms, including things we think we deserve, who we are, and the world around us – we begin to see how harmful and incorrect some of them might have been.

Think about some of the things you might say to yourself in the privacy of your own mind.

'I didn't get the promotion because I'm dumb.'

'The girl didn't like me? That's because I'm basic.'

You would never talk to someone you love and respect like that!

Editing one's inner dialogue might not feel organic or natural; it may even feel forced. Don't believe us? Just 'fake it till you make it.' The more experience you have of working on self-love, giving yourself encouragement, and exploring, the more it becomes hardwired.

Self-help techniques including meditation work wonders for this. There is a saying that 'everybody should meditate for 20 minutes a day, and if you absolutely have no time, you should meditate for one hour a day!'

Some coaches or therapists may have their clients believe that some types of thinking are 'wrong' and 'need to be fixed.'

Storytelling is about understanding how those thoughts came about, locating the first seed that blossomed into a series of thoughts validating the narrative, making it more and more true.

Yener jokingly suggests that at any given moment, he has 17 things on his mind, like:

■ Can you cry underwater?
■ Do animals get bored?
■ Should I keep pretending I understand the double slit experiment?
■ All while Sublime's song 'What I Got' is playing in his brain on repeat.

Just like Beowulf's interactions with his wise father, let's take Yener's interactions with our 12-year-old son. He calls Yener 'Baba,' which is 'Dad' in Turkish, but he often calls him "Baba, Baba, Baba, Baba, Baba."

And when he asks Yener for something a million times and he doesn't respond immediately, our son could feel rejection, maybe abandoned, and could go as far as feeling unloved, unwanted, or like he's a burden.

The way Yener uses his tone and eye contact, saying 'context cues,' makes such a difference. He can yell, 'Context cues,' or say, 'Hey buddy, context cues.' They both take about the same energy, although 'I see you; I love you; I'm working' goes a long way.

Perceptions we form about ourselves in early childhood, especially if we don't receive enough love from the people we need it from, prevent us from being able to live up to our full potential.

Certain narratives like self-sacrifice or submitting to oppressive social norms get passed from generation to generation. When parents don't come to terms with the sacrifices they made for their own children and go through their own trauma, they pass them on. There are so many people who are living with so much of this hurt.

Dysfunctional role archetypes also get passed down – like what it means to be a man or a woman in society: our pre-prescribed roles in parenting, at home, or at work. Our kids learn from watching us and how we interact and move through the world.

When our kid was in kindergarten and Yener would go to pick him up, the staff would be super quick, and they would be out in minutes. But when Duygu would do the pickup, she'd be in there for 30 minutes, chatting with the teachers and other moms and signing them up for six bake sales and a readathon!

The roles people assume shape their behavior. Maureen Murdock describes the heroine journey, dismantles dualistic cultures, and explores a circular, inclusive perspective as a model for living.

At any given moment, we are bombarded with messaging, commercials, viral memes, and dancers doing synchronized moves, not to mention all the political propaganda on the news.

Marketing works because it's designed to tap into our primal lizard brains. The addictive nature of video games and social media is designed by scientists who have studied the mind to explicitly create these addictions.

The developers openly admit this, and yet, the use of social media and the consumption of digital detritus are at an all-time high!

Basic connections between visual stimuli and the emotions they elicit are fully taken advantage of to ensure the organization delivering the message wins. That's the business model.

Some clinicians have even malevolently traded their pledge of 'first do no harm' for a lucrative paycheck in manipulating masses, propagandizing, and deceiving.

It's now more important than ever that we have the ability to learn the language of our mind and body. We must learn to appreciate the signals our physical organs are sending and how our emotional and thinking selves are connected.

As humanity has been increasingly preoccupied over the last three years, we have tragically seen a significant increase in the inability to focus on and pay attention to our bodies and minds. We're constantly being told what to do, how to act, how to think, what to be afraid of, what to buy, what to wear, how to interact, and how to avoid others.

The pandemic was a great traumatic equalizer. Relationships have been impacted, exacerbated by isolation, political rifts, medical misinformation, and the erosion of trust in once highly regarded institutions.

As we come out on the other end of the pandemic, matters such as climate crisis, economic unrest, gender inequality, and multiple wars throughout the world are all weighing heavily on our minds.

Are there some individuals, cultures, or values people have that enable resilience and protect them from this whirlwind? The answer is yes.

What about those who have been sucked into the vortex and want to learn to re-write their narrative and gain a better grasp on their mind and body? To elicit the answers to these questions, we suggest learning the language of yourself.

Healthy editing of your story is exploring 'How did I learn to think like this?' Curiosity and thoughts will organically change when you understand how you learn these things and how these thoughts are debilitating and hold you back.

Because of the nature of how our brains have evolved – designed to conserve as much energy as possible – these patterns and habits and our personalities often go on autopilot.

Like many of the high-tech solutions offered for mental health conditions, we humans are also be able to be programmed and changed. It will take energy, and the information we put into the program will yield what comes out.

Garbage in? Garbage out. Quality information and data in? Quality information and transformative change out.

There are many popular movies these days in which the action is nonstop. Compare the action and male-centric hero from *The Iliad* to today's John Wick. Car chases and crashes and fighter jets whooshing overhead as the pilot jumps out of the plane on a motorcycle!

So cool – but the action alone isn't what creates the memorable impact. Something as simple as the protagonist walking into a bar, ruffling his hair as he orders a drink, and taking a side glance at a beautiful woman with long hair and a red dress by the jukebox.

In three seconds, with these details, you get so much more feeling. Your brain wakes up! You see the person, and you connect emotionally as you access that person in that story and in your own stories. The stories of your ancestors. These small details make you connect.

Even the way we use technology – the apps that are extremely successful – are designed with human motivation and human centeredness to elicit that human contact. With social media, we want to connect with other people; the hunger for learning about other people's lives and being seen in this creative expression is what makes it so delicious.

Think about Gen Z and meme culture, the expression and use of memes to express discontent that they've not been seen or supported. No matter how sterile or robotic an app or a platform may be, people always find a way to personalize it and make it connect to the human experience. It's our human nature.

As James Taylor Gatto once said, 'You either learn your way towards writing your own script in life, or you unwittingly become an actor in someone else's script.'

Think about how you wake up, how you show up to work, what you bring home, how you socialize, how you use your space at home. These are all in your control.

If you notice some patterns in relationships in which you're always pleasing others, you have the ability to re-write your narrative and change those relationship dynamics. You can choose people who you feel energized around, who fulfill you, and who will support your growth.

Consider spending more time in nature – or, as they say on Discord, 'Go touch grass.'

There is so much that is in our control about how we live our day-to-day lives. Story-telling and rewriting the narrative are about taking that power back.

If someone had a securely attached childhood, has a fulfilling relationship, has been taken care of, and is loving, they have more capacity to handle adversity. This is a fact.

Their sense of self is strong, so if they have a bad breakup, because there is no internalized message of 'I'm unworthy of love,' 'No one loves me because I'm insufficient,' or 'Everyone I love leaves me,' they are able to recover and move on.

Since children are so egocentric, narratives developed within attachment wounding become internalized. It's difficult for a child to survive if they think, 'My parents can't take care of me,' or 'My parents are shitty.' It's easier and evolutionarily protective to think, 'I'm bad. I was difficult.'

Their sense of self continues to develop around that – they keep repeating their stories, abandoned in their relationships, seeking out people who will reenact these same dynamics with them.

In secure attachment, they can have, in real time, the appropriate reaction that the incident requires. A breakup is still difficult and will have tears and a tub of ice cream, but the person will have healthier soothing mechanisms overall, and in their story, they have the ability to ask for help and won't think it's only about them. It's a painful breakup but not because they are a horrible person, reinforcing their message.

Understand that your past trauma is not a life sentence and that you are not your symptoms. Whether you have anxiety, depression or post traumatic distress disorder, the symptoms do not identify you or who you are in the world; these are things you can change.

Mindfulness allows for a progressive decrease in sensitivity to stressors and how we react to our triggers. An improved sense of control of our bodies and sensations results in a decreased need for outpatient health care visits, decreased emergency department visits, decreased inpatient medical and psychiatric hospitalizations, and a decreased need for pharmaceuticals.

Bringing attention to your body with mindfulness and labeling and describing the associated feelings are skills that can be achieved. Use these along with other key elements of a story, including your supporting characters and the themes of your life.

Allow yourself to dream. Whenever you notice you have a critical voice telling you something is too much for you, or you don't deserve grandiose dreams, accept the thought and let it float away.

Don't let anyone edit your story – remember, there is no reason to dream small. Anyone who ever accomplished anything dreamed it first.

And when the critical voice comes – and it will – tell the voice it's just a dream, and you can dream as high and magnificently as you want.

We're all in a dream. We are all dreamers. Everything is a dream.

As one of the wisest storytellers we know, Clarissa Pinkola Estes, so eloquently put it:

> I hope you will go out and let stories, that is life, happen to you, and that you will work with these stories from your life – your life – not someone else's life – water them with your blood and tears and your laughter till they bloom, till you yourself burst into bloom. That is the work. The only work!

8.32 Resilience

The ability to adapt, change, and overcome situations of hardship and uncertainty are hallmarks of resilience. We discuss resilience as a factor shown to be protective against developing and worsening anxiety, depression, and stress-related disorders during the pandemic. See Chapter 6, 'COVID, Fear, and Grief,' for in-depth discussion of how the pandemic impacted the world's mental health and well-being.

Resilience involves the ability to recover from adversity and can be viewed as a form of toughness. Being able to bounce back into shape like a rubber band and flexibility are another ways of thinking of the term.

Resilience is a characteristic that can be defined by the individual as well as on a community level. For the individual, it involves the ability to cope with adversity and overcome it. As a person learns they can recover from difficulty, it provides internal reinforcement that they can similarly overcome it in the future, thereby strengthening their resilience.

People with elevated levels of resilience have better emotional regulation ability and, according to studies, did significantly better during the pandemic.

8.33 Secure Attachment

Attachment theory discusses the impact of the style and quality of our earliest relationships with our primary caregivers. Understanding health-promoting attachment styles, specifically secure attachment, allows us to identify our current strengths and work on areas of opportunity.

For the purpose of this section, we will use the term *mother* as the example of a primary caregiver and acknowledge that consistency and love are the main ingredients, rather than the person themselves.

Secure attachment begins when a baby has the sense of being loved in the world. When the mother responds appropriately to the child's distress and their cries for help and provides attention and love, the child internalizes feelings of being safe and secure.

When the mother is calm, available, and consistent yet not overbearing, the child is allowed to explore and go on adventures, knowing the mother is there if needed. The trust and comfort the child develops teaches the child it is OK to take risks as they begin to develop a sense of self and autonomy with a secure base to return to.

Mothers who respond with empathy and validation foster emotional regulation in the child, so when an experience becomes overwhelming or an accident happens, the child intrinsically knows they can express their discomfort and concerns and be acknowledged.

As the child matures, so do their self-image and self-esteem. Securely attached kids have had the opportunity to try things, take risks, make mistakes, and persevere. They develop resilience and a higher sense of self-worth.

The benefits continue exponentially later in life as those with secure attachment develop healthy relationships, including with friends and romantic partners. They are better liked by their teachers and coworkers and have a stronger sense of self, increased empathy, and a stronger ego and are able to enjoy life more. Secure attachment is also predictive of lower levels of anxiety and depression later in life, improved coping skills, and a sense of independence.

Children who grow up securely attached become emotionally regulated parents, empathic and responsive to their child's needs.

If, however, you are realizing that your attachment experience was different, there are steps you can take to improve yourself and your relationships going forward. Reflect on your experiences and consider counseling to explore your past in a safe environment. The exercises and writing prompts in this book, along with the mindfulness practices discussed, are all designed to help strengthen your self-awareness and self-compassion.

8.34 Compassion Versus Kindness

The concepts of compassion and kindness are related, yet they have several differences worth exploring. For example, we talk about self-compassion, but there is no such thing as 'self-kindness.'

Compassion involves empathy and recognizing the experiences of the self or another. Compassion extends past noticing the suffering, pain, and difficulties someone else has and emotionally connects with an understanding and genuine acknowledgement of their circumstances. Coupled with this profound connection to the other comes the desire to help support them and reduce the suffering they feel. Compassion can also include forgiveness as a true sense of caring for the other or self.

> **Tenderness and kindness are not signs of weakness and despair, but manifestations of strength and resolution.**
>
> **—Kahlil Gibran**

Kindness is often described in the context of actions and attitudes towards someone. Generously spending time, energy, or money to improve someone's experience can be an act of kindness. Compared with compassion, kindness doesn't necessarily require an empathic acknowledgement or validation of the other. You can simply hold the door open for someone and be kind without having a deep emotional connection with them.

Both kindness and compassion are pro social, positively impact interactions, and can lead to improved relationships with oneself and others. When we perform acts of kindness or make people happy, we feel a part of a community and feel good in return. Also, as emotions are contagious, someone else's happiness or gratitude will reflect onto us as well.

8.35 Compassion Towards Others

Acts of compassion towards others include:

- Including friends who are being left out because they are new, shy, or different.
- Standing up for somebody who is being mistreated.
- Baking cookies for someone who isn't feeling well.

Use the space provided to write your own examples of compassion towards others:

_____

_____

_____

_____

8.36 Compassion Towards Yourself

Acts of compassion towards yourself include:

- Taking a break when you feel overwhelmed.
- Talking to yourself like you would talk to someone you really care about.
- Cutting yourself some slack when you don't achieve something.

Use the space provided to write your own examples of compassion towards yourself:

_____

_____

_____

_____

8.37 Volunteer Work

An example that often necessitates both compassion and kindness, and something we recommend every person engage in at some point in their lives is volunteer work.

The act of voluntarily providing one's time, energy, and money has many positive mental health values, as well as helping solve other's problems. This is a rare example of a true win-win, in which you can selfishly benefit while selflessly assisting others.

Volunteer work:

- Boosts mood
- Builds empathy
- Builds self-worth
- Decreases anxiety
- Decreases stress
- Develops self-value
- Fosters connections and networks
- Helps focus on others
- Improves confidence
- Improves life satisfaction
- Improves mindfulness and presence
- Improves mood and happiness
- Improves skills
- Increases gratitude
- Increases resilience
- Increases self-esteem
- Increases sense of purpose
- Promotes a sense of belonging
- Provides a sense of accomplishment
- Provides a sense of control
- Reduces feelings of isolation

Depending on your age, skill level, and the amount of time and energy you have, consider volunteer opportunities in your community.

Opportunities include:

- Reading to children at a local library
- Working at soup kitchens
- Collecting and donating books and toys for children in hospitals
- Making 'get well soon' cards
- Spending time with shelter animals

With these many positive reasons to do so, it is well worth your while to try volunteering!

8.38 Writing Prompt

Consider using the space provided to reflect on how you thought and felt when you helped someone else.

_____

_____

_____

_____

_____

_____

_____

_____

8.39 Humor

Humor is a mature defense mechanism and is associated with a healthier, more fulfilling outlook on life. The cognitive and emotional aspects of humor involve a complex interaction between thinking and feeling.

Humor can be situationally based or verbal and always engages the audience by focusing on the concept or meaning of what is being shared. Invariably, humor is social and has the power to bring people closer and to allow bonds and friendships to form. Children grow up using humor as a template to practice social interactions and even problem solving.

Examples of humor include:

- Jokes, riddles, and puns
- Mannerisms, facial expressions, and gestures
- Funny sounds and noises
- Taboo or inappropriate humor
- Humorous stories, anecdotes, and observations

Humor can be wielded as a powerful tool to shed light on the entirety of a topic while putting things in perspective. It can deflate tension between people and allow anxious energy to be released.

8.40 Writing Prompts

What role does humor play in your life?

_____

_____

_____

_____

_____

_____

What are some inside jokes you have with people you are close with?

_____

_____

_____

_____

_____

_____

What makes you laugh?

_____

_____

_____

_____

_____

_____

8.40.1 Self-Benefits of Humor

The stress relief and emotional release associated with practicing and enjoying humor are further associated with:

- Improved mental health
- Improved mood
- Decreased stress
- Decreased anxiety
- Stimulating cognitive function
- Increased creativity
- Increased productivity
- Improved health:

  - Decreased pain perception
  - Improved cardiovascular health
  - Improved immune system health

- Increased resilience
- Improved self-awareness
- Improved self-esteem

8.40.2 Relationship Benefits of Humor

There is clearly a difference between making fun of someone or something and using humor to describe or make an intelligent observation. Simply obtaining laughs from an observer or audience does not make something humorous. Deliberate mockery or bullying is cruel, unwarranted, and unacceptable. There is a fine line between self-deprecation, insulting and hurtful comments, and witty comments that rely on idiosyncrasies.

Constructively used, humor can:

- Be an icebreaker when fostering new relationships
- Foster communication
- Help resolve conflicts
- Improve social bonding
- Increase connection and deepen relationships
- Elevate self-esteem
- Highlight common areas of interest

8.41 Case Example: Yener's Approach

Yener was born with a congenital defect called proximal femoral focal deficiency (PFFD), in which his left leg and left hip were incompletely formed. The result was when he was born, his left leg was significantly shorter, requiring him to receive surgery to remove the malformed left foot so a prosthesis could be used to allow him to ambulate.

Especially during his childhood, when meeting other people, he had to learn to introduce himself and discuss the – obvious – difference he has. Due in large part to his secure attachment with his parents and the modeling of resilience as well as the use of humor in his childhood home, he developed ways to address curious inquiries and mitigate bullying.

As Yener describes it, there are inherent situational anxieties that come with having one leg, walking with a prosthesis, and always being somewhat off balance, with an increased tendency to trip and fall. As he has lived in several countries and speaks multiple languages, he's become more comfortable making friends and creating relationships. The mechanism he uses to reduce anxieties and tensions in social situations, specifically relating to his leg, is humor.

One example is the astonishingly large number of phrases that involve the use of the word 'leg' or 'foot' in the English language to describe various scenarios.

Yener gives the reader *full permission* to enjoy the next section, smirk, giggle, or laugh, knowing that this type of humor has helped him cope with his own journey and, quite frankly, still makes him giggle when he hears the phrases being used.

When somebody wants to start something off appropriately, they say they want to 'start off on the right foot,' and they want to 'put one foot in front of the other' to 'gain footing' and perhaps 'get their foot in the door.' As this person 'gets their feet wet,' they also 'get their sea legs,' especially if they've 'put their best foot forward.' They certainly don't want to be perceived as 'dragging their feet' or 'having cold feet,' and to be able to 'get a leg up,' they must 'shake a leg' and 'think on their feet.'

We wouldn't be 'pulling your leg' when we describe that at work, during presentations, Yener hears that people want to 'avoid land mines' and that some business cases 'cost an arm and a leg.' When asked to 'foot the bill,' he 'leans towards' with generosity. This can be challenging, as he avoids having other people 'pulling the rug from under his feet,' so he works diligently to avoid 'putting his foot in his mouth,' with the desire to 'stand on his own two feet.'

When Yener gets home, he 'puts his foot down' when it is time to relax, wind down, 'put his feet up,' and spend time with his wife and son. Speaking of his loved ones, many years ago, his wife, Duygu, 'swept him off his feet' when they were in theater club together in Istanbul. Interestingly, to wish people luck before going on stage so they wouldn't miss a line or trip as if they 'have two left feet,' they would superstitiously say, 'Break a leg.'

Growing up, he remembers going to all-you-can-eat buffets and eating so much that he was accused of having 'a hollow leg.' As these phrases and silly idioms are running out, he feels he has 'no leg left to stand on' and may even be 'on his last leg.'

In conclusion, think about this exercise and put the 'shoe on the other foot' so you can employ humor that is constructive, appropriate, and acceptable to the person you're with, so you don't 'shoot yourself in the foot.'

8.42 Mimics, Gestures, and Behaviors

We communicate not only with our words, but also with our micro expressions. It is important to notice which gestures we resort to and how they might make others feel. Similarly, it is important to notice what other people's gestures or micro expressions makes us feel and what they trigger.

8.43 Writing Prompts

Use the space provided beneath each prompt to think about how each of the behaviors impact your feelings and how they may affect others.

Part 1: Eyes

When I roll my eyes, I feel:

_____

_____

When I roll my eyes, someone else might feel:

_____

_____

When someone rolls their eyes, I feel:

_____

_____

Part 2: Smile

When I smile, I feel:

_____

_____

When I smile, someone else might feel:

_____

_____

When someone smiles, I feel:

_____

_____

Part 3: Phone

When I fiddle with my phone, I feel:

_____

_____

When I fiddle with my phone, someone else might feel:

_____

_____

When someone fiddles with their phone, I feel:

_____

_____

Part 4: Look Down

When I look at the floor, I feel:

_____

_____

When I look at the floor, someone else might feel:

_____

_____

When someone looks at the floor, I feel:

_____

_____

Part 5: Questions

When I ask a lot of questions, I feel:

_____

_____

When I ask a lot of questions, someone else might feel:

_____

_____

When someone asks a lot of questions, I feel:

_____

_____

Part 6: Interrupting

When I interrupt, I feel:

_____

_____

When I interrupt, someone else might feel:

_____

_____

When someone interrupts me, I feel:

_____

_____

Part 7: Walk Away

When I walk away, I feel:

_____

_____

When I walk away, someone else might feel:

_____

_____

When someone walks away, I feel:

_____

_____

Part 8: Personalize

Use the space provided to write in mimics, gestures, or behaviors you would like to reflect on.

When I _____, I feel:

_____

_____

When I _____, someone else might feel:

_____

_____

When someone _____, I feel:

_____

_____

8.44 Food Is Mood

Throughout this book, you are learning how your body and brain are in constant communication with one another physically, as well as affecting your conscious awareness of what you are thinking and feeling. Your behaviors are motivated and influenced by what you need and want.

As you learn to be an expert listener to your body, you will see the habits and rituals you have created, either intentionally or seemingly on their own. The reality is that everything we do and say and eat and feel is connected.

8.45 Healthy Eating

> **If you eat your food like medicine, you won't have to eat your medicine like food.**
>
> **—Anonymous**

The following is a list of foods that are known to positively influence our moods. In moderation and balance, they are correlated with and often cause improved mood and decreased anxiety and depression, as well as restorative sleep and immune functions. Obviously, consult your doctor before trying something new and if you have any personal concerns. The information provided throughout this book is for informational purposes based on scientific evidence known at the time of writing.

Compare this section with the section discussing dietary links to the development of anxiety, depression, and fatigue, and you can begin making informed choices to succeed in your goals for your overall health.

- Calcium-containing foods: milk, yogurt, cheese, broccoli, spinach
- Omega-3 fatty acids:

    - Fish: tuna, salmon, sardines
    - Nuts: walnuts
    - Vegetables: soybeans, green leafy vegetables

- Carbohydrates:

    - When we feel down or anxious, we reach out to comfort foods, typically high in carbohydrates. We know that low serotonin levels in the body are linked to craving carbohydrates, and that carbs increase serotonin levels.
    - Complex carbohydrates, specifically whole grains: bread, cereals, pasta, rice

- Meat:

    - Meats such as chicken and turkey have been shown to increase serotonin levels.

- Sugars:

- The goal with any health system is to create a balance.
- There are sugars in many foods that are not necessarily harmful in and of themselves. The body breaks down foods into smaller components, one of the main ones being sugars.
- The measurement to compare the amount of sugars in each food is called the glycemic index.
- Comparatively, foods that have a lower glycemic index include fruits and lentils.

■ Vitamin-containing foods:

- Biotin: eggs, cheese, peanuts, cauliflower
- Folic acid: oranges, peas, avocados, cabbage, broccoli, soybeans, turkey
- Magnesium: almonds, spinach, avocados, sunflower seeds, Brazil nuts
- Niacin: chicken, brown rice, tuna, turkey
- Pantothenic acid: yogurt, avocados, salmon, mushrooms, sunflower seeds
- Riboflavin: pork, avocados, mushrooms, milk, yogurt
- Thiamin: wheat, pork, tuna, oats, asparagus, sunflower seeds, white rice
- Vitamin B_{12}: tuna, beef, crab, clams, yogurt
- Vitamin B_6: bananas, mangoes, turkey, tuna, pork, sweet potatoes, sunflower seeds
- Vitamin C: Oranges, strawberries, broccoli, peppers, pineapple, papaya, cauliflower

8.46 Writing Prompt

Consider using the space provided to reflect on what you eat and its impact on your anxiety levels. Specifically, think about when you ate it, when it began to cause anxiety, and how long the anxiety lasted.

As you grow increasingly aware of how your food and your mood are connected, you will learn to adapt and accommodate your own needs.

_____

_____

_____

_____

_____

_____

_____

_____

_____

_____

_____

_____

_____

_____

8.47 Writing Prompt

Make a list of things you are thinking about or dealing with that cause you anxiety
and that you think you can change.

_____

_____

_____

_____

_____

_____

_____

Now think of things that cause you to worry that you likely cannot change.

_____

_____

_____

_____

_____

_____

_____

_____

As you consider the things that you are likely able to influence and make a difference on, what are some of the things you can actually do? How will you go about solving some of your problems or reducing the anxiety associated with these things?

_____

_____

_____

_____

_____

_____

_____

Some of these issues may require additional support. What tools or other things will you need to help you along your way? Are there other people in your life you will need to connect with to help you tackle these issues?

_____

_____

_____

_____

_____

_____

_____

_____

Chapter 9

Safety Planning

9.1 Introduction

In this chapter, we discuss the importance of developing goals, values, and systems in the context of identity formation, anxiety reduction, and building confidence. We continue with the concept of success, as well as the fear of achieving success. The chapter draws these concepts together with instructions on the development of an evidence-based, user-friendly safety plan.

Clinically, a safety plan refers to a set of predetermined goals within a systematic structure of ensuring the physical and emotional safety of the individual. Clinicians often work with their clients to develop a safety plan to ensure adequate information is gathered and reviewed prior to a health emergency.

The process of putting together a safety plan involves deliberate self-reflection and awareness of oneself and one's support networks. The purpose of a safety plan is to reduce the potential of self-injurious behaviors and harmful decisions.

Among the most concerning mental health emergencies involves violence turned inwards. There are many possible causes of such aggression and impulsivity, and the discussion between clinician and client is designed to personalize the tactics and strategies to be easy to remember and follow.

> **It's in vain to recall the past, unless it works some influence upon the present.**
>
> **—Charles Dickens, *David Copperfield***

9.2 Goals, Values, and Systems

In this section, we discuss how goals, values, and systems can be used to mitigate feelings of anxiety and worry. We outline the areas of focus or life domains that these can be thought of in and provide insights into how and when to use them.

DOI: 10.4324/9781003413547-13

Spending time and energy to think about your own goals and systems is valuable for your development, personally and professionally. As you overcome barriers and learn new skills, you build strength and resilience, making the next set of questions or challenges you face less anxiety provoking.

I was only just now starting to exist.
—Barbara Kingsolver, *Demon Copperhead*

9.3 Areas of Focus

The following are areas of focus you can use to think about your goals, values, and systems. Consider how they may be different, depending on the circumstance, yet, in combination, make up who you are and how you plan on getting to where you want to be.

- Home life
- Relationships

    - Family relationships
    - Friend relationships
    - Romantic relationships
    - Parent-child relationships

- Outside the home

    - Educational/school
    - Professional/workplace/career

- Health

    - Physical health
    - Mental health

- Individual growth

    - Spirituality/religion
    - Leisure activities/fun

- Other (add additional areas of focus that are important for you):

    _____

    _____

    _____

    _____

9.4 Goals

Goals are actions you can take; they are something you can accomplish and be done with. Goals are described as being specific, measurable, realistic, and time limited.

Some goals may be aligned with your values while others may not necessarily have to be. By definition, they provide focus in the direction of the task you want to complete.

As goals are outcome oriented, as soon as you complete one goal, the natural next thing to do is begin working on another goal. To some, goals may be motivating, something to look forward to and strive for. For others, the time taken achieving goals may be viewed as a source of frustration. Some may find themselves constantly not having met their goals yet, with them hanging over their head, adding to their anxiety. This is why having goals alone does not round out the strategy for reducing stress, anxiety, and worry.

Examples of goals may include specific things such as 'completing college.' There are clear boundaries around this goal, and it is clear when the goal is achieved. Other types may be something like 'learning a new language.' Levels of proficiency in a language are nuanced, and while taking an exam to see if you are advanced or native equivalent is an option, perhaps a real-world modifier, such as 'learn enough Spanish to enjoy my trip abroad,' may better suit your needs.

9.5 Writing Prompt

Within the framework of the Balan 3-2-1 Method, consider your response to the following:

Using the areas of focus listed earlier, reflect on your current goals.

3: With intention, set your internal and external environment.

- The body: What mindfulness techniques are you choosing to allow your body to heal?

_____

_____

_____

- The setting: How are you intentionally influencing your setting?

_____

_____

_____

■ The breath: Which breathing technique will you use as you prepare for this exercise?

_____

_____

_____

2: What are your thoughts and feelings in response to the writing prompt?

_____

_____

_____

_____

_____

_____

_____

_____

_____

_____

1: What is your one intent, or affirmation in the context of the writing prompt?

_____

_____

_____

9.6 Values

Take a moment to reflect and be honest with yourself. Think about what makes you happy. What makes you angry? Who do you look up to? Who do you admire?

Values can be seen as guiding principles: a long-term journey with no specific end point. Compared to goals, they may not have a measurable outcome.

The purpose of having values, specifically if you are someone with anxiety, is to help guide you through anxious and stressful times. Values will help you focus on what you identify as important. They help you know who you are. Values can inform your goals and their progression as they can help with a sense of purpose and inner awareness.

Examples of values include:

- Accountability
- Altruism
- Authenticity
- Compassion
- Connection
- Courage
- Creativity
- Diversity
- Empathy
- Environmentalism
- Faith
- Family
- Freedom
- Friendship
- Generosity
- Gratitude
- Growth
- Happiness
- Health
- Honesty
- Humility
- Humor
- Independence
- Integrity
- Justice
- Kindness
- Love
- Loyalty
- Mindfulness
- Morality
- Optimism
- Patience
- Perseverance
- Resilience
- Respect
- Responsibility
- Self-discipline
- Spirituality
- Transparency
- Trust
- Other (add additional values):

_____

_____

_____

As with the concept of identity and roles, discussed in Chapter 7, 'Un-Social Media,' values are also developed through one's culture, family, beliefs, and experiences. There is no such thing as an incorrect value – they are personal and relevant to you. While you may share values with your family or support network, they ultimately are what you consider to be important and are aligned with who you are.

9.7 Writing Prompt

Within the framework of the Balan 3-2-1 Method, consider your response to the following:

Using the areas of focus listed, reflect on your current values.

3: With intention, set your internal and external environment.

■ The body: What mindfulness techniques are you choosing to allow your body to heal?

_____

_____

_____

■ The setting: How are you intentionally influencing your setting?

_____

_____

_____

■ The breath: Which breathing technique will you use as you prepare for this exercise?

_____

_____

_____

2: What are your thoughts and feelings in response to the writing prompt?

_____

_____

_____

_____

_____

_____

_____

_____

_____

_____

1: What is your one intent or affirmation in the context of the writing prompt?

_____

_____

_____

9.8 Creative Prompt: Family Crest

(The following creative prompt has been reprinted from our previous book *Re-Write: A Trauma Workbook of Creative Writing and Recovery in Our New Normal*, 2023.)

A creative family activity that we have engaged in and recommended to clients and colleagues is the concept of creating a family crest. Imagine historically, the shields or coats of arms and symbols families would create to wear and display. These would be developed to demonstrate belonging as well as pride. Values, accomplishments, morals, and other important elements would be incorporated. Even in current times, you may have seen some universities that have crests with symbols and words on them in Greek or Latin.

The color, shape, and chosen symbols for this exercise are all up to you and your family. Symbols can be simple line drawings of something like an animal, a plant, or a hobby. Words such as the name chosen for your family and or other phrases you would like to display that are meaningful to you can be added.

For the exercise, especially in the context of the family chapter dealing with trauma and resilience, we suggest initially thinking of who is in your family. It can be a biological family, a chosen family, folks you live with, or those loved ones farther away.

1. Consider listing those you identify as being part of your family:

_____

_____

_____

_____

_____

_____

_____

_____

_____

_____

2. Discuss this exercise with those listed earlier and together, begin brainstorming your collective family values and morals, things you are proud of, and concepts that make you all feel you belong as part of the family. Consider listing those identified; you can use single words or phrases to describe them.

_____

_____

_____

_____

_____

_____

_____

_____

_____

3. We have divided the family crest template into four sections, although feel free to use as many or as few of the items listed in your personal crest. Using the space provided, think with your family about how you will depict and draw or write the elements that symbolize your family. Examples could be something like a lion for bravery or a heart for love. The value in this exercise is less the artistic quality of the product and more the process of discussing and creating together.

_____

_____

_____

_____

_____

_____

_____

_____

_____

4. Now take turns together, using pencils, markers, crayons, and the colors of your choosing to begin your family crest.

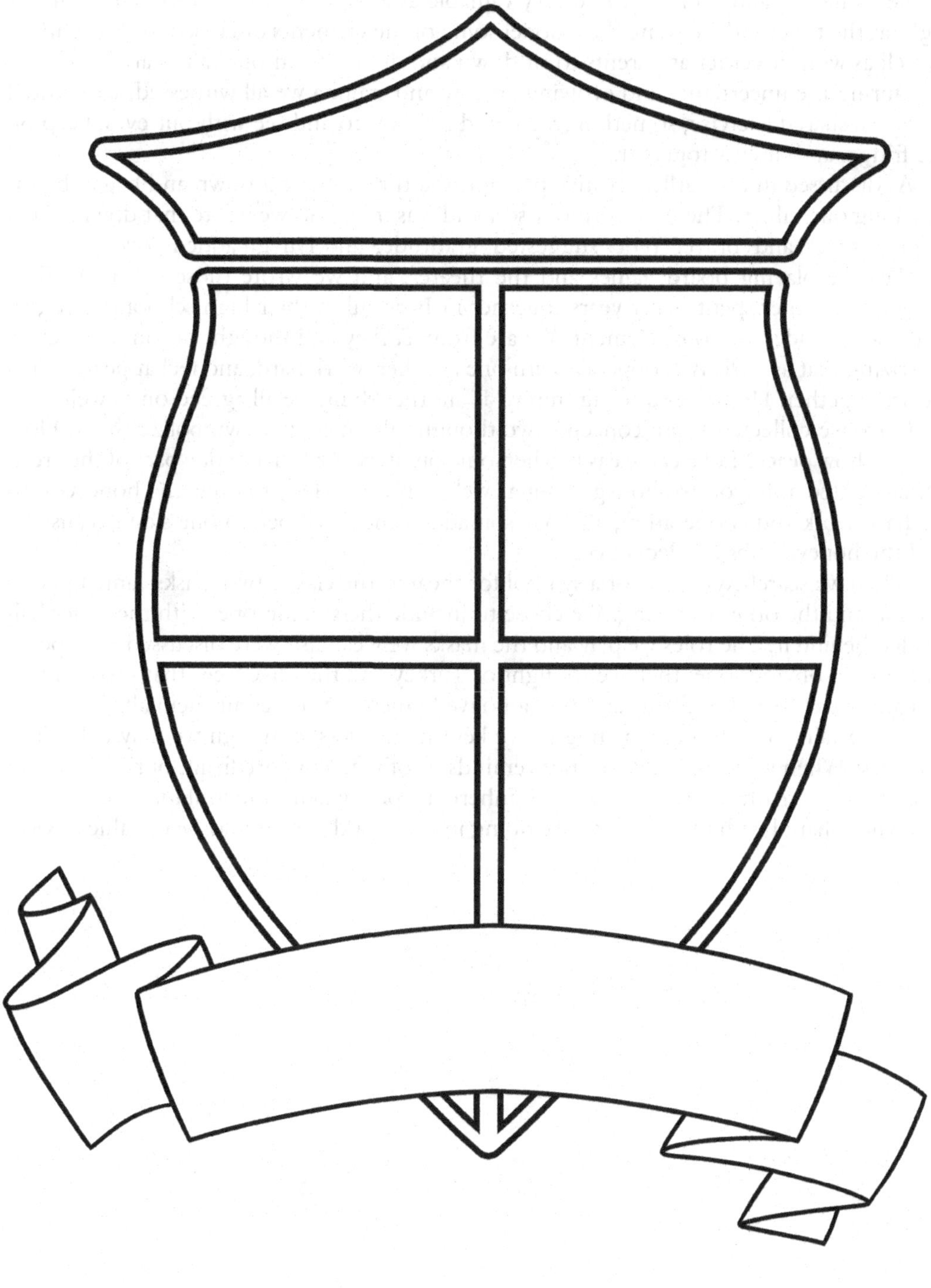

9.9 Example: Balan Family Crest

As a family, we also created our family crest. We began this exercise during the first year of the pandemic and found it to be very valuable as a communication tool. Our son was eight at the time, and we wanted to model some of the elements discussed in this chapter, as well as work together as parents to sit down and discuss what our values are.

During the uncertainty and evolving anxiety and trauma we all witnessed, we wanted to have a shared exercise, something we could hold on to and see with our eyes, keep on the fridge, and discuss together.

As discussed in the earlier creative prompt, the three of us sat down and began brainstorming our values. The first word our son said was 'nice.' So we wrote that down. Then came 'respect' and 'brave.' Yener suggested 'gratitude,' and Duygu added 'love.'

We love playing board games and the theater, and we wrote those down. In fact, Duygu and Yener spent many years together in Istanbul in their high school theater, so that was an added personal element. We are from Turkey and thought of somehow characterizing that as well. We cooperate with one another, work hard, and feel at peace when we are together. Humor and being 'funny' is another thing we all agreed on as well.

Once we collected those concepts, we thought about how to symbolize them. How can we show peace? Love came easily when our son drew the heart in one part of the crest. Yener wanted a dragon to show gaming as well as bravery. Duygu drew the honeycombs for hard work and cooperation, and our son added the small bee to one side because he said the honeycombs needed a bee.

When we searched online for a symbol for theater, the classic two masks came up, one smiling and the other frowning. We chose to include the smiling one, with the other half shaded behind it. The roles we play and the masks we wear also were discussed. The peace sign was an obvious one; then we thought of Turkey and the olive trees that grow in that climate as well as in California and that an olive branch can represent them all.

We certainly had fun completing it; we kept it colorless, although we may color it in someday. When we look at the crest, it reminds us of where we are from, our current values, and some truths we hold sacred. It is inherently personal meaningful for us as a family, and when shared with others, as we are doing in this workbook, it may be of value as well.

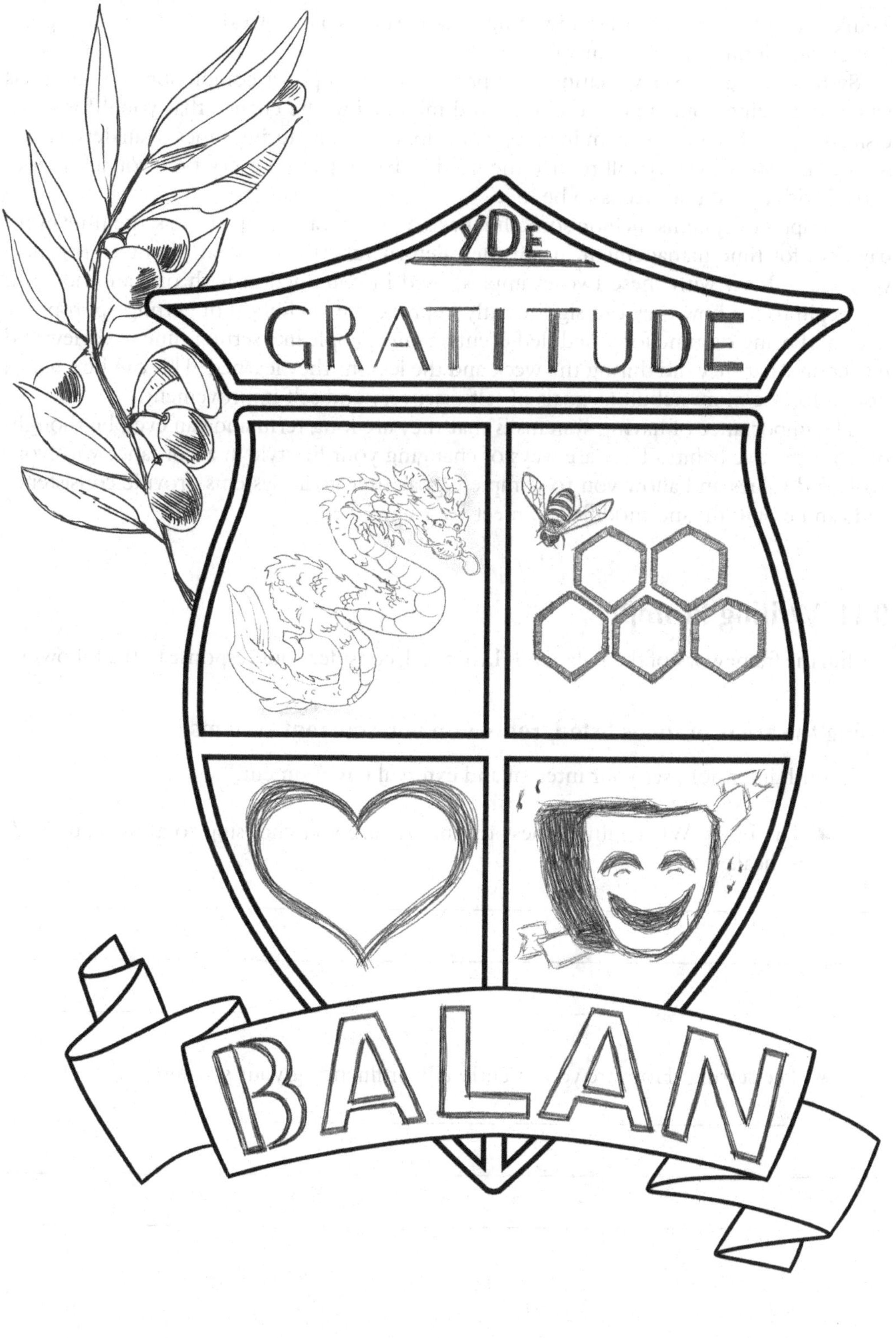
YDE
GRATITUDE
BALAN

9.10 Systems

Think of a system as a way of doing things that ensures you are working towards the goals that are in alignment with your values.

Systems are day-to-day routines and processes that support completion of your goals while optimizing your time and energy and minimizing the chance that you'll forget or dismiss a goal. Having a system in place will help, especially during times of anxiety, stress, self-doubt, and worry. It will reduce the need to be motivated every time you are preoccupied with a goal that needs to be met.

Examples of systems include something as simple as waking up at the same time every day and, for time management, using the calendar function on your phone to organize your tasks. Even with these two examples, used in conjunction with one another, you can begin to see how they can significantly improve the likelihood of getting appropriate sleep and being on time for scheduled events. Some people like setting time to review and reflect on what they did during the week and the lessons they learned. This can be a useful system for the more nebulous goals of self-discovery and self-improvement.

The importance of having systems is that they are long term and can even be thought of as productive habits. They are ways of changing your lifestyle in accordance with your goals and values and allow you to complete goal after goal. Systems provide consistency and can be built on and modified to meet your new needs.

9.11 Writing Prompt

Within the framework of the Balan 3-2-1 Method, consider your response to the following:

Using the areas of focus listed, reflect on your current systems.

3: With intention, set your internal and external environment.

■ The body: What mindfulness techniques are you choosing to allow your body to heal?

_____

_____

_____

■ The setting: How are you intentionally influencing your setting?

_____

_____

_____

■ The breath: Which breathing technique will you use as you prepare for this exercise?

_____

_____

_____

2: What are your thoughts and feelings in response to the writing prompt?

_____

_____

_____

_____

_____

_____

_____

_____

_____

_____

_____

1: What is your one intent or affirmation in the context of the writing prompt?

_____

_____

_____

9.12 Sense of Control

Depending on where we are in life, our level of autonomy, physical health, financial stability, level of resources, and relationships and connections, our ability to control things varies. As a baby, we have minimal control over anything other than going to the bathroom, and even then, we don't have voluntary control over our bodily functions. As a toddler and a child, we have very clear expectations and are told what to do, when to do it, where to go, when to sleep, what to eat, when to go to school, and when to go on vacation. Autonomy and a gradual sense of control develop slowly throughout grade school and advance over the years.

Anxiety is, by nature, a concern about something that may or may not happen in the future. Whether or not we have role in what's going to happen to us, what we will experience, or how we will behave can be variable. There are some very clear things we can control, such as our diet, what we put into our bodies, our sleep schedules, and our physical activities. There are some things we have no control over, and therefore, worrying about them has little to no value as they relate to moving towards our goals or desired outcomes. Things that can make a difference, such as concerns about imminent danger or thinking about doing well on an exam, can be prepared for. What someone might think about us at some point in the future likely is not under our control.

9.13 Writing Prompt

Consider using the space provided to reflect on the areas of focus listed earlier that you have no control over and areas over which you have absolute control.

Areas of focus I have NO control over:

_____

_____

_____

_____

_____

_____

Areas of focus I have ABSOLUTE control over:

_____

_____

_____

_____

_____

_____

9.14 Success

The concept of success is extremely personal, although there are some general terms, especially in Western societies, that include things such as attaining education, a career, a family relationship, and financial stability. Surrounding these are other community, spiritual, and religious concepts.

The purpose of thinking about one's idea of success is to help better reflect on whether or not success is a goal or a value and how it can be incorporated into the concept of having an ongoing system.

Do you define success as something that you feel, something others validate for you, or something that happens without any external awareness? As discussed in Chapter 8, 'Confidence and Recovery,' the pressures of ill-defined success can increase anxiety and lead to distraction, decreased energy, and decreased productivity.

As you go through the exercises and review the concepts in this book, think about the following:

- How much of your concept of success is something that's in the future and always something to be attained?
- Is success something that has happened to you in the past?
- Or is success something you are currently experiencing?

Because there is no one single definition of success, and it's more of a feeling rather than an absolute universal, understanding the fluidity with which you are comfortable with these concepts is also going to be important.

9.15 Fear of Success?

Terms such as 'achieving' a goal or 'accomplishing' something are descriptors of success, and, as discussed in the section on goals, they can also create stress and anxiety themselves.

Having expectations of yourself can be stressful, and achieving success in a domain can generate even more anxiety. Success can bring about change in the way people view you and how you are perceived at school or work, as well as socioeconomic benefits. These can be in the interpersonal relationship domain in which others may be critical or envious of you, which may further exacerbate anxiety.

Some people are concerned about the attention success will bring them while others are anxious about the change itself and the uncertainty it may bring. While this may seem foreign to you, ask yourself if you ever purposely hesitated to complete a goal you set for yourself.

We discuss 'faking it till you make it' earlier in the book, although the flipside to this is imposter syndrome. This is when someone is concerned they are not worthy of their achievements.

The complexities with which anxiety and success are entwined are very interesting, and we encourage you to continue your journey of self-discovery.

9.16 Writing Prompt

Within the framework of the Balan 3-2-1 Method, consider your response to the following:

Using the areas of focus listed, reflect on how you define success.

3: With intention, set your internal and external environment.

- The body: What mindfulness techniques are you choosing to allow your body to heal?

_____

_____

_____

- The setting: How are you intentionally influencing your setting?

_____

_____

_____

- The breath: Which breathing technique will you use as you prepare for this exercise?

_____

_____

_____

2: What are your thoughts and feelings in response to the writing prompt?

_____

_____

_____

_____

_____

_____

_____

_____

_____

_____

1: What is your one intent or affirmation in the context of the writing prompt?

_____

_____

_____

9.17 Safety Plan: Overview

We recommend structuring your safety plan to include as much detail as useful in the event of a crisis. Untreated anxiety and stress can lead to depression and hopelessness, all of which may impact one's insight and judgment. This is why it is important to write down the answers to each section of the safety plan.

Complete this exercise when you are in a state of calm and do your best to be as stigma- and judgment-free in your responses as possible. You can use the space provided in this book and rip the completed page out or take a photo of it and keep a digital copy.

If you are completing the plan alone, consider sharing it with someone you can trust so they are aware of your plan and strategies. If you are working with a clinician, they will likely keep a copy in your file as well.

Effective safety plans typically consist of the following elements:

- Warning signs
- Triggers
- Coping strategies
- Family, social, and professional contacts

Your clinician and other members of your care team may reference your safety plan throughout your treatment and make updates with you as clinically appropriate. This coordination of care and inclusion in the medical records are further reminders that the safety plan is an extremely important part of your treatment journey.

9.18 Section 1: My Warning Signs

This section includes when the safety plan should be used and identifies a list of emotions associated with escalating anxiety and concern about loss of control. As this plan should be as easy to use as possible, spend time thinking about all your emotional, behavioral, physical, and other external cues you may encounter that may suggest you are having a problem.

You may want to write down any past behaviors that are indicative of decreased safety. Think about physical sensations in your body associated with anxiety, panic, stress, and depression and how they have been linked to previous times you felt a loss of control.

Document your emotional reactions, including things such as numbness and feelings of depersonalization or derealization, that may be linked to a decrease in insight and increase in impulsive, reckless behavior.

If using drugs or alcohol is a part of your life, reflect on changes in usage patterns as potential warning signs that may need to be addressed. Think of other signs and symptoms such as fluctuations in mood, sleep schedule, or eating patterns that may reveal clues as to how you are doing.

Regarding interpersonal relationships, think about how you react during times of severe stress. Do you tend to spend more time socializing with others, or do you isolate more? The warning signs should be as specific as possible, so when you review the entire safety plan in the future, you can go down the list and be honest with yourself about how you are doing.

9.19 Writing Prompt

Consider using the space provided to reflect on the following:

What are your warning signs?

_____

_____

_____

_____

_____

_____

_____

_____

_____

_____

9.20 Section 2: My Triggers

This section is an opportunity to review sensations, thoughts, other people, places, and anything else that negatively impacts you. As you continue to learn more about your body and the signals it gives you, the amount of information you can gather from these triggers will be very valuable.

The most useful way to think about the triggers section is to connect the identification of them with coping strategies to minimize their effect on you. As the source of triggers vary between individuals, we include a structure based on category to help you organize your thoughts.

■ **Interpersonal Triggers**

- These may include a specific individual or merely the thought of interacting with them.
- This may be a current dispute or conflict with someone.
- A history of mistrust or betrayed loyalty may be a trigger.
- Interactions such as public speaking, going to a party, or meeting someone new may all be sources of anxiety and stress as well.

■ **Experiential Triggers**

- People, places, or situations associated with prior traumatic experiences may be current triggers.
- Specific dates, anniversaries, and times of the year such as holidays may all impact mood and stress.
- Looming deadlines, financial difficulties, and decisions that must be made as well as uncertainties are all stressors that may be triggering.

■ **External Triggers**

- Some people are sensitive to loud noises or bright lights.
- Specific locations or modes of transportation, especially where the sense of lack of control is predominant, may be triggers, such as being in a crowded area, being outdoors, or being in a car or on a plane or an elevator.
- Activities such as school performance, a presentation at work, or competing in sports may all cause anxiety and stress.
- Exposure to social media, violence on television, dismal news, or weather reports of climate disaster may all elicit fear and stress.

■ **Physical and Health Triggers**

- Sensations such as increased heart rate, sweating, feeling cold or warm, ringing in the ears, and a sore throat may all be associated with prior feelings of unease, anxiety, or panic and may be triggers.

- Having concerns about one's own health-related issues, such as a new condition or chronic illness, are potential sources of apprehension and may be triggering.
- Not getting enough sleep may be an issue.
- Things you eat, including caffeine and alcohol; stimulants; and nicotine may all cause bodily sensations that the mind interprets as threats and may be triggering.
- Fear of getting sick, especially seen during the pandemic, and any mention of lack of access to health-care providers are potential triggers.

9.21 Writing Prompt

Consider using the space provided to reflect on the following:

What are your triggers?

_____

_____

_____

_____

_____

_____

_____

_____

_____

_____

_____

_____

9.22 Section 3: My Coping Strategies

Brainstorming coping strategies during times of calm and ease will allow you to refer back to them during times of anxiety and unease. Think of coping strategies as straightforward actions that can be taken to reduce the effects of panic or extreme sadness. They are meant to ensure continued mental and physical safety and reduce self-injurious thoughts and behaviors.

As these are meant to be personalized, think about what has worked for you in the past, such as self-soothing strategies or coping skills. During a time of crisis, the main goal is to exit the crisis to safety, so action items that serve as distractions towards safety are fine.

Examples of coping strategy domains may include:

■ **Mindfulness Techniques**

- Meditation, yoga, or simply going out for a walk can all help you remove yourself from fight-or-flight mode and begin calming down.
- Grounding techniques, such as the ones reviewed in Chapter 2, 'Identifying and Treating Anxiety,' can help bring your focus back to the present so you may decide on action items to stay safe.
- Affirmations or things you can repeat to yourself during times of stress can be very effective. Think of them as ways of reducing your negative self-talk and increasing confidence. Examples of affirmations include:
  - 'I am worthy of feeling calm.'
  - 'I am resilient.'
  - 'I am safe right now.'

■ **Breathing Techniques**

- Chapter 3, 'Balan 3-2-1 Method,' describes several evidence-based breathing techniques that engage the vagus nerve and help soothe your mind.
- Deep breathing will help decrease your heart rate and begin to unwind the anxiety-that-causes-physical-symptoms-that-trigger-more-anxiety loop.

■ **Movement and Distraction Techniques**

- As mentioned earlier, during a crisis, the main goal is to get to safety. Deeper analysis of why it occurred and the use of long-term life skills should be done later. Think of ways to physically remove yourself from the situation.
- Do you play sports, skateboard, or dance? Think of how you can incorporate physical activities into your distraction strategy.
- Listening to music, looking at photo albums, coloring, or playing your piano can all be things you can do to help yourself.
- Self-soothing activities such as taking a warm bath, sitting on grass, or watching the fireplace or the ocean may all be things you can use to enhance your calmness.

Your coping strategy may include reaching out to trusted friends or loved ones. If you are in treatment, calling your therapist may be a great coping strategy as well. We discuss these in the following sections in detail.

These coping strategies are geared towards increasing a sense of control and allowing your rational brain to think of next steps to get you on your way from crisis to safety. Even the feedback from successfully adhering to coping strategies will further reinforce your ability to care for yourself and provide hope and confidence for the future.

9.23 Writing Prompt

Consider using the space provided to reflect on the following:

What are your coping strategies?

_____

_____

_____

_____

_____

_____

_____

_____

_____

_____

_____

9.24 Section 4: Family, Social, and Professional Contacts

Think about someone you know, someone you respect who you perceive as calm and confidently chill. What are their attributes? What is it about them that allows them to portray themselves as calm and in control of their feelings of anxiety?

This section is used specifically to think about and document the names and contact information of your main social support network. This may include family members, your coach, a teacher, a neighbor, your friends, a romantic partner, your therapist, the school counselor, and other clinicians, as well as religious or spiritual advisors.

When you think of these people, think specifically about what they have demonstrated to you and others that shows their ability to acknowledge their own fears and maintain their own composure under stress. Think about how you might be able to talk with them about how they manage their own stress.

Consider discussing beforehand the reality that you are putting together a safety plan for your feelings of anxiety and stress. Ask them if there is a specific phone number or time that you can call them and let them know that stress might come up at any time of the day, and depending on what your needs are, you want to be able to reach out to them for help. Think about how you would express your feelings of anxiety and the words you can say to this person, especially when you are in time of need.

Learn everything you can from people who are willing to spend time with you – about their experience in life, their wisdom, and their courage. Consider their recommendations, advice, and view of the world. Remember that each of us is in possession of logic, common sense, and the capacity to reason. Learn from others you feel safe around who can make you feel calm just being in their presence so you can evolve your own strengths and relationships.

For this section in the safety plan, think about those individuals who are trustworthy, considerate, and supportive; can help decrease your anxiety; are optimistic and consistent; and can get you to safety, including an emergency room if needed.

If you experience alcohol- or substance-use issues and that is one of your triggers or unhealthy coping mechanisms, consider including someone in this section who is familiar with either treatment options or ways to remove you from a triggering circumstance.

We recommend that you list the people in order of priority: for example, who you would call first in a situation and which professional agency you would connect with for which specific needs.

Towards the end of the book, we also include a comprehensive list of websites and contact information resources for individuals, families, and allies.

9.25 Writing Prompt

Consider using the space provided to reflect on the following:

Who do you feel comfortable sharing your emotions with? Think of members of your family, your friends, and your school or work contacts, and write their names and how they can help you if you need to connect.

_____

_____

_____

_____

_____

_____

_____

_____

_____

_____

9.26 Section 5: Keeping Me Safe

This section continues the exercise of practicing safety behaviors with easy-to-follow actions. These can include:

- Going somewhere safe, calling 911, or going to the nearest emergency department in the event of an emergency.
- Going to a crisis shelter or drug detox unit if those are among the issues you are dealing with.
- If there are firearms or other items with potential for high lethality around you, think about how you can keep safe through environmentally securing them.
- Similarly, consider reducing access to pills, drugs, or medications that may worsen the situation in a time of crisis.

Rehearsing or even role-playing these measures to keep yourself safe may be a great way to practice these behaviors. Documenting them for future reference will further solidify the memory and awareness of the many tools and strengths you have available.

9.27 Writing Prompt

Consider using the space provided to reflect on the following:

What behaviors can you use to keep yourself safe?

_____

_____

_____

_____

_____

_____

_____

_____

_____

_____

9.28 Section 6: Signature Section

Brainstorming, discussing, and then documenting your warning signs, triggers, coping strategies, family and professional contacts, and action items to keep yourself safe are the most important steps in your safety plan. Signing and dating the document serves to memorialize and add accountability to your words.

As you refine and update your plan, sign it again with the current date. Consider discussing your safety plan with a trusted loved one, as well as your therapist. Make them aware of your plans and how they can help you succeed.

We provide space later in the chapter for a safety plan you can remove from the book and keep with you. You can also take a photo of it and refer to it later.

You are now increasingly empowered to care for yourself and know when and how to reach out for help if needed. Congratulations.

9.29 Writing Prompt

Consider using the template provided to reflect on each of the prompts to draft your entire safety plan.

This can be done with a clinician or on your own. Consider sharing with your clinician if you are working with one.

9.30 Safety Plan

My Warning Signs

_____

_____

_____

_____

_____

_____

_____

_____

_____

_____

_____

My Triggers

_____
_____
_____
_____
_____
_____
_____
_____
_____
_____

My Coping Strategies

_____
_____
_____
_____
_____
_____
_____
_____
_____
_____
_____
_____
_____

Family, Social, and Professional Contacts
(Include names and contact phone numbers)

_____

_____

_____

_____

_____

_____

_____

_____

_____

_____

Keeping Me Safe

_____

_____

_____

_____

_____

_____

_____

_____

_____

_____

_____

_____

_____   _____

Signature   **Date**

Chapter 10

Confidently Chill in Our New Normal

10.1 Our Journey Together

Congratulations once again for diving deep into understanding more about yourself and taking these steps on your healing journey.

Throughout this book, we have learned we have the power and freedom to choose how to interpret our reality and re-write our narrative. We have also learned to treat our anxiety with humility and respect. All our emotions are informative and allow us access to our inner minds.

We have explored many subjects relating to anxiety and improving confidence. We set the stage for our current state and introduced the stress diathesis model of anxiety. We defined anxiety, risks and protective factors, the medical diagnostic criteria of multiple conditions, and their impact on day-to-day living. We reviewed grounding skills and culturally sensitive anxiety care, as well as pharmacological treatment options.

We discussed the Balan 3-2-1 Method with an emphasis on setting the conscious stage for self-care and introduced additional breathing techniques proven to help reduce anxiety.

In the context of post-pandemic mental health needs, we discussed the rapid growth in demand for care and provided recommendations for equitable access.

We discussed the mental, physical, personal, and financial benefits of treating anxiety and related disorders and investing in mental health in general. A detailed analysis of the pros and cons of having anxiety was provided in combination with guidelines for preparing to heal, navigating one's environment, and recruiting a support network.

Through writing prompts and exercises, we provided guidance for creative explorations and thoughtful interactive experiences.

How the body responds to and regulates emotions through the lens of the autonomic nervous system and various neurotransmitters was discussed. We provided clinical case examples and relevant exercises to improve physical activity and sleep hygiene. We also included a compilation of external causes of anxiety ranging from one's environment to the food and drink they consume.

DOI: 10.4324/9781003413547-14

We explored the impact of the pandemic on school systems, faculty well-being, and LGBTQIA+ communities, as well as issues that impact having and caring for a newborn.

In the section on social media, we provided a balanced and evidence-based thesis on the risks of social media addiction, the consequences of misuse, and the impact always being online has on identity. We explored cyber bullying and provided useful recommendations and preventative measures for individuals, family systems, schools, and communities to utilize.

Themes of confidence, resilience, humor, and gratitude have been the golden threads that wove throughout this book.

Risk factors that worsen anxiety and protective factors to mitigate symptoms were explored. Safety planning within a framework of community and value systems was discussed. We provided tools for setting the stage for mindfulness, autonomy, and hope.

This brief review of our path so far gets us to this chapter, where we explore our new normal and reinforce self-care, self-advocacy, healthy boundaries, and an empowering sense of self-love.

> **Antifragility is beyond resilience or robustness.**
> **The resilient resists shocks and stays the same; the antifragile gets better.**
>
> —Nassim Nicholas Taleb

10.2 Equitable Access to Mental Health

Striving for equitable access to services is critical in promoting mental health and wellness and reducing the harmful effects of stressors, trauma, anxiety, and depression.

Removing barriers involves being able to identify, diagnose, and treat those in need, regardless of their socioeconomic status, race, gender, ethnicity, or background. As discussed, the best way to reduce the effects of mental illness is by prevention and expanding available options for care.

While the pandemic has changed our lives forever, increased use of telehealth has largely been positive, allowing those in remote areas or with mobility issues to access care from service providers who have the experience and background to meet specific needs. However, there continue to be significant barriers in access to reliable internet service and digital platforms in lower socioeconomic communities, which is why a hybrid model including in-person availability continues to be important.

The buzz around our previous book *Re-Write* (2023) is a clear indication that there has been a conscious shift, and more and more people are beginning to be vocal about their mental health struggles. As there is still room for growth, we need to continue to reduce stigma and raise awareness of mental health.

Throughout the book, we also discussed the importance of culturally competent care and respect for diverse backgrounds, languages, and belief systems. Evidence shows that authentic connection yields better health outcomes.

Continued research and collection of data on the financial and societal impact of anxiety and other stress-related disorders are critical, especially in underserved populations. Collaborative care models such as those discussed in this book improve the availability of early diagnosis and intervention at the primary care level.

Ongoing mental health education in schools and workplaces is important to promote informed consent and educated consumers of the health care system. Availability of care such as guidance counselors, employee-assistance programs, and stigma-reducing programs is invaluable. The earlier we can intervene, the better the outcomes.

10.3 Reducing Disparities

To help identify and manage anxiety, we reviewed the bio-psychosocial models. It is imperative, however, to ensure that we remove disparities in access to care and improve the availability of clinically sound information.

We discussed adverse childhood experiences (ACEs) in great detail in our prior book *Re-Write* (2023) and encourage you to review those sections. It is well known that traumatic experiences early in life lead to decreased coping skills and resilience later.

It is critical to build awareness of the sources of one's anxiety in order to process adverse experiences and take necessary preventative measures. In school and workplace settings, it is critical to prevent bullying and harassment.

In an attempt to create a culture that empowers the individual, we included practical techniques for analyzing values – for oneself and one's family system. Having a clear set of goals and values and a system with which to navigate them allows one to recognize threats and remain resilient.

Many schools claim they have a 'zero violence' policy, and workplaces declare a 'speak up' environment, and we applaud them and implore that they adhere to their policies. Being able to intervene, speak up, and ask for help is critical, and we must do everything in our power to support this.

Having a set of techniques and tools to regulate emotions will help manage stress. Improved mental health and stigma-reduction training will result in better screening outcomes at doctor visits, decrease disparities in care, and increase sensitivity to marginalized groups.

10.4 Writing Prompt

Consider using the space provided to reflect on the following prompt:

On an individual level, what can you do to reduce anxiety and worry?

_____

_____

_____

_____

On a family level, what can you do to reduce anxiety and worry?

_____

_____

_____

_____

_____

_____

_____

_____

_____

On a school or workplace level, what can you do to reduce anxiety and worry?

_____

_____

_____

_____

_____

_____

_____

_____

_____

On a community level, what can you do to reduce anxiety and worry?

_____

_____

_____

_____

_____

_____

_____

_____

_____

_____

The tools provided in this book will empower you and facilitate the ongoing development of your personal strengths. As you recognize these strengths, consider how you can further reinforce them. Similarly, we recommend you identify your weaknesses and areas of growth opportunity and experiment with the coping skills discussed.

Continue to learn how to process your emotions while exploring your patterns and habits so you can protect the ones that work and incorporate healthier strategies in place of ones that don't.

10.5 Writing Prompt

Consider using the space provided to reflect on the following prompt:

How will you reinforce your healthy behaviors?

_____

_____

_____

_____

_____

_____

_____

_____

_____

_____

10.6 Writing Prompt

Within the framework of the Balan 3-2-1 Method, consider your response to the following:

How do you dream your future?

3: With intention, set your internal and external environment.

- ■ The body: What mindfulness techniques are you choosing to allow your body to heal?

_____

_____

_____

- ■ The setting: How are you intentionally influencing your setting?

_____

_____

_____

- ■ The breath: Which breathing technique will you use as you prepare for this exercise?

_____

_____

_____

2: What are your thoughts and feelings in response to the writing prompt?

_____

_____

1: What is your one intent or affirmation in the context of the writing prompt?

10.7 Climate Change and Eco-Anxiety

There is an increasing amount of information and literature regarding the impact climate change has on mental health. In addition to the very real differences experienced in our day-to-day lives, with increased carbon dioxide, radical weather patterns, fires, hurricanes, and flooding, we are also hearing more about it on the news, on social media, and in schools.

The reality is that climate change itself, as well as witnessing disasters, has real mental health impacts that require identification and treatment.

Temperatures are rising globally, and there is evidence that this is caused by humans – our destructive, careless, reckless, and short-term capitalistic mindsets. We are past the point of naivete and ignorance as corporations are aware of their carbon footprints and have levers they can pull to reduce their burden.

Along the spectrum of anxieties, we have discussed the myriad of treatment options available, from talk-based therapeutics to exercise and diet to medication options. The cognitive aspect of handling anxiety involves recognizing triggers and discovering practices for symptomatic relief.

In some circumstances, we may not be able to make any changes to the anxiogenic stimuli and may have to remove ourselves from the situation. Some things that destabilize us and increase our anxiety are in our control, such as food and diet options and alcohol and drug use. However, climate change, for instance, is not something that is in our control, and this knowledge and incorporating ways to manage our emotions in practical way are critical.

It is important that the information provided to children about climate change is age appropriate. Exposing children to scientific knowledge they can understand and are developmentally able to fit within their framework of the world will empower them rather than scaring them.

Prematurely introducing information with messaging instilling apocalyptic fear of the end of the world because of increased temperatures to a kindergartener is counterproductive to their mental health.

A very young child has minimal control of their own autonomy, let alone other people's behaviors or the environment. Their day-to-day lives – when they eat and sleep, what they wear, what activities they participate in, where they live – are all dictated by the adults in their lives.

Adults are responsible for teaching their children bodily autonomy, such as recognizing when they need to go to the bathroom and when they are hungry and how to manage their body temperature. The temperature of their thermostat-controlled homes isn't even subject to the young child's initiative, let alone the temperature of the planet.

Similar to the fears and anxieties adults have exposed children to at school regarding COVID, which we discussed previously, we recommend that responsible adults and schools provide age-appropriate information regarding doom-and-gloom scenarios that are likely very real but of no use to a young child.

Actionable information, with real-world options to exert some control – whether real or imaginary/inconsequential – is important to provide.

When can a child learn how to actively influence their environment by doing things such as:

- Cleaning up trash?
- Recycling appropriately?
- Gardening sustainably?
- Being good stewards of the water systems?
- Shopping locally and supporting farmers and sustainable practices?

Each of these examples entails achievable goals that may actually have an impact on the world and climate change and, more importantly, make the child feel they are doing what is scientifically and morally ethical for our planet. It is, however, a shame when children and other vulnerable populations are injected with fear and terror, without any opportunity for empowerment.

The studies, including a brilliant article by Léger-Goodes et al. (2022), describe the emotions connected with climate change, including:

- Anger

  - Studies discuss how learning about corporation-related pollution resulting in increased carbon emissions and the possible lack of or inadequate responses by governmental regulators results in feelings of frustration and anger.

- Anxiety, fear, distress, and depression

  - Becoming informed of climate change at premature, age-inappropriate times can lead to anxiety.

■ Despair

  – Chronic fear of environmental disasters and one's imminent demise can instill despair in individuals, especially the more vulnerable.

■ Existential questioning

  – The fear of the inevitability of death is described in an article by Guthrie (2023), in the context of needing to appreciate the catastrophic yet rational fear that is eco-anxiety. The author reframes eco-anxiety as a death anxiety and illustrates examples of healing through acceptance and commitment therapy, grief, and focus on end-of-life care.

■ Feeling powerless

  – Disempowerment can occur when exposed to age-inappropriate information.

■ Grief

  – The grief described by individuals is for themselves, their loved ones, and the planet.
  – The term 'eco-grief' has been used in literature discussing this phenomenon.

■ Guilt

  – Internalizing the potential causes of climate change may instill feelings of causation by self, resulting in guilt.

■ Hopelessness

  – This may lead to the feeling that things may not be worth doing anymore and that one can have no real impact on the environment.

■ Learned helplessness

  – This may lead to apathy.
  – The term 'eco-paralysis' has been used to describe the inability to perform or provide pro-environmental, adaptive solutions

■ Feeling overwhelmed

  – 'Activism fatigue' is another term used in the literature for the feeling of being overwhelmed with information, media messages, and the desire to help.

■ Panic

  – An acute sense of overwhelming anxiety that they and their loved ones will imminently perish due to rising temperatures.

- ▪ Sadness and pessimism

  - – Crying
  - – Sleep disturbances, including nightmares

- ▪ Sense of doom and gloom

  - – Resulting in decreased attention and ability to focus, general sadness, and decrease in life satisfaction.

- ▪ Substance use

  - – Coping mechanisms, including denial, are less than constructive and may lead to worsening mental health outcomes.

- ▪ Stress and worry

  - – Thinking that one has minimal to no ability to impact the issues can lead to feelings of worry and anxiety.

Eco-anxiety is a real term in the literature that describes anxieties about climate change and the accompanying existential angst. What we find objectionable is the fear instilled in those who have no say in the matter. Captive audiences at schools, for example, have nowhere to go, are expected to appease the teachers/administrators, and have no option other than to go along with the authoritative narrative.

Studies that survey school-aged children show that inappropriate and premature exposure results in students' feeling a constant sense of doom, as if the world will end before they grow to be adults! As in any situation, the individual has the (subconscious) option to face the fears head on, express the worry, and try to get better or to push the feelings down and deny there is any problem.

As clinicians, we see that suppressing emotions regarding climate change manifests unhealthily in adults, as well as in those who may or may not even understand climate science. When fear and anxiety peak, a defense mechanism, albeit maladaptive, is to avoid intense thoughts such as imminent death due to climate crisis. This often is a learned/modeled behavior in families and social circles, resulting in increased misinformation and unhelpful messaging.

According to studies, eco-anxiety is more common than initially thought, with a majority of those describing their eco-anxiety as causing significant distress in their day-to-day lives. As mental health demand increases, people are finding it increasingly difficult to connect with a clinician, let alone one with expertise in treating climate change–related existential anxieties.

If, on the other hand, the journey of understanding the bond humans have with earth and our connections with wildlife is taught in a naturalistic way, inspired with vision and hope, children will be more constructively sensitive to the messages of climate change.

Top-down messaging is minimally helpful and, according to the studies, appears to do more (mental health) harm than (real-world) good.

An article by Liu et al. (2022) discusses the importance of tailored public information campaigns to educate and shift attitudes relating to climate change and the risk it poses.

The suggested targeted information should be developed based on the specific needs and vulnerabilities of the groups. The value of such an approach would be to appropriately influence attitudes regarding perception of risk while ensuring the audience receiving the message has actionable resources available to make necessary changes.

We have discussed the relationship between anxiety and hope in other parts of the book as well, and it is valuable to see that not all anxiety in the setting of the environment is negative. When hope is instilled, creative solutions can emerge. Personal implications can be assessed, and personal corrective measures can be taken. Similarly, communal and societal implications can be studied, and appropriate pro-environmental measures can be taken. Healthy mentors and learning communities have the ability to empower the individual and move towards change.

10.8 Writing Prompt

Consider using the space provided to reflect on the following prompt:

What have you done for yourself today?

_____

_____

_____

_____

_____

_____

_____

_____

What have you done for your family today?

_____

_____

_____

_____

_____

_____

_____

_____

_____

What have you done for your community today?

_____

_____

_____

_____

_____

_____

_____

_____

_____

What have you done for the planet today?

_____

_____

_____

_____

_____

_____

_____

_____

_____

Anxiety is the dizziness of freedom.

—Soren Kierkegaard

10.9 Final Thoughts

You are amazing for having made it this far – you are certainly ahead of the curve!
Here are a few final thoughts to consider as you progress on your healing journey:

■ You possess common sense, intelligence, logic, and the capacity for rational thinking.
■ Continue to learn, study, be curious, engage, and question.

   – Read long-form, actual physical books.
   – Play.
   – Move.
   – Laugh.
   – Go to bed on time.

■ Acquire knowledge from others with relevant experience and expertise, but do not outsource your common sense.

   – Learn to spot blatant contradictions and reason logically.
   – Notice when things don't add up.
   – Keep asking questions.
   – Always inquire, 'Who benefits?'
   – You have the right to ask, 'Why are we doing this?' at any time. If someone cannot produce an answer that you believe, don't do it.
   – Form your own perspectives.

■ As you understand the 'why' . . .

   – You will not be as afraid.
   – You will see why things may appear threatening or why some forces may wish to keep you in fear.
   – You will not be as confused.
   – You will be less anxious and depressed.
   – You will see the reasons and causality and be able to acknowledge stressors and decide how you will react.
   – You will develop the courage to stand up for yourself.

■ Model these behaviors at home.

   – If you are a parent or caregiver, it's never too early to start. Even before kindergarten, children's inquisitive and perceptive nature will allow them to pick up on your cues and mimic emotion regulation.
   – Also remember it's never too late to begin healing and incorporating healthy coping mechanisms.

- Develop and document your values for yourself and your family. Refer back to them during times of stress.

■ Create spaces free from extreme judgment.
■ Empower rational discussions and debates.
■ There are no quick solutions:

  - To love
  - To learning
  - To wisdom
  - To health
  - To experience

■ Think of how you can move . . .

  - From feeling the threat of being cancelled to having the space for open communication.
  - From constantly filtering what you say to open discussions.
  - From mind-numbing social media to mindful inquiry and in-person connection.
  - From stopping thoughts to allowing ideas to take their evolutionary course.
  - From toxic anxiety to creative, expressive positive energy.
  - From social conformity to social inclusion.
  - From fear- and threat-based mandates to informed consent, true bodily autonomy, and choice.
  - From allowing inappropriate exposure to social and digital media to becoming digitally literate parents and teachers.
  - From digital babysitting to caring for children without resorting to addictive garbage.
  - From chemical substitutes to natural remedies.
  - From waiting for someone to save you to learning to be autonomous and self-sufficient.
  - From waiting for someone to tell you how to live your life to reading and learning about your options and choosing a like-minded community where everyone can live their best lives.
  - From social distancing and mistrusting people to learning how to calculate risk through education and trust.
  - From unbalanced diets of fast food, video games, social media, and mass media propaganda to healthy eating, exercise, and increased time in nature.
  - From isolation to building friendships and meaningful connections.
  - From online presence to face-to-face interactions.
  - From feeling powerless to contributing to your community and neighborhoods, even if only in small ways.
  - From repetitive, uninspiring work to a dignified, productive, energizing presence.
  - From being stuck on a hamster wheel to living an active, fulfilling, creative life.

Remember, no matter how hard the winds may be blowing in a certain direction, your future is not set in stone. Small pushes can steer large courses.

The universe acts, but it also listens.

Appendix: Websites and Phone Numbers

If you or someone you know is having a psychiatric emergency, including suicidal thoughts, in the United States, dial 911 and or go to the nearest emergency room.

Helplines, Hotlines, and Websites

United States

1-800-Children

A parenting helpline for local resources and support such as housing, food, employment, childcare, health, education, safety, and legal.

- kcsl.findhelp.com
- (800) 244-5373

All Options National Talk Line

- all-options.org
- (888) 493-0092

Alzheimer's Association Helpline

- alz.org
- (800) 272-3900

Amala Muslim Youth Helpline

- amala.mas-ssf.org
- Text: 85595

American Cancer Society

- cancer.org
- (800) 227-2345

American Psychological Association

- APA.org/topics/trauma

American Psychiatric Association

- Psychiatry.org

Anxiety and Depression Association of America

- adaa.org/understanding-anxiety/posttraumatic-stress-disorder-ptsd/resources

Caregiver Action Network

- caregiveraction.org
- (855) 227-3640

Crisis Text Line

- Text CHAT to 741741

The Deaf Hotline

- thedeafhotline.org
- (206) 812-1001

Disaster Distress Helpline

- samhsa.gov
- Call and text: (800) 985-5990

Exhale Pro-Voice

Emotional support, information, and resources for all people who have had abortions. Also available to the people who want to better support them, including partners, family, and care providers.

- exhaleprovoice.org
- Call or text: (617) 749-2948

Federal Emergency Management Agency (FEMA)

■ FEMA.gov

Games and Online Harassment Hotline

■ gameshotline.org
■ Text SUPPORT to 23368 to get connected.

Healthy Children

This is a link on the American Academy of Pediatrics' parenting website, also available in Spanish, which walks families through a media use plan based on age and specific goals for the individual.

■ Healthychildren.org/mediauseplan

Hey Sam

Peer-to-peer texting service for people up to 24 years old.

■ samaritanshope.org
■ Text: 439726

International Association for Suicide Prevention

■ iasp.info

LGBT National Youth Talk Line

■ lgbthotline.org/youth-talkline
■ (800) 246-7743

LGBT National Coming-Out Support

■ lgbtcomingout.org
■ (888) 688-5428

Love Is Respect

■ loveisrespect.org
■ (866) 331-9474
■ Text: LOVEIS to 22522

National Abortion Hotline

- prochoice.org
- (800) 772-9100

Mothers Against Drunk Driving (MADD)

- madd.org
- (877) MADD-HELP
- (877) 623-3435

Military Helpline

- militaryhelpline.org
- (888) 457-4838
- Text: 839863

National Alliance on Mental Illness

- NAMI.org
- (800) 950-NAMI
- (800) 950-6264
- Text: 62640

National Center for Missing and Exploited Children 24-Hour Hotline

- missingkids.org
- (800) 843-5678

National Center for PTSD

- ptsd.va.gov

National Child Abuse Hotline

- childhelphotline.org
- (800) 4-A-CHILD
- Call or Text: (800) 422-4453

National Child Traumatic Stress Network (NCTSN)

- Nctsnet.org

National Domestic Violence Hotline

- thehotline.org
- (800) 799-SAFE

- (800) 799-7233
- Text: 22522

National Eating Disorders Association

- Nationaleatingdisorders.org

National Grad Crisis Line

- gradresources.org
- (877) 472-3457

National Human Trafficking Hotline

- humantraffickinghotline.org
- (888) 373-7888
- Text: 233733

National Maternal Mental Health Hotline

- mchb.hrsa.gov
- Call or Text: (833) 943-5746

National Parent Helpline

- nationalparenthelpline.org
- (855) 4-A-PARENT
- (855) 427-2736

National Problem Gambling Helpline

- Ncpgambling.org
- Call or Text: (800) 522-4700

National Sexual Assault Hotline

- rainn.org
- (800) 656-HOPE
- (800) 656-4673

National Suicide Prevention Lifeline:

- 988
- (800) 273-TALK
- (800) 273-8255

Physician Support Line

- physiciansupportline.com
- (888) 409-0141

Postpartum Support International

- postpartum.net
- Call or text: (800) 944-4773

Psych Central

- Psychcentral.com

Psychology Today

- Psychologytoday.com

PTSD Foundation of America

- ptsdusa.org
- (877) 717-7873

RAINN: Rape, Abuse, and Incest National Network

- Rainn.org

Su Familia

Spanish and bilingual support

- healthyamericas.org
- (866) 783-2645

Substance Abuse and Mental Health Services Administration

- samhsa.gov
- (800) 487-4889
- Text: 435748

STOMP Out Bullying

- stompoutbullying.org

Stop It Now!

Support and information for victims of abuse, domestic violence, and sexual abuse of children.

- stopitnow.org
- (888) 773-8368

StrongHearts Native Helpline

Culturally appropriate domestic and sexual violence helpline.

- Strongheartshelpline.org
- (844) 762-8483

Teen Line

- teenline.org
- (800) 852-8336
- Text: 839863

Trans Lifeline

Available in the US and Canada.

- translifeline.org
- (877) 565-8860

Trauma Survivors Network

- Traumasurvivorsnetwork.org

Trevor Lifeline

- thetrevorproject.org
- (866) 488-7386
- Text: 678678

TXT 4 HELP

- nationalsafeplace.org
- Text: 44357

Canada

Canadian Mental Health Association

- cmha.ca
- (833) 456-4566

Kids' Help Phone

- kidshelpphone.ca

Talk Suicide Canada

- talksuicide.ca
- (833) 456-4566

United Kingdom

Campaign Against Living Miserably

- thecalmzone.net
- 0800 58 58 58

Lifeline

- lifelinehelpline.info
- 0808 808 8000

National Suicide Prevention Helpline UK

- spuk.org.uk/bristol-projects/suicide-prevention-bristol
- 0800 689 5652

Papyrus Prevention of Young Suicide

Papyrus-uk.org
0800 068 4141
Text: 07860039967

PTSD UK

- ptsduk.org

Shout

- giveusashout.org
- Text: 85258

SOS Silence of Suicide

- sossilenceofsuicide.org
- 0300 1020 505

Australia

Beyond Blue

Information and support regarding anxiety, depression, and suicide.

- 1 300 22 4636

Kids' Helpline

- 1 800 55 1800

Phoenix Australia

- phoenixaustralia.org

Please use the space provided to write your own resources and contact information you find useful for your situation and country.

_____

_____

_____

_____

_____

_____

_____

_____

Appendix: But Wait, There's More!

Dearest reader! You've made it this far in your journey of exploring the depths of anxiety and healing. Congratulations on your tenacity – clearly, you are a person who is motivated and well on your way to your goals.

As we were conceptualizing *Confidently Chill*, we were in discussion with our colleague Kristine Mednansky at Taylor & Francis, who suggested we also connect with our readers through another medium: the graphic novel!

First Ever

> Our dreams make us large.
>
> —Jack Kirby

Duygu initially had the story in mind for an upcoming novel, and through collaborating with Yener and Nadir, we decided to use the strengths of the comic book medium.

This heralded the first medical textbook that is accompanied by a fully illustrated visual exploration of an emotional, psychological journey. And that is how *Kader's Quest* became a reality.

Unique Combination

Both *Confidently Chill* and *Kader's Quest* have been thoughtfully produced and published together, simultaneously, as companion pieces.

We strongly recommend that you see them as relating to one another – one feeds into the other.

Although they stand alone in their messaging, content, and usefulness, they augment one other. The two books and the two different mediums help each other, complement each another, and work in tandem in the same way that certain coping and healing mechanisms work with each another.

Greater Than Their Parts

> Everybody is special. Everybody. Everybody is a hero, a lover, a fool, a villain. Everybody. Everybody has their story to tell.
>
> —Alan Moore

The two works in combination add more value than they do individually as the written words as literature and the drawn images speak to different parts of your brain. The symbiosis of these mediums help you understand and appreciate at a higher level than simply reading written words alone.

The reason we put these together in this way is that one speaks to your visual brain, threading the emotional impact with light, shadow, and archetypal symbols. The written messaging and creative expressive writing prompts in the textbook feed into the themes of the graphic novel, and, experienced together, they become greater than their individual parts. This is what an artist always hopes for in whatever their chosen medium, and we look forward to hearing from you about your experience reading them.

Our effort has been to maximize the effect of the medium being used, so if the book or the graphic novel were to be adapted into an animation or a live-action movie, it would have to be reinterpreted. Our books are specially tailored to speak to you in the medium they are intended to be viewed through.

Visual Exploration

> The glass is always completely full – half air and half liquid.
>
> —Mark Millar

The visual exploration of the psychological journey *Kader's Quest* transcends the conventional boundaries of storytelling through the distinctive medium of illustrations that forge a profound connection with the reader.

You can spend time with a printed set of images and review the interplay and harmony of the represented depictions and pacing as you delve into the intricacies of the human emotions of our hero. Each frame, each panel, each page has been meticulously crafted by Nadir to serve as a visual landscape with intentional pacing that reflects the multifaceted elements of the psyches of the characters. This allows for a different level of connection with the reader as the artwork speaks to the conscious and the subconscious.

What may have been apparent early on may become obfuscated later, and there similarly may be answers revealed to questions alluded to at the onset of the story.

Empathic Connections

> No one has a perfect life. Everybody has something that he wishes was not the way it is.
>
> —Stan Lee

The graphic novel is a visual exploration of how an individual's experiences that might be easily overlooked from the outside – for example, something as banal or typical as a kid with family issues – can be connected to empathically. Through attention to critical moments in the story and purposeful manipulation of the visual rhythm, the artwork can bring to light internal experiences that may have been invisible.

Everybody is living their own journey; everyone is experiencing stresses and traumas that are life altering and yet typical to the human condition. We all have had or will have experiences or traumas that will alter us forever. From the outside, it may be easy to overlook such a common occurrence in humanity. No one has an easy ride; no one has a simple journey. Everyone is going through huge ups and downs that are not obvious from the outside. They are only obvious when we are going through them ourselves.

Consider, for example, a death in the family. When someone you love dies, you experience insurmountable grief. From the outside, from a zoomed-out, societal perspective, however, this is incredibly ordinary. Through our work in the graphic novel, in combination with the textbook, we are taking something that is incredibly easy to overlook and bringing you the individual's experience, so you can now experience it through their mind's eye. You can understand how your personal experiences map with those of the human family at large.

Therein lies the idea – the point is to take something that appears simple from the outside and show what the hero and what the reader are going through. That is why we chose to explore difficult concepts in a visual manner.

Healing Relationships

> Read comics. All comics. And then cut them open to steal their power.
> —Warren Ellis

Another way the textbook and the graphic novel intertwine and synergistically add value for the reader is that they explore issues that people may need help, solutions, and guidance with. The illustrated story discusses different ways that someone might come to points in their life where they might need guidance or help if they are unable to find it naturally. Everyone copes and heals in different ways; some people are more fortunate than others.

Friendship as a substitute for family to help cope with trauma is a main theme in the graphic novel. The protagonist comes to terms with and deals with his family dynamics as he finds acceptance and friendship outside his family. This is an example of several of the topics that are woven across and can be cross-referenced in the textbook.

The concept of the mentor as being the person in the right place at the right time is explored in the context of a central character who allows himself to be helped. The mentor is a totem in a location that becomes a symbol for the hero who only has the power that he has because the hero allows it. When we are open to the experience of being mentored, to being helped – it must come from within, not from without – we can experience their guidance, wisdom, and help. If you are not ready or available to explore, it is so easy to overlook or dismiss an available mentor in your life.

Our protagonist is in such an environment and mind space that he needs help. Through the inspiration he finds from the friends he makes in theater club, the hero becomes receptive to having a mentor. He is the adult figure who is there; it is important that he is there, but he's not the deus ex machina saving the day. Our hero learns to accept and utilize his environment and supporting characters to ultimately save himself – a lesson we should heed as we work to save ourselves.

So Many Choices

The visual representation of the choices that we make and the end results are spread throughout. Sometimes we must go up or down. Must we die, survive, or enter our own selves to get through what we are dealing with? Do we have to keep going up and up? Is salvation internal or external? Are the decisions we make good or bad? Do we have to go down and die before rebirth? Try not to deny yourself the possibility of those decisions.

In the graphic novel, up and down are directionally represented as movement; neither is good nor bad. Through elements such as height, ladders, and stairs, we explore what our options are as dimension becomes increasingly important in different ways. Shadow, rain, the way lines are used, and the quality of the lines are all intentional and important.

Think about how much information is incorporated into any given image. How much time are you asked to spend on each panel? Determined by how much detail is put in, the composition is also going to be important. Will you need to jump from one panel to another quickly to understand what is happening? Or will you need to spend time on a specific panel or page to appreciate another? Each page is consciously used as a new sentence, a concept that adds to the journey.

Your Path

> Sometimes, all it takes is a few words to change your life.
>
> —Scott Snyder

At any moment, you may begin a life-altering journey that you have no control over or even a concept of readiness for. This is literally life. That is how it begins; then you are thrust into the journey that you didn't choose, but you must find ways through to the other end. You're either going to come out better or worse. All your experiences along the way are what determine that: the decisions you've made on your path so far and the choices that lie ahead.

The graphic novel explores emotional growth, maturity, happiness, depression, and shock. The illustrations use light and dark to work with the reader to interpret the environment. What might not seem interesting at one moment becomes a focal point, similar to the way we experience real life. How our world can change on a dime with a tiny bit of new information on the page mirrors exactly what happens in our world. It is what always happens – it is always a tiny bit of information that changes our world.

As varying amounts of time pass from panel to panel, we also explore the masks we wear. Our bodies change physically, and we literally become different people from moment to moment. Different aspects of our personality become who we are. There are also aspects of ourselves that we don't know. We don't know how we might react; we have no way to prepare for some things. The story, as in life, reveals that it is more about discovering who we are than about preparing for an event.

Becoming whole and having an appreciation of your boundaries and limitations involve the ability to use the information you have discovered to become better, to cope, to deal. We can almost never anticipate something to such an extent that we can change ourselves before the event. We must have strategies to understand and accept ourselves and work with what we have to become the most capable version of ourselves.

The End?

You clearly aren't at the beginning of your path, and a new journey might start tomorrow. You might even be in the middle of four journeys right now!

We don't need to convince you or sell you on any solutions. You already are the type of reader who knows what they want, and it is up to you to continue to find where you fit in the journey of your life and where in the story you currently are.

You have the power – the power was in you all along! There is no magic bullet; there isn't a prescription or a cure-all – it is through exploring yourself and understanding yourself that you can best help yourself.

The impetus behind our writing, the artifacts we create, our illustrations, and our musings is to impart the reality that you don't need to be looking for someone to help you. You must know what works best for you. Ultimately, we are all individually, separately working with our own histories and our own interpretations. No two stories are going to be alike, and no two solutions will be equally effective.

Don't listen to authority figures who may tell you otherwise. Learn to self-heal. Learn to listen to yourself. Listen to your body. Use the tools that are available that you have made an effort to learn. By getting to the end of this book, you are above and beyond the vast majority of people on earth. You are obviously above average in emotional intelligence, and we commend you for how your mind works. You clearly have an enormous amount of ability to self-explore and are open to new and different ideas. You know what's going on. Please continue to explore, question, and accept what you learn about yourself as you go through this journey.

Be well, be safe, and enjoy!

—**Duygu, Yener, and Nadir**
January 2024

Bibliography

Abramowitz J. *Getting Over OCD – 10 Step Workbook for Taking Back Your Life*. New York: The Guilford Press, 2018.

Agård AS, Lomborg K. Flexible family visitation in the intensive care unit: Nurses' decision-making. *Journal Clinical Nursing*. 2011;20(7–8):1106–1114.

Akbari M, Seydavi M, Palmieri S, Mansueto G, Caselli G, Spada MM. Fear of missing out (FoMO) and internet use: A comprehensive systematic review and meta-analysis. *Journal Behavioral Addictions*. 2021;10(4):879–900.

Akhther N, Sopory P. Seeking and sharing mental health information on social media during COVID-19: Role of depression and anxiety, peer support, and health benefits. *Journal Technol Behavioral Science*. 2022;7(2):211–226.

Aldao A, Nolen-Hoeksema S, Schweizer S. Emotion-regulation strategies across psychopathology: A meta-analytic review. *Clinical Psychology Review*. 2010;30(2):217–237.

Al Kazhali M, Shahwan M, Hassan N, Jairoun AA. Social media use is linked to poor sleep quality: The opportunities and challenges to support evidence-informed policymaking in the UAE. *Journal of Public Health (Oxford)*. 2021:fdab372.

American Psychological Association. Fear. In *APA Dictionary of Psychology* (2nd edition). Washington, DC: American Psychological Association, 2015.

Andreassen CS. Online social network site addiction: A comprehensive review. *Current Addiction Reports*. 2015;2:175–184. https://doi.org/10.1007/s40429-015-0056-9

Arzamani N, Soraya S, Hadi F, Nooraeen S, Saeidi M. The COVID-19 pandemic and mental health in pregnant women: A review article. *Frontiers Psychiatry*. 2022;13:949239.

Awao S, Park CL, Russell BS, Fendrich M. Social media use early in the pandemic predicted later social well-being and mental health in a national online sample of adults in the United States. *Behavioral Medicine*. 2022:1–10.

Azhari A, Toms Z, Pavlopoulou G, Esposito G, Dimitriou D. Social media use in female adolescents: Associations with anxiety, loneliness, and sleep disturbances. *Acta Psychologica*. 2022;229:103706.

Balcombe L, De Leo D. The impact of YouTube on loneliness and mental health. *Informatics*. 2023;10(2):39.

Barlow DH. *Anxiety and Its Disorders: The Nature and Treatment of Anxiety and Panic* (2nd edition). New York: The Guilford Press, 2004.

Bartholomew RE, Wessely S, Rubin GJ. Mass psychogenic illness and the social network: Is it changing the pattern of outbreaks? *Journal of the Royal Society of Medicine*. 2012;105(12):509–512.

Bell IH, Nicholas J, Alvarez-Jimenez M, Thompson A, Valmaggia L. Virtual reality as a clinical tool in mental health research and practice. *Dialogues in Clinical Neuroscience*. 2020;22(2):169–177.

Bentley TGK, Seeber C, Hightower E, Mackenzie B, Wilson R, Velazquez A, Cheng A, Arce NN, Lorenz KA. Slow-breathing curriculum for stress reduction in high school students: Lessons learned from a feasibility pilot. *Frontiers in Rehabilitation Sciences*. 2022;3:864079.

Bian C, Zhao WW, Yan SR, Chen SY, Cheng Y, Zhang YH. Effect of interpersonal psychotherapy on social functioning, overall functioning and negative emotions for depression: A meta-analysis. *Journal Affective Disorders*. 2022;320:230–240.

Billieux J, Maurage P, Lopez-Fernandez O, Kuss D, Griffiths M. Can disordered mobile phone use be considered a behavioral addiction? An update on current evidence and a comprehensive model for future research. *Current Addiction Reports*. 2015;2:156–162.

Bilodeau-Houle A, Morand-Beaulieu S, Bouchard V, Marin MF. Parent-child physiological concordance predicts stronger observational fear learning in children with a less secure relationship with their parent. *Journal of Experimental Child Psychology*. 2022;226:105553.

Bozzola E, Spina G, Agostiniani R, Barni S, Russo R, Scarpato E, Di Mauro A, Di Stefano AV, Caruso C, Corsello G, Staiano A. The use of social media in children and adolescents: Scoping review on the potential risks. *International Journal of Environmental Research and Public Health*. 2022;19(16):9960.

Braghieri L, Levy R, Makarin A. Social media and mental health. *American Economic Review*. 2022;112(11):3660–3693.

Breuning L. *Tame Your Anxiety: Rewiring Your Brain for Happiness*. Rowman and Littlefield, 2019.

Bridge JA, Ruch DA, Sheftall AH, Hahm HC, O'Keefe VM, Fontanella CA, Brock G, Campo JV, Horowitz LM. Youth suicide during the first year of the COVID-19 pandemic. *Pediatrics*. 2023;151(3):e2022058375.

Brooks HL, Rushton K, Lovell K, Bee P, Walker L, Grant L, Rogers A. The power of support from companion animals for people living with mental health problems: A systematic review and narrative synthesis of the evidence. *BMC Psychiatry*. 2018;18:31.

Callender R, Canales JM, Avendano C, Craft E, Ensor KB, Miranda ML. Economic and mental health impacts of multiple adverse events: Hurricane Harvey, other flooding events, and the COVID-19 pandemic. *Environmental Research*. 2022;214(Pt 3):114020.

Cameron EE, Joyce KM, Delaquis CP, Reynolds K, Protudjer JLP, Roos LE. Maternal psychological distress & mental health service use during the COVID-19 pandemic. *Journal of Affective Disorders*. 2020;276:765–774.

Campbell J. *The Hero with a Thousand Faces*. Novato, CA: New World Library, 2008.

Caner N, Efe YS, Başdaş Ö. The contribution of social media addiction to adolescent life: Social appearance anxiety. *Current Psychology*. 2022:1–10.

Carrol JM, Maughan B, Goodman R, Meltzer H. Literacy difficulties and psychiatric disorders: Evidence for comorbidity. *Journal of Child Psychology and Psychiatry*. 2005;46:524–532.

Celik D, Alpay EH, Celebi B, Turkali A. Intolerance of uncertainty, rumination, post-traumatic stress symptoms and aggression during COVID-19: A serial mediation model. *European Journal Psychotraumatology*. 2021;12(1):1953790.

Chassiakos YR, Radesky J, Christakis D, Moreno MA, Cross C. Children and adolescents and digital media. *Pediatrics*. 2016;138(5):e20162593.

Chevalier G. The effect of grounding the human body on mood. *Psychological Reports*. 2015;116(2):534–542.

Chiu M, Gatov E, Fung K, Kurdyak P, Guttmann A. Deconstructing the rise in mental health-related ED visits among children and youth in Ontario, Canada. *Health Affairs (Millwood)*. 2020;39(10):1728–1736.

Cho IK, Ahmed O, Lee D, Cho E, Chung S, Günlü A. Intolerance of uncertainty mediates the influence of viral anxiety on social distancing phobia among the general Korean population during the coronavirus disease 2019 pandemic. *Psychiatry Investigation*. 2022;19(9):712–721.

Chung S, Ahn M, Lee S, Kang S, Suh A, Shin Y. The stress and anxiety to viral epidemics-6 items (SAVE-6) scale: A new instrument for assessing the anxiety response of general population to the viral epidemic during the COVID-19 pandemic. *Frontiers in Psychology*. 2021;12:705805.

Clark D, Beck A. *Anxiety and Worry Workbook*. New York: The Guildford Press, 2012.

Coplan JD, Hodulik S, Mathew SJ, Mao X, Hof PR, Gorman JM, Shungu DC. The relationship between intelligence and anxiety: An association with subcortical white matter metabolism. *Frontiers in Evolutionary Neuroscience*. 2012;3:8.

Czeisler MÉ, Lane RI, Petrosky E, Wiley J, Christensen A, Njai R, Weaver M, Robbins R, Facer-Childs E, Barger L, Czeisler C, Howard M, Rajaratnam S. Mental health, substance use, and suicidal ideation during the COVID-19 pandemic—United States, June 24–30, 2020. *MMWR Morbidity Mortality Weekly Report*. 2020;69:1049–1057.

Daimer S, Mihatsch LL, Neufeld SAS, Murray GK, Knolle F. Investigating the relationship of COVID-19 related stress and media consumption with sociotype, depression, and anxiety in cross-sectional surveys repeated throughout the pandemic in Germany and the UK. *Elife.* 2022;11:e75893.

Dalpati N, Jena S, Jain S, Sarangi PP. Yoga and meditation, an essential tool to alleviate stress and enhance immunity to emerging infections: A perspective on the effect of COVID-19 pandemic on students. *Brain, Behavior, & Immunity—Health.* 2022;20:100420.

Dubey H, Sharma RK, Krishnan S, Knickmeyer R. SARS-CoV-2 (COVID-19) as a possible risk factor for neurodevelopmental disorders. *Frontiers Neuroscience.* 2022;16:1021721.

Edmonds M, Hadjistavropoulos HD, Schneider LH, Dear BF, Titov N. Who benefits most from therapist-assisted internet-delivered cognitive behaviour therapy in clinical practice? Predictors of symptom change and dropout. *Journal of Anxiety Disorders.* 2018;54:24–32.

Elbarazi I, Saddik B, Grivna M, Aziz F, Elsori D, Stip E, Bendak E. The impact of the COVID-19 "infodemic" on well-being: A cross-sectional study. *Journal Multidisciplinary Healthcare.* 2022;15:289–307.

Elhai JD, Hall BJ, Erwin MC. Emotion regulation's relationships with depression, anxiety and stress due to imagined smartphone and social media loss. *Psychiatry Research.* 2018;261:28–34.

Elharake JA, Akbar F, Malik AA, Gilliam W, Omer SB. Mental health impact of COVID-19 among children and college students: A systematic review. *Child Psychiatry Human Development.* 2022:1–13.

Espelage DL, Van Ryzin MJ, Holt MK. Trajectories of bully perpetration across early adolescence: Static risk factors, dynamic covariates, and longitudinal outcomes. *Psychology of Violence.* 2018;8:141–150.

Espinoza G. Personal and witnessed cyber victimization experiences among adolescents at the beginning of the COVID-19 pandemic. *Journal of Child & Adolescent Trauma.* 2022:1–8.

Fani N, Tone EB, Phifer J, Norrholm SD, Bradley B, Ressler KJ, Kamkwalala A, Jovanovic T. Attention bias toward threat is associated with exaggerated fear expression and impaired extinction in PTSD. *Psychological Medicine.* 2012;42:533–543.

Farooqui SI, Khan AA, Rizvi J, Hassan B, Adnan QU. Impact on mental health of families during Covid-19: A cross-sectional survey. *Ethiopian Journal of Health Sciences.* 2021;31(6):1125–1132.

Favotto L, Michaelson V, Pickett W, Davison C. The role of family and computer-mediated communication in adolescent loneliness. *PLoS One.* 2019;14(6):e0214617.

Fekih-Romdhane F, Away R, Jahrami H, Cheour M. Internet addiction is associated with psychological distress in highly schizotypal students. *Early Intervention in Psychiatry.* 2023;17(7):681–691.

Forbes MK, Fitzpatrick S, Magson NR, Rapee RM. Depression, anxiety and peer victimization: Bidirectional relationships and associated outcomes transitioning from childhood to adolescence. *Journal of Youth and Adolescence.* 2019;48:692–702.

Forsyth JP, Eifert G. *The Mindfulness & Acceptance Workbook for Anxiety: A Guide to Breaking Free from Anxiety, Phobia & Worry Using Acceptance & Commitment Therapy* (2nd edition). Oakland, CA: New Harbinger Publications, 2016.

Freedman G, Dainer-Best J. Who is more willing to engage in social rejection? The roles of self-esteem, rejection sensitivity, and negative affect in social rejection decisions. *The Journal of Social Psychology.* 2022:1–20.

Fremer C, Szejko N, Pisarenko A, Haas M, Laudenbach L, Wegener C, Müller-Vahl KR. Mass social media-induced illness presenting with Tourette-like behavior. *Frontiers in Psychiatry.* 2022;13:963769.

Gabarrell-Pascuet A, Koyanagi A, Félez-Nobrega M, Cristóbal-Narváez P, Mortier P, Vilagut G, Olaya B, Alonso J, Haro JM, Domènech-Abella J. The association of age with depression, anxiety, and posttraumatic stress symptoms during the COVID-19 pandemic in Spain: The role of loneliness and pre-pandemic mental disorder. *Psychosomatic Medicine.* 2023;85(1):42–52.

Gazendam N, Cleverley K, King N, Pickett W, Phillips SP. Individual and social determinants of early sexual activity: A study of gender-based differences using the 2018 Canadian Health Behaviour in School-aged Children Study (HBSC). *PLoS One.* 2020;15(9):e0238515.

Gazi MA, Çetin M, Çaki, C. The research of the level of social media addiction of university students. *International Journal of Social Sciences and Education Research.* 2017;3:549–559.

Gerdes ME, Aistis LA, Sachs NA, Williams M, Roberts JD, Rosenberg Goldstein RE. Reducing Anxiety with Nature and Gardening (RANG): Evaluating the impacts of gardening and outdoor activities on anxiety among U.S. adults during the COVID-19 pandemic. *International Journal of Environmental Research and Public Health.* 2022;19(9):5121.

Gill EK, McQuillan MT. LGBTQ+ students' peer victimization and mental health before and during the COVID-19 pandemic. *International Journal of Environmental Research and Public Health.* 2022;19(18):11537.

Gong Z, Lv Y, Jiao X, Liu J, Sun Y, Qu Q. The relationship between COVID-19-related restrictions and fear of missing out, problematic smartphone use, and mental health in college students: The moderated moderation effect of resilience and social support. *Frontiers in Public Health.* 2022;10:986498.

González-Nuevo C, Cuesta M, Postigo Á, Menéndez-Aller Á, García-Fernández J, Kuss DJ. Using social networking sites during lockdown: Risks and benefits. *Psicothema.* 2022;34(3):365–374.

Gonzalez-Sanguino C, Ausin B, Castellanos MA, Saiz J, Lopez-Gomez A, Ugidos C, Munoz M. Mental health consequences during the initial stage of the 2020 coronavirus pandemic in Spain. *Brain, Behavior, & Immunity.* 2020;87:172–176.

Gotlib I, Miller G, Borchers L, Coury S, Costello L, Garcia J, Ho, T. Effects of the COVID-19 pandemic on mental health and brain maturation in adolescents: Implications for analyzing longitudinal data. *Biological Psychiatry Global Open Science.* 2023;3(4):912–918.

Granberg A, Engberg IB, Lundberg D. Acute confusion and unreal experiences in intensive care patients in relation to the ICU syndrome. Part II. *Intensive Critical Care Nursing.* 1999;15(1):19–33.

Gregg D, Somers CL, Pernice FM, Hillman SB, Kernsmith P. Sexting rates and predictors from an urban Midwest high school. *Journal of School Health.* 2018;88(6):423–433.

Guerfali Y, Zdanowicz N. Depression during COVID-19 pandemic: Is there an emergency? *Psychiatria Danubina.* 2022;34(Suppl 8):14–17.

Guthold R, Stevens GA, Riley LM, Bull FC. Global trends in insufficient physical activity among adolescents: A pooled analysis of 298 population-based surveys with 1.6 million participants. *Lancet Child Adolescent Health.* 2020;4:23–35.

Guthrie D. How I learned to stop worrying and love the eco-apocalypse: An existential approach to accepting eco-anxiety. *Perspectives on Psychological Science.* 2023;18(1):210–223.

Haidt J. *The Anxious Generation: How the Great Rewiring of Childhood Is Causing an Epidemic of Mental Illness.* London: Penguin Press, 2024.

Håkansson A, Moesch K, Kenttä G. COVID-19-related impact on mental health and career uncertainty in student-athletes-data from a cohort of 7,025 athletes in an elite sport high school system in Sweden. *Frontiers in Sports and Active Living.* 2022;4:943402.

Hamilton M. The assessment of anxiety states by rating. *British Journal of Medical Psychology.* 1959;32:50–55.

Heeren A, Hanseeuw B, Cougnon LA, Lits G. Excessive worrying as a central feature of anxiety during the first COVID-19 lockdown-phase in Belgium: Insights from a network approach. *Psychologica Belgica.* 2021;61(1):401–418.

Heeren A, Mouguiama-Daouda C, McNally RJ. A network approach to climate change anxiety and its key related features. *Journal Anxiety Disorders.* 2022:102625.

Hinduja S, Patchin JW. Connecting adolescent suicide to the severity of bullying and cyberbullying. *Journal of School Violence.* 2018;18:333–346.

Hodgson CR, DeCoteau RN, Allison-Burbank JD, Godfrey TM. An updated systematic review of risk and protective factors related to the resilience and well-being of indigenous youth in the United States and Canada. *American Indian and Alaska Native Mental Health Research.* 2022;29(3):136–195.

Hoffmann MS, McDaid D, Salum GA, Silva-Ribeiro W, Ziebold C, King D, Gadelha A, Miguel EC, Mari JJ, Rohde LA, Pan PM, Bressan RA, Mojtabai R, Evans-Lacko S. The impact of child psychiatric conditions on future educational outcomes among a community cohort in Brazil. *Epidemiology and Psychiatric Sciences*. 2021;30:e69.

Hoge E, Bickham D, Cantor J. Digital media, anxiety, and depression in children. *Pediatrics*. 2017;140(Suppl 2):S76–S80.

Hoge EA, Bui E, Marques L, Metcalf CA, Morris LK, Robinaugh DJ, Worthington JJ, Pollack MH, Simon NM. Randomized controlled trial of mindfulness meditation for generalized anxiety disorder: Effects on anxiety and stress reactivity. *The Journal of Clinical Psychiatry*. 2013;74(8):786–792.

Hossain MM, Nesa F, Das J, Aggad R, Tasnim S, Bairwa M, Ma P, Ramirez G. Global burden of mental health problems among children and adolescents during COVID-19 pandemic: An umbrella review. *Psychiatry Research*. 2022;317:114814.

Hutson E, Mazurek Melnyk B. An adaptation of the COPE intervention for adolescent bullying victimization improved mental and physical health symptoms. *Journal of the American Psychiatric Nurses Association*. 2022;28(6):433–443.

Iuso S, Petito A, Ventriglio A, Severo M, Bellomo A, Limone P. The impact of psycho-education on school-children's homophobic attitudes. *International Review of Psychiatry*. 2022;34(3–4):266–273.

Jarman HK, Marques MD, McLean SA, Slater A, Paxton SJ. Social media, body satisfaction and well-being among adolescents: A mediation model of appearance-ideal internalization and comparison. *Body Image*. 2021;36:139–148.

Joseph, N, De los Santos, T, Amaro, L. Naturalistic social cognitive and emotional reactions to technology-mediated social exposures and cortisol in daily life. *Biological Psychology*. 2022;173:108402.

Kapil V, Collett G, Godec T, Gupta J, Maniero C, Ng SM, McIntosh I, Kumar A, Nair S, Kotecha A, Janmohamed A, Antoniou S, Khan R, Khanji MY, Siddiqui I, Gupta A. Longitudinal comparisons of mental health, burnout and well-being in patient-facing, non-patient-facing healthcare professionals and non-healthcare professionals during the COVID-19 pandemic: Findings from the CoPE-HCP study. *BJPsych Open*. 2022;8(5):e173.

Keith DR, Tegge AN, Stein JS, Athamneh LN, Craft WH, Chilcoat HD, Le Moigne A, DeVeaugh-Geiss A, Bickel WK. Struggling with recovery from opioids: Who is at risk during COVID-19? *Journal of Addiction Medicine*. 2023;17(3):e156–e163.

Khajeheian D, Colabi AM, Ahmad Kharman Shah NB, Bt Wan Mohamed Radzi CWJ, Jenatabadi HS. Effect of social media on child obesity: Application of structural equation modeling with the Taguchi method. *International Journal of Environmental Research and Public Health*. 2018;15(7):1343.

Kim MJ, Shin D, Ahn YM. Association between the number of hours of sleep during weekdays and suicidality among Korean adolescents: Mediating role of depressive and anxiety symptoms. *Journal Affective Disorders*. 2022;320:74–80.

Kornor H, Winje D, Ekeberg O, Weisaeth L, Kirkehei I, Johansen K, Steiro A. Early trauma-focused cognitive behavioral therapy to prevent chronic post-traumatic stress disorder and related symptoms: A systematic review and meta-analysis. *BMC Psychiatry*. 2008;8:81.

Kovačić Petrović Z, Peraica T, Kozarić-Kovačić D, Palavra IR. Internet use and internet-based addictive behaviours during coronavirus pandemic. *Current Opinion in Psychiatry*. 2022;35(5):324–331.

Kuester A, Niemeyer H, Knaevelsrud C. Internet-based interventions for post traumatic stress: A meta-analysis of randomized controlled trials. *Clinical Psychology Review*. 2016;43:1–16.

Lal S, Tremblay S, Starcevic D, Mauger-Lavigne M, Anaby D. Mental health problems among adolescents and young adults with childhood-onset physical disabilities: A scoping review. *Frontiers in Rehabilitation Sciences*. 2022;3:904586.

Lambert J, Barnstable G, Minter E, Cooper J, McEwan D. Taking a one-week break from social media improves well-being, depression, and anxiety: A randomized controlled trial. *Cyberpsychology, Behavior, and Social Networking.* 2022;25(5):287–293.

Lang Q, Roberson-Moore T, Rogers KM, Wilson WE Jr. Cultural considerations in working with black and African American youth. *Child and Adolescent Psychiatric Clinics of North America.* 2022;31(4):733–744.

Lavoie L, Dupéré V, Dion E, Crosnoe R, Lacourse É, Archambault I. Gender differences in adolescents' exposure to stressful life events and differential links to impaired school functioning. *Journal of Abnormal Child Psychology.* 2019;47(6):1053–1064.

Layug A, Krishnamurthy S, McKenzie R, Feng B. The impacts of social media use and online racial discrimination on Asian American mental health: Cross-sectional survey in the United States during COVID-19. *JMIR Formative Research.* 2022;6(9):e38589.

Lee JH, Maeng S, Lee JS, Bae JN, Kim WH, Kim H. The difference in the quality of life of Korean children with attention-deficit/hyperactivity disorder between before and after COVID-19. *Soa Chongsonyon Chongsin Uihak.* 2022;33(4):113–121.

Léger-Goodes T, Malboeuf-Hurtubise C, Mastine T, Généreux M, Paradis PO, Camden C. Eco-anxiety in children: A scoping review of the mental health impacts of the awareness of climate change. *Frontiers in Psychology.* 2022;13:872544.

Lewin KM, Kaur A, Meshi D. Problematic social media use and impulsivity. *Current Addictions Report.* 2023;10:553–562.

Lewin KM, Meshi D, Schuster AM, Cotten SR. Active and passive social media use are differentially related to depressive symptoms in older adults. *Aging and Mental Health.* 2022:1–8.

Lewis C, Roberts NP, Simon N, Bethell A, Bisson JI. Internet-delivered cognitive behavioural therapy for posttraumatic stress disorder: Systematic review and meta-analysis. *Acta Psychiatrica Scandinavica.* 2019;140:508–521.

Listernick ZI, Badawy SM. Mental health implications of the COVID-19 pandemic among children and adolescents: What do we know so far? *Pediatric Health Medicine and Therapeutics.* 2021;12:543–549.

Liu T, Shryane N, Elliot M. Attitudes to climate change risk: Classification of and transitions in the UK population between 2012 and 2020. *Humanities and Social Sciences Communications.* 2022;9(1):279.

Mahamid FA, Veronese G, Bdier D. Fear of coronavirus (COVID-19) and mental health outcomes in Palestine: The mediating role of social support. *Current Psychology.* 2021:1–10.

Mateu A, Pascual-Sánchez A, Martinez-Herves M, Hickey N, Nicholls D, Kramer T. Cyberbullying and post-traumatic stress symptoms in UK adolescents. *Archives of Disease in Childhood.* 2020;105(10):951–956.

Mathiak K, Weber R. Toward brain correlates of natural behavior: fMRI during violent video games. *Human Brain Mapping.* 2006;27(12):948–956.

McClean CP, Asnaani A, Litz BT, Hofmann SG. Gender differences in anxiety disorders: Prevalence, course of illness, comorbidity and burden of illness. *Journal of Psychiatric Research.* 2011;45(8):1027–1035.

McCurdy J. *I'm Glad My Mom Died.* New York: Simon & Schuster, 2022.

McDaid D, Park AL, Wahlbeck K. The economic case for the prevention of mental illness. *Annual Review of Public Health.* 2019;40:373–389.

McKenna P. *I Can Make You Sleep.* New York: Sterling Publishing, 2009.

McLaughlin KA, Sheridan MA, Gold AL, Duys A, Lambert HK, Peverill M, Heleniak C, Shechner T, Wojcieszak Z, Pine DS. Maltreatment exposure, brain structure, and fear conditioning in children and adolescents. *Neuropsychopharmacology.* 2016;41(8):1956–1964.

Meshberg-Cohen S, Svikis D, McMahon TJ. Expressive writing as a therapeutic process for drug-dependent women. *Substance Abuse.* 2014;35(1):80–88.

Minghelli B. Sleep disorders in higher education students: Modifiable and non-modifiable risk factors. *Northern Clinics of Istanbul.* 2022;9(3):215–222.

Moghtaderi A, Zocchi MS, Pines JM, Venkat A, Black B. Estimating the uncertain effect of the COVID pandemic on drug overdoses. *PLoS One.* 2023;18(8):e0281227.

Moncrieff J, Cooper RE, Stockmann T, Amendola S, Hengartner MP, Horowitz MA. The serotonin theory of depression: A systematic umbrella review of the evidence. *Molecular Psychiatry.* 2022.

Mougharbel F, Goldfield GS. Psychological correlates of sedentary screen time behaviour among children and adolescents: A narrative review. *Current Obesity Reports.* 2020;9(4):493–511.

Moulin F, Jean F, Melchior M, Patanè M, Pinucci I, Sijbrandij M, van der Waerden J, Galéra C. Longitudinal impact of the COVID-19 pandemic on mental health in a general population sample in France: Evidence from the COMET study. *Journal of Affective Disorders.* 2022;320:275–283.

Mughal AY, Devadas J, Ardman E, Levis B, Go VF, Gaynes BN. A systematic review of validated screening tools for anxiety disorders and PTSD in low to middle income countries. *BMC Psychiatry.* 2020;20:338.

Murdock M. *Heroine's Journey: Woman's Quest for Wholeness.* CO, Shambhala Publications, 1990.

Murthy P, Narasimha VL. Effects of the COVID-19 pandemic and lockdown on alcohol use disorders and complications. *Current Opinion in Psychiatry.* 2021;34(4):376–385.

Muth L, Leven KH, Moll G, Kratz O, Horndasch S. Effects of the COVID-19 restrictions on eating behaviour and eating disorder symptomology in female adolescents. *International Journal of Environmental Research and Public Health.* 2022;19(14):8480.

Nakhaei MRS, Noorbala AA, Haghighi AS, Arbabi M. Neuropsychiatric symptoms in the psychiatric counseling of patients admitted with COVID-19 infection. *Psychiatry Research.* 2022;317:114855.

Neuspiel, D. Bullying: Effects on physical and emotional health. *AAP Grand Rounds.* 2001;6(5):50–51.

Newman, MG, Jacobson, NC, Zainal, NH, Shin, KE, Szkodny, LE, Sliwinski, MJ. The effects of worry in daily life: An ecological momentary assessment study supporting the tenets of the contrast avoidance model. *Clinical Psychological Science.* 2019;7(4):794–810.

Niles LL. The influence of social media on adolescent suicide: Is it all bad? *Journal of Psychosocial Nursing and Mental Health Services.* 2022:1–6.

Noh D, Kim H. Effectiveness of online interventions for the universal and selective prevention of mental health problems among adolescents: A systematic review and meta-analysis. *Prevention Science.* 2022:1–12.

Olafiranye O, Jean-Louis G, Zizi F, Nunes J, Vincent M. Anxiety and cardiovascular risk: Review of epidemiological and clinical evidence. *Mind Brain.* 2011;2(1):32–37.

Olenik-Shemesh D, Heiman T. Cyberbullying victimization in adolescents as related to body esteem, social support, and social self-efficacy. *Journal of Genetic Psychology.* 2017;178(1):28–43.

Panchal U, Salazar de Pablo G, Franco M, Moreno C, Parellada M, Arango C, Fusar-Poli P. The impact of COVID-19 lockdown on child and adolescent mental health: Systematic review. *European Child & Adolescent Psychiatry.* 2021:1–27.

Patel V, Saxena S, Lund C, Thornicroft G, Baingana F, Bolton P, Chisholm D, Collins PY, Cooper JL, Eaton J, Herrman H, Herzallah MM, Huang Y, Jordans MJD, Kleinman A, Medina-Mora ME, Morgan E, Niaz U, Omigbodun O, Prince M, Rahman A, Saraceno B, Sarkar BK, De Silva M, Singh I, Stein DJ, Sunkel C, UnÜtzer J. The Lancet Commission on global mental health and sustainable development. *Lancet.* 2018;392(10157):1553–1598.

Pickering L, Hadwin JA, Kovshoff H. The role of peers in the development of social anxiety in adolescent girls: A systematic review. *Adolescent Research Review.* 2020;5:341–362.

Pokhrel P, Lipperman-Kreda S, Wills TA, Kaholokula JK, Kawamoto CT, Amin S, Herzog TA. Ethnicity, COVID-related stress, and e-cigarette use and cigarette smoking among young adults: A longitudinal study. *Nicotine & Tobacco Research.* 2023:ntad095.

Primack BA, Perryman KL, Crofford RA, Escobar-Viera CG. Social media as it interfaces with psychosocial development and mental illness in transitional-age youth. *Child and Adolescent Psychiatric Clinics of North America.* 2022;31(1):11–30.

Probst G, Vîslă A, Flückiger C. Patients' symptoms and strengths as predictors of long-term out-comes of CBT for generalized anxiety disorder—A three-level, multi-predictor analysis. *Journal of Anxiety Disorders*. 2022;92:102635.

Quinn A, Grant JE, Chamberlain SR. COVID-19 and resultant restrictions on gambling behaviour. *Neuroscience & Biobehavioral Reviews*. 2022;143:104932.

Racine N, McArthur BA, Cooke JE, Elrich R, Zhu J, Madigan S. Global prevalence of depressive and anxiety symptoms in children and adolescents during COVID-19: A meta-analysis. *JAMA Pediatrics*. 2021;175:1142–1150.

Radovic A, Li Y, Landsittel D, Odenthal KR, Stein BD, Miller E. A social media website (supporting our valued adolescents) to support treatment uptake for adolescents with depression or anxiety: Pilot randomized controlled trial. *JMIR Mental Health*. 2022;9(10):e35313.

Rawal T, Mishra VK, Sharda SG, Sharma K, Mehta R, Kulkarni MM, Goel S, Arora M. Impact of closure of educational institutions due to COVID-19 lockdown on overall subjective wellbeing of adolescents and youth: Cross-sectional survey, India. *Frontiers in Psychology*. 2022;13:903044.

Ritzert TR, Forsyth JP, Sheppard SC, Boswell JF, Berghoff CR, Eifert GH. Evaluating the effectiveness of ACT for anxiety disorders in a self-help context: Outcomes from a randomized wait-list controlled trial. *Behavior Therapy*. 2016;47(4):444–459.

Roberti E, Giacchero R, Grumi S, Biasucci G, Cuzzani L, Decembrino L, Magnani ML, Motta M, Nacinovich R, Pisoni C, Scelsa B, Provenzi L; MOM-COPE Study Group. Post-partum women's anxiety and parenting stress: Home-visiting protective effect during the COVID-19 pandemic. *Maternal and Child Health Journal*. 2022:1–10.

Ruyak S, Roberts MH, Chambers S, Ma X, DiDomenico J, De La Garza R 2nd, Bakhireva LN. The effect of the COVID-19 pandemic on substance use patterns and physiological dysregulation in pregnant and postpartum women. *Alcohol (Hoboken)*. 2023;47(6):1088–1099.

Sankar K, Gould MK, Prescott HC. Psychological morbidity after COVID-19 critical illness. *Chest*. 2023;163(1):139–147.

Schab L. *The Anxiety Workbook for Teens*. Oakland, CA: New Harbinger, 2021.

Schacter HL, Marusak HA, Borg BA, Jovanovic T. Facing ambiguity: Social threat sensitivity mediates the association between peer victimization and adolescent anxiety. *Development and Psychopathology*. 2022:1–9.

Schwab C, Frenzel AC, Daumiller M, Dresel M, Dickhäuser O, Janke S, Marx AKG. "I'm tired of black boxes!": A systematic comparison of faculty well-being and need satisfaction before and during the COVID-19 crisis. *PLoS One*. 2022;17(10).

Schwandt H, Currie J, von Wachter T, Kowarski J, Chapman D, Woolf SH. Changes in the relationship between income and life expectancy before and during the COVID-19 pandemic, California, 2015–2021. *JAMA*. 2022.

Shabahang R, Shim H, Aruguete MS, Zsila Á. Oversharing on social media: Anxiety, attention-seeking, and social media addiction predict the breadth and depth of sharing. *Psychological Reports*. 2024;127(2):513–530.

Shakiba N, Perlstein S, Powell T, Rodriguez Y, Waller R, Wagner NJ. Prospective associations between pandemic-related adversity, harsh parenting, and the development of prosociality across middle to late childhood. *Developmental Psychology*. 2023;59(3):538–548.

Simon NM, Hofmann SG, Rosenfield D, Hoeppner SS, Hoge EA, Bui E, Khalsa SBS. Efficacy of yoga vs cognitive behavioral therapy vs stress education for the treatment of generalized anxiety disorder: A randomized clinical trial. *JAMA Psychiatry*. 2021;78(1):13–20.

Sinanovic S, Vidacek A, Muftic M. Impact of yoga practice on level of stress during COVID-19 pandemic. *Materia Socio Medica*. 2022;34(2):118–120.

Small G. *The Small Guide to Anxiety*. Boca Raton, FL: Humanix Books, 2019.

Somerville LH. The teenage brain: Sensitivity to social evaluation. *Current Directions in Psychological Science*, 2013;22:121–127.

Stein SR, Ramelli SC, Grazioli A, Chung JY, Singh M, Yinda CK, Winkler CW, Sun J, Dickey JM, Ylaya K, Ko SH, Platt AP, Burbelo PD, Quezado M, Pittaluga S, Purcell M, Munster VJ, Belinky F, Ramos-Benitez MJ, Boritz EA, Lach IA, Herr DL, Rabin J, Saharia KK, Madathil

RJ, Tabatabai A, Soherwardi S, McCurdy MT; NIH COVID-19 Autopsy Consortium; Peterson KE, Cohen JI, de Wit E, Vannella KM, Hewitt SM, Kleiner DE, Chertow DS. SARS-CoV-2 infection and persistence in the human body and brain at autopsy. *Nature.* 2022;612(7941):758–763.

Stobbe E, Sundermann J, Ascone L, Kühn S. Birdsongs alleviate anxiety and paranoia in healthy participants. *Scientific Reports.* 2022;12:16414.3

Stossel S. *My Age of Anxiety: Fear, Hope, Dread, and the Search for Peace of Mind.* New York: Alfred Knopf, 2013.

Stuart J, O'Donnell K, O'Donnell A, Scott R, Barber B. Online social connection as a buffer of health anxiety and isolation during COVID-19. *Cyberpsychology, Behavior, and Social Networking.* 2021;24(8):521–525.

Su W, Han X, Yu H, Wu Y, Potenza M. Do men become addicted to internet gaming and women to social media? A meta-analysis examining gender-related differences in specific internet addiction. *Computers in Human Behavior.* 2020;113:106480.

Szuhany KL, Malgaroli M, Miron CD, Simon NM. Prolonged grief disorder: Course, diagnosis, assessment, and treatment. *Focus: The Journal of Lifelong Learning in Psychiatry.* 2021;19(2):161–172.

Takizawa R, Maughan B, Arseneault L. Adult health outcomes of childhood bullying victimization: Evidence from a five-decade longitudinal British birth cohort. *American Journal of Psychiatry.* 2014;171(7):777–784.

Tan L, Ng SH, Omar A, Karupaiah T. What's on YouTube? A case study on food and beverage advertising in videos targeted at children on social media. *Childhood Obesity.* 2018;14(5):280–290.

Tang A, Harrewijn A, Benson B, Haller SP, Guyer AE, Perez-Edgar KE, Stringaris A, Ernst M, Brotman MA, Pine DS, Fox NA. Striatal activity to reward anticipation as a moderator of the association between early behavioral inhibition and changes in anxiety and depressive symptoms from adolescence to adulthood. *JAMA Psychiatry.* 2022;79(12):1199–1208.

Tanir Y, Karayagmurlu A, Kaya İ, Kaynar TB, Türkmen G, Dambasan BN, Meral Y, Coşkun M. Exacerbation of obsessive compulsive disorder symptoms in children and adolescents during COVID-19 pandemic. *Psychiatry Research.* 2020;293:113363.

Tarar ZI, Farooq U, Zafar Y. Burden of anxiety and depression among hospitalized patients with irritable bowel syndrome: A nationwide analysis. *Irish Journal of Medical Science.* 2023;192(5):2159–2166.

Taylor SC, Smernoff ZL, Rajan M, Steeman S, Gehringer BN, Dow HC, Barzilay R, Rader DJ, Bucan M, Almasy L, Brodkin ES. Investigating the relationships between resilience, autism-related quantitative traits, and mental health outcomes among adults during the COVID-19 pandemic. *Journal of Psychiatric Research.* 2022;148:250–257.

Thai H, Davis CG, Mahboob W, Perry S, Adams A, Goldfield GS. Reducing social media use improves appearance and weight esteem in youth with emotional distress. *Psychology of Popular Media.* 2024;13(1):162–169.

Thielemann JFB, Kasparik B, König J, Unterhitzenberger J, Rosner R. A systematic review and meta-analysis of trauma-focused cognitive behavioral therapy for children and adolescents. *Child Abuse & Neglect.* 2022;134:105899.

Thornton BW, Faires A, Robbins M, Rollins E. The mere presence of a cell phone may be distracting. *Social Psychology.* 2014;45:479–488.

Torous J, Bucci S, Bell IH, Kessing LV, Faurholt-Jepsen M, Whelan P, Carvalho AF, Keshavan M, Linardon J, Firth J. The growing field of digital psychiatry: Current evidence and the future of apps, social media, chatbots, and virtual reality. *World Psychiatry.* 2021;20(3):318–335.

Tóth R, Turner MJ, Kökény T, Tóth L. "I must be perfect": The role of irrational beliefs and perfectionism on the competitive anxiety of Hungarian athletes. *Frontiers in Psychology.* 2022;13:994126.

Trenton, N. *Stop Negative Thinking.* Las Vegas: Pkcs Media, Inc. 2022.

Tu W, Jiang H, Liu Q. Peer Victimization and adolescent mobile social addiction: Mediation of social anxiety and gender differences. *International Journal of Environmental Research and Public Health.* 2022;19(17):10978.

Upenieks L, Ford-Robertson J. Childhood abuse, goal-striving stress and self-esteem: An explanatory role for perceptions of divine control? *Journal of Religion & Health.* 2023;62(2):906–931.

Usmani SS, Sharath M, Mehendale M. Future of mental health in the metaverse. *General Psychiatry.* 2022;35(4):e100825.

van Loon AWG, Creemers HE, Vogelaar S, Saab N, Miers AC, Westenberg PM, Asscher JJ. Trajectories of adolescent perceived stress and symptoms of depression and anxiety during the COVID-19 pandemic. *Scientific Reports.* 2022;12(1):15957.

Varma P, Junge M, Meaklim H, Jackson ML. Younger people are more vulnerable to stress, anxiety and depression during COVID-19 pandemic: A global cross-sectional survey. *Progress in Neuro-Psychopharmacology and Biological Psychiatry.* 2021;109:110236.

Viaux-Savelon S, Maurice P, Rousseau A, Leclere C, Renout M, Berlingo L, Cohen D, Jouannic JM. Impact of COVID-19 lockdown on maternal psychological status, the couple's relationship and mother-child interaction: A prospective study. *BMC Pregnancy and Childbirth.* 2022;22(1):732.

Vieira YP, Viero VDSF, Saes-Silva E, Silva PAD, Silva LSD, Saes MO, Demenech LM, Dumith SC. Excessive use of social media by high school students in southern Brazil. *Revista Paulista de Pediatria.* 2022;40:e2020420.

Weersing VR, Gonzalez A, Hatch B, Lynch FL. Promoting racial/ethnic equity in psychosocial treatment outcomes for child and adolescent anxiety and depression. *Psychiatric Research and Clinical Practice.* 2022;4(3):80–88.

Wegmann E, Stodt B, Brand M. Addictive use of social networking sites can be explained by the interaction of internet use expectancies, internet literacy, and psychopathological symptoms. *Journal of Behavioral Addictions.* 2015;4(3):155–162.

Wehbe AT, Costa TE, Abbas SA, Costa JE, Costa GE, Wehbe TW. The effects of the COVID-19 confinement on screen time, headaches, stress and sleep disorders among adolescents: A cross sectional study. *Chronic Stress.* 2022;6.

Weinstein E. The social media see-saw: Positive and negative influences on adolescents' affective well-being. *New Media & Society.* 2018;20(10):3597–3623.

Wen X, Zhu F, Yuan Z, Mao Z. Relationship between physical activity, screen-related sedentary behaviors and anxiety among adolescents in less developed areas of China. *Medicine (Baltimore).* 2022;101(39):e30848.

Whittington R, Aluh DO, Caldas-de-Almeida J-M. Zero tolerance for coercion? Historical, cultural and organisational contexts for effective implementation of coercion-free mental health services around the world. *Healthcare.* 2023;11(21):2834.

Wicks C, Barton J, Orbell S, Andrews L. Psychological benefits of outdoor physical activity in natural versus urban environments: A systematic review and meta-analysis of experimental studies. *Applied Psychology Health and Well-Being.* 2022;14:1037–1061.

Woessmann L. The economic case for education. *Education Economics.* 2016;24(1):3–32.

Wolfers LN, Utz S. Social media use, stress, and coping, *Current Opinion in Psychology.* 2022;45:101305.

Wood CJ, Barton JL, Wicks CL. The impact of therapeutic community gardening on the wellbeing, loneliness, and life satisfaction of individuals with mental illness. *International Journal of Environmental Research and Public Health.* 2022;19(20):13166.

Wu T, Jia X, Shi H, Niu J, Yi X, Xie J, Wang X. Prevalence of mental health problems during the COVID-19 pandemic: A systemic review and meta-analysis. *Journal of Affective Disorders.* 2021;281:91–98.

Young KS, Purves KL, Hübel C, Davies MR, Thompson KN, Bristow S, Krebs G, Danese A, Hirsch C, Parsons CE, Vassos E, Adey BN, Bright S, Hegemann L, Lee YT, Kalsi G, Monssen D, Mundy J, Peel AJ, Rayner C, Rogers HC, Ter Kuile A, Ward C, York K, Lin Y, Palmos AB, Schmidt U, Veale D, Nicholson TR, Pollak TA, Stevelink SAM, Moukhtarian T,

Martineau AR, Holt H, Maughan B, Al-Chalabi A, Chaudhuri KR, Richardson MP, Bradley JR, Chinnery PF, Kingston N, Papadia S, Stirrups KE, Linger R, Hotopf M, Eley TC, Breen G. Depression, anxiety, and PTSD symptoms before and during the COVID-19 pandemic in the UK. *Psychological Medicine.* 2022:1–14.

Zhang X, Li J, Xie F, Chen X, Xu W, Hudson NW. The relationship between adult attachment and mental health: A meta-analysis. *Journal of Personality and Social Psychology.* 2022;123(5):1089–1137.

Zhao N, Zhang X, Noah J, Tiede M, Hirsch J. Separable processes for live "in-person" and live "zoom-like" faces. *Imaging Neuroscience.* 2023;1:11–17.

Zimmer-Gembeck MJ, Rudolph JI, Gardner AA. Are you looking at me? A longitudinal vignette study of adolescent appearance rejection sensitivity and coping with peer evaluation. *Body Image.* 2022;43:253–263.

Matthews A, [illegible] H, [illegible] R, [illegible] A, [illegible] R, [illegible] M, [illegible] [illegible] L, Kingston N, Pakianathan [illegible] [illegible] [illegible] [illegible] M, [illegible]. Depression, anxiety, and [illegible] [illegible] before and during the COVID-19 pandemic in the UK. *[illegible] Medicine*. 2023:1–14.

Zhang X, [illegible] J, Xie Z, [illegible] X, Xu W, Hutchinson W. The relationship between adolescents' [illegible] and mental health [illegible]. *Journal of [illegible]*. [illegible] 10.1123/[illegible].

Zhao M, Zhang [illegible], [illegible], Tiede M, [illegible]. Separable [illegible] [illegible] and [illegible] [illegible]. *[illegible]*. [illegible]:111–[illegible].

Zimmermann [illegible], [illegible] [illegible] A. [illegible] [illegible] [illegible] [illegible] [illegible] [illegible] and [illegible] [illegible]. [illegible] [illegible].

Index

B

F

G

H

I

J

K

L

M

N

Q

R

U

Printed in the United States
by Baker & Taylor Publisher Services